Affect, Interest and Political Entrepreneurs in Ethnic and Religious Conflicts

In the current environment, most political violence occurs between internal communities, such as ethnic and religious groups, rather than between states. Such inter-communal conflict threatens both internal political stability and interstate relations. In this edited volume, a multidisciplinary and multinational group of scholars analyze the bases of inter-communal conflict and its domestic and international consequences.

The authors focus on inter-communal conflict through the lenses of political struggles in the Middle East and Asia, which provide fertile grounds for assessing the viability of new social constructions and the continuing impact of ancestral ties. Containing theoretical, regional, and country studies, the chapters tackle such issues as: the implications of changes in the institutional rules for political competition; how explanatory narratives for conflict are selected when multiple attributions are possible; the bases of ideological conflict that have arisen within Islam; the problems of ethnic competition that remain unresolved in powersharing arrangements; the consequences for international relations when national boundaries do not circumscribe ethnic and religious communities; and the subordination of women's interests to religious conflict and its resolution. Since identities are shaped by multiple qualities, the contributions examine the role of ideologies, institutions, and politicians in shaping political cleavages, communities, and conflicts.

This book was originally published as a special issue of *Ethnic and Racial Studies*.

Arthur A. Stein is Professor of Political Science at UCLA, California, USA. He is the author of *The Nation at War* (1980) and *Why Nations Cooperate* (1990); and co-editor of *The Domestic Bases of Grand Strategy* (1993, with Richard N. Rosecrance), and of *No More States?: Globalization, National Self-Determination, and Terrorism* (2006, with Richard N. Rosecrance).

Ayelet Harel-Shalev is Senior Lecturer in the Conflict Management and Resolution Program and the Department of Politics and Government at Ben-Gurion University of the Negev, Israel. Her interests and publications are at the intersection of politics, conflict studies and feminist international relations, and focus mainly on ethnic-conflicts and women in the military.

Ethnic and Racial Studies

Series editors:
Martin Bulmer, *University of Surrey, UK*
John Solomos, *University of Warwick, UK*

The journal *Ethnic and Racial Studies* was founded in 1978 by John Stone to provide an international forum for high quality research on race, ethnicity, nationalism and ethnic conflict. At the time the study of race and ethnicity was still a relatively marginal sub-field of sociology, anthropology and political science. In the intervening period the journal has provided a space for the discussion of core theoretical issues, key developments and trends, and for the dissemination of the latest empirical research.

It is now the leading journal in its field and has helped to shape the development of scholarly research agendas. *Ethnic and Racial Studies* attracts submissions from scholars in a diverse range of countries and fields of scholarship, and crosses disciplinary boundaries. It is now available in both printed and electronic form. From 2015 it will publish 15 issues per year, three of which will be dedicated to *Ethnic and Racial Studies Review* offering expert guidance to the latest research through the publication of book reviews, symposia and discussion pieces, including reviews of work in languages other than English.

The Ethnic and Racial Studies book series contains a wide range of the journal's special issues. These special issues are an important contribution to the work of the journal, where leading social science academics bring together articles on specific themes and issues that are linked to the broad intellectual concerns of *Ethnic and Racial Studies*. The series editors work closely with the guest editors of the special issues to ensure that they meet the highest quality standards possible. Through publishing these special issues as a series of books, we hope to allow a wider audience of both scholars and students from across the social science disciplines to engage with the work of *Ethnic and Racial Studies*.

Most recent titles in the series include:

Immigrant Incorporation in Political Parties
Exploring the diversity gap
Edited by Ricard Zapata-Barrero, Iris Dähnke and Lea Markard

Racialized Bordering Discourses on European Roma
Edited by Nira Yuval Davis, Georgie Wemyss and Kathryn Cassidy

Affect, Interest and Political Entrepreneurs in Ethnic and Religious Conflicts
Edited by Arthur A. Stein and Ayelet Harel-Shalev

Celebrating 40 Years of Ethnic and Racial Studies
Classic Papers in Context
Edited by Martin Bulmer and John Solomos

Affect, Interest and Political Entrepreneurs in Ethnic and Religious Conflicts

Edited by
Arthur A. Stein and Ayelet Harel-Shalev

Routledge
Taylor & Francis Group

LONDON AND NEW YORK

ETHNIC
◄ AND ►
RACIAL
STUDIES

First published 2018
by Routledge

2 Park Square, Milton Park, Abingdon, Oxfordshire OX14 4RN
52 Vanderbilt Avenue, New York, NY 10017

Routledge is an imprint of the Taylor & Francis Group, an informa business

First issued in paperback 2020

British Library Cataloguing in Publication Data
A catalogue record for this book is available from the British Library

ISBN 13: 978-0-8153-9611-6 (hbk)
ISBN 13: 978-0-367-51942-1 (pbk)

Typeset in Myriad Pro
by RefineCatch Limited, Bungay, Suffolk

Publisher's Note
The publisher accepts responsibility for any inconsistencies that may have
arisen during the conversion of this book from journal articles to book chapters,
namely the possible inclusion of journal terminology.

Disclaimer
Every effort has been made to contact copyright holders for their permission to
reprint material in this book. The publishers would be grateful to hear from any
copyright holder who is not here acknowledged and will undertake to rectify
any errors or omissions in future editions of this book.

Contents

Citation Information   vii
Notes on Contributors   ix

Introduction

Ancestral and instrumental in the politics of ethnic and religious
conflict   1
Arthur A. Stein and Ayelet Harel-Shalev

**Part I: Domestic and International Sources of Political Competition
and Conflict**

1. When and why do some social cleavages become politically salient
   rather than others?   21
   Daniel N. Posner

2. Ethnicity, extraterritoriality, and international conflict   40
   Arthur A. Stein

Part II: Ethnic and Religious Conflict in the Middle East

3. Representation, minorities and electoral reform: the case of the
   Palestinian minority in Israel   59
   Rebecca Kook

4. The paradox of power-sharing: stability and fragility in postwar
   Lebanon   78
   Amanda Rizkallah

5. Changing Islam, changing the world: contrasting visions within
   political Islam   97
   Nimrod Hurvitz and Eli Alshech

CONTENTS

Part III: Ethnic and Religious Conflict in Asia

6. The "ethnic" in Indonesia's communal conflicts: violence in Ambon, Poso, and Sambas   116
   Kirsten E. Schulze

7. Gendering ethnic conflicts: minority women in divided societies – the case of Muslim women in India   135
   Ayelet Harel-Shalev

   Index   155

Citation Information

The chapters in this book were originally published in *Ethnic and Racial Studies*, volume 40, issue 12 (October 2017). When citing this material, please use the original page numbering for each article, as follows:

Introduction
Ancestral and instrumental in the politics of ethnic and religious conflict
Arthur A. Stein and Ayelet Harel-Shalev
Ethnic and Racial Studies, volume 40, issue 12 (October 2017), pp. 1981–2000

Chapter 1
When and why do some social cleavages become politically salient rather than others?
Daniel N. Posner
Ethnic and Racial Studies, volume 40, issue 12 (October 2017), pp. 2001–2019

Chapter 2
Ethnicity, extraterritoriality, and international conflict
Arthur A. Stein
Ethnic and Racial Studies, volume 40, issue 12 (October 2017), pp. 2020–2038

Chapter 3
Representation, minorities and electoral reform: the case of the Palestinian minority in Israel
Rebecca Kook
Ethnic and Racial Studies, volume 40, issue 12 (October 2017), pp. 2039–2057

Chapter 4
The paradox of power-sharing: stability and fragility in postwar Lebanon
Amanda Rizkallah
Ethnic and Racial Studies, volume 40, issue 12 (October 2017), pp. 2058–2076

Chapter 5
Changing Islam, changing the world: contrasting visions within political Islam
Nimrod Hurvitz and Eli Alshech
Ethnic and Racial Studies, volume 40, issue 12 (October 2017), pp. 2077–2095

Chapter 6
The "ethnic" in Indonesia's communal conflicts: violence in Ambon, Poso, and Sambas
Kirsten E. Schulze
Ethnic and Racial Studies, volume 40, issue 12 (October 2017), pp. 2096–2114

Chapter 7
Gendering ethnic conflicts: minority women in divided societies – the case of Muslim women in India
Ayelet Harel-Shalev
Ethnic and Racial Studies, volume 40, issue 12 (October 2017), pp. 2115–2134

For any permission-related enquiries please visit:
http://www.tandfonline.com/page/help/permissions

Notes on Contributors

Eli Alshech is associated with the Preventing, Interdicting and Mitigating Extremism (PRIME) project, based in The Criminology Institute at the Hebrew University, Jerusalem, Israel. He also serves as a private consultant for the Israeli government. His research touches on an array of topics, including privacy in Islamic legal thought, Jihad in Islamic law, martyrdom, and cyber-terrorism.

Ayelet Harel-Shalev is Senior Lecturer in the Conflict Management and Resolution Program and the Department of Politics and Government at Ben-Gurion University of the Negev, Israel. Her interests and publications are at the intersection of politics, conflict studies and feminist international relations, and focus mainly on ethnic-conflicts and women in the military.

Nimrod Hurvitz is Senior Fellow in the Department of Middle East Studies at Ben-Gurion University of the Negev, Israel. His research focuses on medieval and modern Muslim religious movements and the politics of religiosity. He is the author of *The Formation of Hanbalism: Piety into Power* (2002). He is also the co-founder of The Forum for Regional Thinking.

Rebecca Kook is Senior Lecturer in Politics and Government at Ben-Gurion University of the Negev, Israel. Her research focuses on liberal nationalism, the politics of memory, and the interaction between immigration and citizenship. She is the author of *The Logic of Democratic Exclusion: African Americans in the U.S. and Palestinian Citizens of Israel* (2002).

Daniel N. Posner is Professor of International Development at UCLA, California, USA. His research focuses on ethnic politics, research design, distributive politics, and the political economy of development in Africa. He is the co-author of *Coethnicity: Diversity and the Dilemmas of Collective Action* (with James Habyarimana, Macartan Humphreys and Jeremy M. Weinstein, 2009).

Amanda Rizkallah is Assistant Professor of International Studies at Pepperdine University, California, USA. Her research interests include Middle Eastern politics, civil war, international intervention in civil war settlement, and post-conflict politics. She is currently writing a book on the long-term political consequences of civil war, with a focus on Lebanon.

Kirsten E. Schulze is Associate Professor in the Department of International History at the London School of Economics, UK. Her research focuses on armed conflict; communal and separatist violence; and political Islam and militant jihadism in Indonesia and the Middle East. She is the author of *The Arab-Israeli Conflict* (3rd ed., 2016).

Arthur A. Stein is Professor of Political Science at UCLA, California, USA. He is the author of *The Nation at War* (1980) and *Why Nations Cooperate* (1990); and co-editor of *The Domestic Bases of Grand Strategy* (1993, with Richard N. Rosecrance), and of *No More States?: Globalization, National Self-Determination, and Terrorism* (2006, with Richard N. Rosecrance).

Ancestral and instrumental in the politics of ethnic and religious conflict

Arthur A. Stein ⓘ and Ayelet Harel-Shalev ⓘ

ABSTRACT
Ethnicity, like race, religion, and nationality, is a feature of group identity that is contested. There are literatures devoted to each, and in each there are those who see the origins of identity and affiliation in ancestry and deeply rooted affect and those who see these as socially constructed and instrumentally used by elites. Yet all recognize that the ancestral is socially constructed and that social constructions make use of existing cultural features, and that the vertical cleavages of race, religion, ethnicity, and nationality dominate the horizontal ones of class. This generates implications for institutional changes, for the pursuit of extraterritorial interests, for the selection of explanatory narratives for conflict when multiple attributions are possible, for intra-communal conflict, and for policies for ethnic conflict regulation.

Introduction

Ethnicity is a feature of group identity whose nature, origins, and consequences remain contested. As to its nature and origins, academics debate
its primordial and essentialist roots in contrast to its constructed, strategic,
or modern evolvements; and as to its consequences, they argue about its
importance as a basis for competition and conflict. Although the word is
less than half a century old, ethnicity is a long-standing as well as contemporaneous feature of political and social life. Social life embodies different forms of
conflict. Scarcity is the basis for economic competition, and the collective
character of political rule underlies political competition for power. Such com-
petitions and the conflicts they can generate may or may not reflect ethnic
bases of affiliation, organization, and mobilization.

Political competition reflects the organization of politics, which represents
both the cleavages in society, and the mobilizational strategies of political

elites. Given a world in which there exist a multiplicity of ethnic groups and the fact that many, if not most, extant nation-states are ethnically hetero-geneous, political contestation is likely to reflect, to some degree, conflicting ethnic policy preferences. Yet neither political competition nor political con-flict need necessarily revolve around ethnicity. Political alliances and clea-vages can reflect ethnicity, but they can also reflect race, religion, region, nationality, ideology, or material interest.[1] But in each case, boundaries are demarcated between those in the group and those outside of it.[2]

Most political violence in the current global political environment is internal, and governments must cope with inter-communal conflict that threatens both internal political stability and interstate relations. By dealing with minority communities, governments must perforce balance consider-ations of internal governance with concerns about international spillovers. Ethnic conflict is a staple of internal and international politics in many parts of the globe. This special issue focuses on these matters through the lenses of political struggles in the Middle East and Asia, in order to comprehend the dynamics of ethnic politics. In most states in these areas, since the political regime is typically not ethnically neutral, certain levels of ethnic exclusion are implemented by the political system in both formal and non-formal ways. In many states, ethnic competition becomes ethnic conflict. And in an inter-national system numerically dominated by relatively fragile states in which ethnicities spill across national borders and states have extraterritorial inter-ests, severe conflicts and instability are frequent. The regulation of such con-flict perforce depends on the bases of ethnicity and both the internal and international sources of political competition and conflict. As described below, the papers draw upon and transcend the standard debates in the field and focus on the bases of political competition and the political use of particular identities for framing political contestation and conflict.

The relationship between ethnicity and politics is developed in general terms yet instantiated in regional and national histories and analyses. Scho-larly work on ethnicity initially "drew on the works of those who sought to describe and explain the rise of modern Europe" (Bates 2006, 168), but con-cerns about the universality of that experience and the different paths of pol-itical development in the non-Western parts of the world resulted in shifting the focus to post-colonial societies, a shift reflected in this special issue as well.

Through the myriad ways that ethnicity conceptually informs each contri-buting author's research, collectively these pieces examine the deep intercon-nectedness of political competition and ethnicity at the international, national, local, and individual level. This issue emphasizes the multiple ways ethnic and religious conflicts intersect with political competition and political violence. The contributory disciplinary perspectives range from anthropology to political geography, history, political science, international relations, psychology, and sociology. The pieces reflect, in part, different attitudes and approaches to the study of political, religious, and ethnic conflicts.

A stale debate: primordialism versus constructivism

Scholars debate the relationship between ethnicity, race, religion, and nationality. As Brubaker (2009, 22) notes, although "the literature on ethnicity, race, and nations and nationalism [has been] fragmented and compartmentalized", it can be construed "as a single integrated family of forms of cultural understanding, social organization, and political contestation".[3] Moreover, the concept of ethnicity, like those of race, religion, and nationality, has been essentially contested. Regarding each, scholars have addressed two questions: where identities come from and what impact they have. As to origins, a debate has pitted primordial accounts versus constructivist ones. The former stress the long-standing and deep-seated nature of these elements of identity and interest,[4] whereas the latter stress the malleability and socially constructed features of identification. As to the impact of identity, there is a presumption by all scholars that it matters, but for some the impact of these features becomes an issue of how they are used. A subset of constructivists are instrumentalists who argue that social constructions reflect the instrumental choices of elites mobilizing supporters or of individuals selecting ethnic status for social advantage.[5] Since identities and groupings can be socially constructed without the presumption of instrumentality, in this section we just use constructivism to characterize this perspective, and the role of instrumental choice is discussed below.

Race

Race was widely used in the past as an analytic category, but came under assault, and is now thought of quite differently. The case for a primordial basis of identification is the easiest to make for characteristics that are genetically transmitted, and so race can be characterized as a biological category. The use of racial classification, however, has a problematic history (Banton 1998) and associated with pernicious policies and practices that are now widely rejected. Race came to be criticized on factual grounds, that genetic research did not provide a basis for racial classification, and on epistemic grounds, that there are "no effective criteria to establish membership in races" (Gracia 2007, 3). The epistemic challenge resulted in the widespread view that race is a social construct.[6]

Nevertheless, race continues to be used as a category of identification.[7] The US has included race as a category since its first census in 1790, but over the years the number of categories has grown, the labels have changed, ethnicity has been added, and the system moved in 1960 from having enumerators classify people to having people choose their own racial (and ethnic) identity (Ahmad and Hagler 2015).[8]

The debate about race is evident in the area of public health. Race and ethnicity "are among the most commonly used epidemiological variables" (Afshari and Bhopal 2010), with ethnicity increasingly replacing race (Afshari and Bhopal 2002, 2010; also see Bhopal 2004), but nevertheless generating a debate about whether "research into ethnicity and health [is] racist, unsound, or important science" (as in the title of Bhopal 1997), whether "as an epidemiological determinant? it is "crudely racist or crucially important" (as in the title of Chaturvedi 2001).

Ethnicity

Although ethnicity replaced race in much academic work because the latter was seen as socially constructed, a similar debate exists regarding ethnicity.[9] Primordialists point to the continuity of features of group identity, such as language and religion, as items that are culturally rather than genetically transmitted across generations. As such, irrespective of how these came into being, they function, and thus can be treated, as the equivalent of naturalized categories. Indeed, some go so far as to argue that there is a biological basis to ethnicity to the extent that human beings acquire their ethnic status cognitively and their "ethnic cognition is at core primordialist" (Gil-White 1999, 789; more on cognition below). That is, if people are biologically hard-wired to categorize one another in particular ways, then the groups into which they sort themselves can be thought of as primordial.

The common and multi-pronged retort to primordial conceptions of ethnicity is that they are socially constructed.[10] First, ethnic categories have shifted over time. The scale of human organization has grown over time and this has shaped the nature of identification, moving from those who are biological kin to tribe to larger groupings that come to be seen as brethren.[11] Second, elites have often used ethnic appeals instrumentally for social mobilization and thus activated sentiments that are not at the forefront of consciousness in many cases (Brass 1985). Third, individuals in many cases have a choice of group affiliation, can shift their alignment as needed, and thus the politics that emerges is not inherent in any society but an emergent property of aggregated individual choices (Posner 2004, 2005).

Nationality

Finally, the same debate exists regarding nationality and has been characterized as that between perennialists versus modernists (Smith 1986).[12] The former are those who point to long-standing historical nations. They point to the existence of nations before there were states,[13] of even modern

4

states drawing on ethnic origins, and nationality as a core aspect of identity that transcends individuals and generations.[14]

Here too constructivists and modernists fundamentally disagree. They point to the recency of modern nationalism and the self-conscious creation of traditions and rituals in efforts to construct a sense of nationality. There is much evidence of the creation of nation-states and nationality as an emergent identity in the past two centuries (among others, Ben-Israel 1992, 1994). Projects of nation-building are replete with the creation of founding myths, rituals, and a host of created symbols (Hobsbawm and Ranger 1983).[15]

Numerous examples exist of nation-building exercises, of efforts to construct and imprint new categories of identification on residents, on the construction of citizenship. Indeed, citizenship laws themselves vary, and some states use blood ties as the basis for membership.[16] Rwanda provides a recent example of an attempt to reconstruct the bases of identity through citizenship rules and discourse. Initially following independence, citizenship was limited to ethnic Hutus and excluded Tutsis. Following the genocidal conflict of the 1990s, the government has undertaken the construction of a national identity with citizenship based on Rwandanness and the elimination of ethnic differences in public discourse (Buckley-Zistel 2006).

Problems and truths

In short, the scholarly debates about race, ethnicity, and nationality, all reflect a division between primordialists and constructivists. Both schools of thought contain cores of truth, yet remain problematic. On the one hand, primordialists rely on conceptions of ancestry, with race relying on perceived physical features, ethnicity focusing on beliefs and practices culturally transmitted across generations, and nationality dependent on these combined with geographic location. The social groupings of identity and affiliation – race, religion, ethnicity, nationality – have survived centuries and millennia. They are social constructions, but they are rooted in the past, in sustained physical and cultural differences. To suggest that such forms of identification can be reconfigured and recombined as needed at will is to miss a dominant feature of continuity of human communities.

On the other hand, the categories of identification and affiliation are indeterminate and subject to change, to construction and reconstruction. People have multiple characteristics that can be the basis for identity and alignment. Amartya Sen (2006) argues against what he calls the "solitarist" approach to human identity in which individuals belong to just one group. Second, even the features of identity that are transmitted across generations are also subject to transformation. And the multiplicity of bases of identification and affiliation imply that there are multiples axes along which competition might occur and conflict might arise.

Finally, the social constructivist position regarding group identity is reinforced by the social identity approach from psychology, which presumes that people make us-and-them distinctions based on social identity in categorizing themselves. Although the experiments that gave rise to the literature suggested that purely arbitrary group identities could be constructed, "SIT [self-identity theory] argued that intergroup relations were governed by an interaction of cognitive, motivational, and socio-historical considerations" (Hornsey 2008, 207).[17]

In short, race, ethnicity, religion, and nationality are social constructions which typically have roots in long-standing self-conceptions of community.

An alternative formulation: ancestral and instrumental

The features emphasized in the debate, however, point to a different analytic cleavage. On the one hand, there are those who point to affective ties as the bases for cleavage, for conflict and alignment. Such vertical cleavages of race, ethnicity, nationality, and religion provide the affective glue for the construction of community, alignment and interest, while also establishing the bases of difference and conflict. Were political divisions and alignments driven solely by material interest, the horizontal cleavage of class or interest group should dominate. Yet modern politics provides recurrent evidence of the centrality of vertical rather than horizontal cleavages.[18] That is the point that underlies arguments about the long-standing, if not necessarily primordial, character of religious conflict, ethnic conflict, and racial conflict. Characterized in this way, these are conflicts of affect and of identity.[19]

The contrast is with those who point to interests and political mobilization. Conflicts are about competing interests and not conflicting identities. Individuals are mobilized by political appeals by elites interested in emerging triumphant in a contest for power and control. Changing interests imply changing coalitions. This argument is akin to an electoral one of constructing a winning coalition. The necessary components will change as a function of group size and the appeals, or combination of appeals, may change as a function of the requisites for at least a minimum winning coalition.

The contrast can be seen in the bases for political parties. There are parties that are loose coalitions, which in some institutional settings are regularly reconfigured and created to win power. Elites assess the characteristics and interests of their citizens at any point in time and construct mobilization strategies to secure the requisite support to come to, or to stay in, power. In the 1960 election in the US, the electorate was broken down into 480 groups, dramatized in the novel by political scientist, Eugene Burdick (1964). Over time, marketers of products and politicians have divided the US population into dozens of clusters that cut across gender, race, ethnicity, and wealth (Weiss 1988, 2000) and have given us phrases such as narrowcasting and microtargeting. In this view, politicians cobble together coalitions from numerous clusters whose composition is ever changing, and individuals are presumed to vote for the candidates whose policy positions are closest to them. There is no affective component underlying alignment, it is merely a matter of interest.

But there are also parties built on cross-generational affective ties. In some countries, there are ethnic and religious parties, in which deep affective ties are the basis for interest alignments and identity.[20] Even in societies without ethnic and religious parties, one finds ethnic groups, for example, who systematically support one party and whose affective ties to the party are transmitted across generations. More broadly, there is a sociological model of voting in which people are thought to vote their party identification, which is transmitted across generations, and in which they adopt the positions of their party. In such cases, people do not vote their narrow material interests. Rather, the affective tie of party determines one's allies and one's policy positions. This stands in contrast to a political economy view in which interests shape one's party ties, which are merely temporary links of convenience.

The two perspectives can agree that both affect and interest matter, but they disagree on their causal priority. Ancestralists emphasize affect and argue that interests derive from affective bases of identity. Races, religions, ethnicities, and nationalities can have conflicting interests, but those derive from their affective ties. And at any point in time, religion, ethnicity, nationality, and their markers are exogenous and underly interests.

In contrast, instrumentalists emphasize that interests drive identity. Shared interests create categories of identification, but these can be as readily changed as suits of clothing by either the mobilizational efforts of leaders or changing circumstances and how they affect individuals.

Those using an economic or rational choice approach to ethnic conflict require some logic for why the horizontal cleavages of class which underly material divisions and interests are overwhelmed by affective concerns. Bates (2006, 169) argues that "ethnic groups provide low-cost means for rallying constituents". An alternative argument is provided by Esteban and Ray (2008, 2186) who argue that the rich have few material incentives for class conflict while the opportunity costs for engaging in such conflict are high for the poor. In contrast, ethnic alignments sustain within-group economic inequality in which the poor provide the labor and the rich provide the resources for conflict. The result is "a definite bias in favor of ethnic conflict" over class conflict.[21]

Although many couch the debates regarding race, ethnicity, and nationality as conflicts of isms, primordialism versus constructivism, there are those who combine the ancestral and the instrumental. They recognize that race, ethnicity, and nationality are social constructions, many of which are quite modern. But they are built on existing features on which appeals to group identity can be founded. As Gellner (1964, 168) notes, "Nationalism is not the awakening of nations to self-consciousness: it invents nations where they do not exist – but it does need some pre-existing differentiating marks to work on." Put differently, "the social structural environment constitutes what is 'ethnically realizable'" (Arfi 1998, 198).[22]

This has been reinforced by what can be called the cognitive turn. A recognition that people categorize themselves and others and on the basis of some pre-existing attributes has led to a focus on the cognitive underpinnings of identity and affiliation. As Brubaker, Loveman, and Stamatov (2004, 47) put it,

> what cognitive perspectives suggest, in short, is that race, ethnicity, and nation are not things in the world but ways of seeing the world. They are ways of understanding and identifying oneself, making sense of one's problems and predicaments, identifying one's interests, and orienting one's action. They are ways of recognizing, identifying, and classifying other people, of construing sameness and difference, and of 'coding' and making sense of their actions.[23]

A world of regions

The study of ethnicity, like that of religious conflict, state formation, nationalism, modernization, development, governance, democracy, and capitalism, among others, has been affected by the historical experience of modern Europe. Based on this setting, scholars developed a variety of propositions, presumed to be universal, about politics and ethnicity (Bates 2006).

Yet the historical experience outside of Europe differed. Many countries in the world today achieved autonomy and independence only after centuries of European colonization and settlement.[24] Their borders and institutions are external creations and their path to their contemporary condition historically foreshortened. Just as scholars contrast late industrializers to initial industrializers, so too it is important to assess independently the experience of late state-developers, late nationalizers, and late democratizers.

Analysing the politics of ethnicity in areas that have achieved their independence recently provides fertile grounds for assessing the viability of new social constructions and the continuing impact of the ancestral (and how far back it extends). It makes possible an assessment of universal elements of political organization and competition as well as that of the combination of circumstances and features that are characterized as unique. The Middle East and the Asian cases of Indonesia and India provide an opportunity to assess the impact of both intra-religious and inter-religious conflict on ethnic politics and conflict.

Contributions

The articles in this special issue delineate the implications of both the ancestral and instrumental, of the affective and material, bases of ethnicity.

Ancestral communal identities pose a challenge to international politics. In many instances, national boundaries do not circumscribe ethnic and religious communities. And in such cases, Arthur Stein points out in "Ethnicity, Extraterritoriality, and International Conflict", it is not unusual for interstate relations to reflect more than the pursuit of narrow state survival, as in the realist argument that states define survival as the maintenance of the physical and territorial integrity of the state. Rather, those who control the state pursue extraterritorial interests on behalf of ethnic kin or co-religionists. In such cases, they define the core interest of the country to be the survival of a transnational community and not merely the maintenance of the physical and territorial integrity of the state. Although realist arguments can be provided for supporting particular factions in other countries, the pursuit of extraterritorial concerns on behalf of those seen as communal brethren constitutes a case in which ancestral affiliation defines identity and drives interest. As Stein also notes, people are willing to fight and die on behalf of those seen as kin and in order to transmit cultural values, and implicitly not on behalf of purely material interests.

In contrast, Daniel Posner, in "When and Why Do Some Social Cleavages Become Politically Salient Rather than Others?", articulates a model of political competition in which individuals have a repertoire of identities, which are both situational and instrumental. Individuals choose the social identity which lands them in a group with the highest return that is also part of a minimum winning political coalition. In Posner's parsimonious model, social identity is not about affect or a product of deep attachments, rather it is about the utility of a mobilizable coalition (as also in Posner 2004, 2005), which is solely a function of its relative size in a particular political setting. One implication of Posner's analysis is that the "depth of attachment may be more productively viewed as a product of identity mobilization rather than as a prior, innate condition that can be treated as an input to the identity choices we observe", and thus "group labels become simply conveyors of information about the coalition to which a person belongs".

At the extreme, constructivists and instrumentalists argue that ethnic groups and ethnic attachments are endogenous to the political process. Posner's claim is more limited. First, at any point in time, people already have pre-existing categories of social identification and thus the issue is one of the salience of cultural difference and social cleavages and the limited recombination of alignments and categories that are possible. Central to his argument is the assumption that powerholders share, or are believed to share, resources with only members of their own social group (evidence of this is in Horowitz 1985 and Posner 2005), because this excludes the possibility of cross-group coalitions.[25]

One implication of the kind of instrumental approach described by Posner is that changes in the institutional rules of representation change the nature of political alignment and both identification and interest. Rebecca Kook, in "Representation, Minorities and Electoral Reform: The Case of the Palestinian Minority in Israel", shows that a change in the electoral threshold for representation in Israel provided an incentive for the unification of what had been smaller minority parties representing Palestinians. But she shows that this did more than change the *form of representation*, but also the very *claims of representation*. A change in the rules had the instrumental impact of leading to a more inclusive representational form which in turn resulted in more inclusive claims which reflected more of Palestinian society in Israel.

Communal competition can lead to ethnic conflicts which become violent, and at the extreme, result in civil war. Such conflicts demonstrate in a heightened sense the impact of affect, interest, and the organizations that embody them. The communal divisions and conflicts that characterize Lebanon resulted in a prolonged civil war and a tense postwar settlement. In "The Paradox of Powersharing: Stability and Fragility in Postwar Lebanon", Amanda Rizkallah focuses on the strength and longevity of the organizations that have represented different sectarian communities in Lebanon during and after the civil war. She demonstrates that postwar power sharing arrangements that simply leave intact the representational arms of previously warring communities simply retain sectarian networks and sow the possibility for mobilization and subsequent violence. Violent conflict presupposes more than competing communities, but also the organizations and resources that can be marshaled in a confrontation. Sectarian communities that fought successfully with their own militias in a civil war retain their resources and bases of support in a powersharing arrangement that ends the civil war. In contrast, new political post-conflict constructions (i.e. new political parties) have neither the resources nor the mobilizational possibilities of more long-standing sectarian associations. This difference gets played out in any subsequent crisis or conflict that arises.

Not only can individuals select from a multiplicity of social identities, but when conflicts occur in such a setting, there are multiple possibilities for framing the conflicts. This implication of competing frames for conflict is addressed in Kirsten Schulze's paper, "The 'Ethnic' in Indonesia's Communal Conflicts: Violence in Ambon, Poso and Sambas". Communal conflicts broke out around the same time in three Indonesian provinces, all evinced ethnic targeting and motivation, and were all initially characterized as ethnic conflicts. In the conflicts that were sustained, non-Muslims advanced an ethnic narrative, while Muslims advanced a religious narrative and in both cases one of the reasons was the way in which the regional conflicts would be seen and the implications for wider support from within Indonesia. The arrival of outside fighters served to recast the conflict as a narrative of religious conflict which better served the interests of elites than one of ethnic conflict. Both communities adopted a religious frame as one side sought support from Muslims from other parts of Indonesia and as Christians looked for support from the international community. Schulze shows that in situations in which multiple attributions and narratives are possible, there is a strategic element in the framing of a conflict.

Even in regions with a common religion (and ethnicity), deeply rooted ideological and affective differences can create profound cleavages, competing visions of the past, and deep and violent political conflicts. In "Changing Islam, Changing the World: Contrasting Visions within Political Islam", Eli Alshech and Nimrod Hurvitz assess disputes among Muslim movements in Muslim-majority states and characterize a profound religious schism between moderates and militants. The two are distinguished by their views of the legitimacy of using violence to achieve social and political change, and also by their attitudes towards non-Muslim social and political institutions, such as "modern states, political parties, the contemporary global order, or pre-Islamic social entities such as tribes and ethnic groups". These ideological differences, between "violent purifiers" who reject Western ideas and espouse violence to reform society and "pacific unifiers" who accept ideas such as political parties and reject violence, are rooted in competing religious interpretations and views of the past that go back to the founding of the religion. Islam always had to deal with "pre-Islamic ethnic and tribal worldviews and loyalties", and in modern times has also had to confront the challenge of non-Muslim institutions. Not only has the acceptability of political parties and democracy been contested, but so have nationalism and international institutions, including international law. Alshech and Hurvitz bring into stark relief the relationship between religion and ethnicity in the Middle East and North Africa, and the religious cleavages that shape political contestation in the region. They highlight areas in which Muslim movements have made their accommodations with modern realities, and which groups and on what issues have fundamentally rejected the possibility of adapting to both the ancient realities of tribe and the modern realities of states and parties.

Gender is a basis for interest and mobilization and yet is typically subordinated to the vertical cleavages of race, ethnicity, religion, and nation. In "Gendering Ethnic Conflicts: Minority Women in Divided Societies and the Case of Muslim Women in India", Ayelet Harel-Shalev brings this into stark relief in her analysis of women in India. She demonstrates that the cleavage between

Hindus and Muslims predominated in post-colonial India and that there was a failure to incorporate women's interests in post-colonial negotiations.

Moreover, she points out that ethnic conflicts are often resolved through the provision of group rights for previously suppressed ethnic communities, and that this often subordinates the individual rights of women. Although the conflict between Hindus and Muslims in India was not in general resolved by providing group rights, religious autonomy was guaranteed and thus each community retained its distinct approach to family law and no uniform civil code was adopted.[26] The result adversely affected the interests of women. Religion trumped gender and women had to fight within their respective communities for their rights.

Ethnicity and conflict regulation

The contributions in this special issue highlight the roles of affect and interest not only in ethnic conflict, but in the prospects and possibilities for ethnic conflict resolution and regulation. *"Structural prevention strategies* … includ[ing] electoral system design, autonomy arrangements, [and] power-sharing arrangements", have been proffered as policies for mitigating, if not resolving, conflict (Bennett, Stern, and Walker 2003, 89). Yet with each solution, the divisions that are the basis of conflict remain and bedevil efforts at conflict resolution.

Partition has been recommended as a way of resolving inter-communal conflict. The argument is plausible in as much as most conflict in the world is intra-state rather than inter-state and this suggests that the problem of deterring war between states has been resolved and the problem that remains is that of preventing internal conflict between factions. Transforming inter-communal conflicts into inter-state ones via partition then has a certain appeal. The contributions in this issue point out obvious problems with partition. Posner notes that partitions simply redistribute the number and distribution of groups within any society. This does not do away with cleavages but simply changes them. Moreover, given the multiplicity of identities and the heterogeneity of population distributions, partition is likely to still result in the existence of communities splayed across borders and this raises the extra-territorial concerns for co-ethnics and co-religionists discussed in the Stein article.

Much the same can be said of changes in institutional rules. These too transform the nature of mobilizational strategies and alignments, but these are built on existing bases of identity and affect. In Posner's analysis and in Kook's, changes in institutional rules change ethnic alignment, but the ethnic identities remain. Kook's analysis of the emergence of a unified Arab party in Israel in the wake of a change in the electoral rules provides an example. What do not emerge are the kind of coalitions across group lines that are evident in societies with little evident ethnic competition and conflict.[27]

Power sharing is also considered to be one of the most prominent solutions for ethnic conflicts in deeply divided societies (Lijphart 1968). Yet power sharing agreements retain and reinforce the very divisions that led to conflict and which power sharing is intended to ameliorate and resolve. Rizkallah's analysis emphasizes how power-sharing agreements enabled participation of militias-turned-parties in politics, which gave them access to state resources, but left their population networks and organizations intact. Powersharing between armed communities leaves intact the very organizational structures that sustained violence during a civil war.

Another structural strategy for ethnic conflict is the provision of autonomy. The assumption is that grievances of particular communities can be politically assuaged by the provision of a degree of community control. This solution simply maintains and sustains the cleavages and bases of mobilization in the hope of avoiding direct inter-communal conflict. Yet this can function in much the same way as a partition, simply refocusing power disparities, cleavages, and alignments to those within each area of autonomous community control. Harel-Shalev's argument about the subordination of gender concerns in family law through the provision of autonomy to the conservative Muslim elite, provides one example.[28]

Conclusion

Political mobilization draws on both affect and interest. Self-interested political entrepreneurs use the resources available to them to animate the support of individuals. Affective attachments of ethnicity and religion both generate group interests on their own, but also prove useful as bases for political mobilization. Thus, even as elites can select from a range of extant social identities with which to mobilize and are able to reconfigure and recombine them at the margins, they also use the affective sentiments of group identity and not purely material incentives.

Notes

1. There is a "fluidity between the conceptual borders" of race, ethnicity, and nationality (Morning 2008, 242) and ethnicity has replaced race (Fenton 2010) and also often subsumes religion and region as well. Moreover, "the boundary between nationalism and ethnicity remains ill-defined" (Bates 2006, 167).
2. For boundary making in constructing identity, see Barth (1969), Eisenstadt and Giesen (1995), and Wimmer (2008).

3. In noting the ill-defined boundary between ethnicity and nationalism, Bates (2006, 168) notes that "the logic mobilised by the students of the one often parallels that invoked by students of the other".

4. Primordialism is an unfortunate term for something long-standing and even naturalistic, for the word technically means something existing from the beginning of time, and no primordialist actually means that.

5. See the discussion in Gil-White (1999) for the evolution of the views of anthropologists regarding ethnicity.

6. The factual challenge is subject to empirical results and a vigorous debate continues to rage among geneticists as to whether race is a useful category, with arguments about how measures of genetic similarity and genetic variation are to be assessed in determining whether there is such a thing as race and its utility in various fields (Jorde and Wooding 2004). For entry into this debate, see Andreasen (1998, 2000, 2005), Glasgow (2003), Sesardic (2010), Smaje (1997), Smedley and Smedley (2005), and Yudell et al. (2016). Using genetic similarity and variation to define a race, Ostrer (2012) concludes that Jews are a race, a view that can be seen as quite troubling and contested (Lebens 2012).

7. Although the racial and ethnic enumeration practices of countries vary, the practice remains widespread (Kertzer and Arel 2002; Morning 2008).

8. The process has been criticized and politicized and each recent census has made changes. For an assessment by a former head of the census, see Prewitt (2013).

9. For reviews of the extensive literature on ethnicity, see, in addition to items referenced elsewhere in this article, Calhoun (1993), Chandra (2006), Cordell and Wolff (2016), Kaufmann (2005), Varshney (2007), and Yinger (1985).

10. See the essays in Chandra (2012).

11. This occurs either in how individuals identify themselves, or how others identify them, or both.

12. For the subtle difference between Smith's distinction and that between primordialism and instrumentalism, see Conversi (2007).

13. There are many examples of people who see themselves as nations and are in search of a state (Rosecrance and Stein 2006a). Moreover, nations pre-existed modern nationalism (Armstrong 1982).

14. For this position, Walker Connor (1978, 1992, 1993, 1994, 2004) and Anthony Smith (1986, 1989, 1991, 1994, 2004) are critical figures, only some of whose works are referenced here. In addition, among others, see Gat with Yakobson (2013) and Roshwald (2006).

15. The predominant view of nationalism as a social construction is in Anderson (1983), Gellner (1983), and Hobsbawm (1990).

16. On citizenship rules and identity, see, among others, Brubaker (1992).

17. In a famous set of experiments, psychologists assigned participants to purely arbitrary groups, ones that had no history, would have no future, and in which individuals did not know who else was in the group and with whom they had no interaction. Nevertheless, participants allocated more of some distributable resource to members of their own group. There was an evolution in the analytic arguments made to explain the results. Henri Tajfel (1978) settled on an argument he called social identity theory, and his student John Turner extended it in social categorization theory (Turner et al. 1987). For reviews see Ellemers and Haslam (2012), Hogg (2006), and Turner and Reynolds (2012), and for a critical examination see Huddy (2001). The two are quite similar and can usefully be characterized as the social identity approach (Hornsey 2008).

Numerous experiments by economists and psychologists have sought to assess the bases of group discrimination. For a meta-analysis of the experiments done by economists, see Lane (2016).

18. At the outbreak of the First World War, for example, workers of the world did not unite, but fought for their nation-states.

19. In addition to material interests, identity concerns include dignity, self-respect, and recognition (Varshney 2003), as well as linguistic and cultural interests.

20. Even if such parties reflect the manipulative self-interested mobilizational choices of politicians, they make use of affective ties for their impact.

21. It may also be that the class or ethnic basis of preference differs by issue area and its assessment is affected by the prospect for preference falsification (Corstange 2013).

22. Or as Eisenstadt (2002, 40) puts it, elites engage in the "activation of the predispositions to and search for some such order which are inherent, even if not fully articulated, among all, or at least most, people". Also see Geary (2002).

23. Whereas Brubaker, Loveman, and Stamatov (2004) see the cognitive turn as a result of the triumph of constructivism and the view that classification is inherently subjective, Gil-White (2001) argues that cognitively individuals are essentialists.

24. This led to a scholarly shift that is broadly evident not only in the analytic approach and substantive focus of many scholars, but even the labels of "post-colonial" and "decolonial" theory adopted by those with the aim of "decentering" the West.

25. Cross-group alignments being an implication of the argument about clustering in US politics (Weiss 1988, 2000).

26. For more on autonomy and family law/personal law, see Harel-Shalev (2009), and Stopler (2007).

27. For the argument about the role of cross-cutting cleavages in reducing social conflict, see Coser (1956), Lipset (1960), and the more recent empirical contribution of Dunning and Harrison (2010).

28. The provision to Scotland, at the time of unification, of autonomy in matters of law and religion, provided the groundwork for a subsequent renewal of Scottish nationalism centuries later (Rosecrance and Stein 2006b).

Acknowledgements

We thank the contributors as well as Paul Brass, Vinay Lal, David Newman, Joel Peters, Oren Yiftachel, and Dror Ze'evi.

Disclosure statement

No potential conflict of interest was reported by the authors.

Funding

Thanks to the Sol Leshin Program for Ben-Gurion University of the Negev-UCLA Academic Cooperation and the UCLA Academic Senate for financial support.

ORCID

Arthur A. Stein ⓘ http://orcid.org/0000-0002-1955-2898
Ayelet Harel-Shalev ⓘ http://orcid.org/0000-0001-9502-0095

References

Afshari, R., and R. S. Bhopal. 2002. "Changing Pattern of Use of 'Ethnicity' and 'Race' in Scientific Literature." *International Journal of Epidemiology* 31 (5): 1074.

Afshari, Reza, and Raj S. Bhopal. 2010. "Ethnicity Has Overtaken Race in Medical Science: Medline-Based Comparison of Trends in the USA and the Rest of the World, 1965–2005." *International Journal of Epidemiology* 39 (6): 1682–1683.

Ahmad, Farah Z., and Jamal Hagler. 2015. "The Evolution of Race and Ethnicity Classifications in the Decennial Census." Center for American Progress, February 6. https://www.americanprogress.org/issues/race/news/2015/02/06/102798/the-evolution-of-race-and-ethnicity-classifications-in-the-decennial-census/

Anderson, Benedict R. 1983. *Imagined Communities: Reflections on the Origin and Spread of Nationalism*. London: Verso.

Andreasen, Robin O. 1998. "A New Perspective on the Race Debate." *British Journal for the Philosophy of Science* 49 (2): 199–225.

Andreasen, Robin O. 2000. "Race: Biological Reality or Social Construct?" *Philosophy of Science* 67 (Supplement): S653–S666.

Andreasen, Robin O. 2005. "The Meaning of 'Race': Folk Conceptions and the New Biology of Race." *Journal of Philosophy* 102 (2): 94–106.

Arfi, Badredine. 1998. "Ethnic Fear: The Social Construction of Insecurity." *Security Studies* 8 (1): 151–203.

Armstrong, John A. 1982. *Nations Before Nationalism*. Chapel Hill: University of North Carolina Press.

Banton, Michael. 1998. *Racial Theories*. 2nd ed. Cambridge: Cambridge University Press.

Barth, Fredrik, ed. 1969. *Ethnic Groups and Boundaries: The Social Organization of Culture Difference*. London: Allen & Unwin.

Bates, Robert H. 2006. "Ethnicity." In *The Elgar Companion to Development Studies*, edited by David Alexander Clark, 167–173. Northampton, MA: Edward Elgar Pub.

Ben-Israel, Hedva. 1992. "Nationalism in Historical Perspective." *Journal of International Affairs* 45 (2): 367–397.

Ben-Israel, Hedva. 1994. "Nationalism: Animal, Vegetable, Mineral, or Cultural?" *Australian Journal of Politics & History* 40 (s1): 134–143.

Bennett, Andrew, Paul C. Stern, and Edward W. Walker. 2003. "A Typology of Identity Conflicts for Comparative Research." In *Conflict and Reconstruction in Multiethnic Societies: Proceedings of a Russian-American Workshop*, edited by National Research Council, 86–92. Washington, DC: National Academies Press.

Bhopal, Raj. 1997. "Is Research Into Ethnicity and Health Racist, Unsound, or Important Science?" *BMJ: British Medical Journal* 314 (7096): 1751–1756.

Bhopal, Raj. 2004. "Glossary of Terms Relating to Ethnicity and Race: For Reflection and Debate." *Journal of Epidemiology and Community Health* 58 (6): 441–445.

Brass, Paul R., ed. 1985. *Ethnic Groups and the State*. Totowa, NJ: Barnes & Noble Books.

Brubaker, Rogers. 1992. *Citizenship and Nationhood in France and Germany*. Cambridge, MA: Harvard University Press.

Brubaker, Rogers. 2009. "Ethnicity, Race, and Nationalism." *Annual Review of Sociology* 35: 21–42.

Brubaker, Rogers, Mara Loveman, and Peter Stamatov. 2004. "Ethnicity as Cognition." *Theory and Society* 33 (1): 31–64.

Buckley-Zistel, Susanne. 2006. "Dividing and Uniting: The Use of Citizenship Discourses in Conflict and Reconciliation in Rwanda." *Global Society* 20 (1): 101–113.

Burdick, Eugene. 1964. *The 480.* New York, NY: McGraw-Hill.

Calhoun, Craig. 1993. "Nationalism and Ethnicity." *Annual Review of Sociology* 19: 211–239.

Chandra, Kanchan. 2006. "What is Ethnic Identity and Does it Matter?" *Annual Review of Political Science* 9: 397–424.

Chandra, Kanchan, ed. 2012. *Constructivist Theories of Ethnic Politics.* New York: Oxford University Press.

Chaturvedi, Nish. 2001. "Ethnicity as an Epidemiological Determinant – Crudely Racist or Crucially Important?" *International Journal of Epidemiology* 30 (5): 925–927.

Connor, Walker. 1978. "A Nation Is a Nation, Is a State, Is an Ethnic Group Is a … ." *Ethnic and Racial Studies* 1 (4): 377–400.

Connor, Walker. 1992. "The Nation and Its Myth." *International Journal of Comparative Sociology* 33 (1–2): 48–57.

Connor, Walker. 1993. "Beyond Reason: The Nature of the Ethnonational Bond." *Ethnic and Racial Studies* 16 (3): 373–389.

Connor, Walker. 1994. *Ethnonationalism: The Quest for Understanding.* Princeton, NJ: Princeton University Press.

Connor, Walker. 2004. "The Timelessness of Nations." *Nations and Nationalism* 10 (1–2): 35–47.

Conversi, Daniele. 2007. "Mapping the Field: Theories of Nationalism and the Ethnosymbolic Approach." In *Nationalism and Ethnosymbolism: History, Culture and Ethnicity in the Formation of Nations*, edited by Athena S. Leoussi, and Steven Grosby, 15–30. Edinburgh: Edinburgh University Press.

Cordell, Karl, and Stefan Wolff, eds. 2016. *The Routledge Handbook of Ethnic Conflict.* 2nd ed, London: Routledge, Taylor & Francis Group.

Corstange, Daniel. 2013. "Ethnicity on the Sleeve and Class in the Heart." *British Journal of Political Science* 43 (4): 889–914.

Coser, Lewis A. 1956. *The Functions of Social Conflict.* Glencoe, IL: Free Press.

Dunning, Thad, and Lauren Harrison. 2010. "Cross-Cutting Cleavages and Ethnic Voting: An Experimental Study of Cousinage in Mali." *American Political Science Review* 104 (1): 21–39.

Eisenstadt, S. N. 2002. "The Construction of Collective Identities and the Continual Reconstruction of Primordiality." In *Making Sense of Collectivity: Ethnicity, Nationalism, and Globalisation*, edited by Siniša Malešević, and Mark Haugaard, 33–87. London: Pluto Press.

Eisenstadt, Shmuel Noah, and Bernhard Giesen. 1995. "The Construction of Collective Identity." *European Journal of Sociology* 36 (1): 72–102.

Ellemers, Naomi, and S. Alexander Haslam. 2012. "Social Identity Theory." In *Handbook of Theories of Social Psychology*, edited by Paul A. M. Van Lange, Arie W. Kruglanski and E. Tory Higgins, vol. 2, 379–398. Los Angeles, CA: SAGE Publications.

Esteban, Joan, and Debraj Ray. 2008. "On the Salience of Ethnic Conflict." *American Economic Review* 98 (5): 2185–2202.

Fenton, Steve. 2010. *Ethnicity.* 2nd ed. Cambridge: Polity Press.

Gat, Azar, with Alexander Yakobson. 2013. *Nations: The Long History and Deep Roots of Political Ethnicity and Nationalism.* Cambridge: Cambridge University Press.

Geary, Patrick J. 2002. *The Myth of Nations: The Medieval Origins of Europe*. Princeton, NJ: Princeton University Press.

Gellner, Ernest. 1964. *Thought and Change*. London: Weidenfeld and Nicolson.

Gellner, Ernest. 1983. *Nations and Nationalism*. Ithaca, NY: Cornell University Press.

Gil-White, Francisco J. 1999. "How Thick is Blood? The Plot Thickens … : If Ethnic Actors Are Primordialists, What Remains of the Circumstantialist / Primordialist Controversy?" *Ethnic and Racial Studies* 22 (5): 789–820.

Gil-White, Francisco J. 2001. "Are Ethnic Groups Biological "Species" to the Human Brain?: Essentialism in Our Cognition of Some Social Categories." *Current Anthropology* 42 (4): 515–536.

Glasgow, Joshua M. 2003. "On the New Biology of Race." *Journal of Philosophy* 100 (9): 456–474.

Gracia, Jorge J. E. 2007. "Race or Ethnicity?: An Introduction." In *Race or Ethnicity? On Black and Latino Identity*, edited by Jorge J. E. Gracia, 1–16. Ithaca, NY: Cornell University Press.

Harel-Shalev, Ayelet. 2009. "The Problematic Nature of Religious Autonomy to Minorities in Democracies – the Case of India's Muslims." *Democratization* 16 (6): 1261–1281.

Hobsbawm, E. J. 1990. *Nations and Nationalism Since 1780: Programme, Myth, Reality*. Cambridge: Cambridge University Press.

Hobsbawm, Eric, and Terence Ranger, eds. 1983. *The Invention of Tradition*. Cambridge: Cambridge University Press.

Hogg, Michael A. 2006. "Social Identity Theory." In *Contemporary Social Psychological Theories*, edited by Peter J. Burke, 111–136. Stanford, CA: Stanford University Press.

Hornsey, Matthew J. 2008. "Social Identity Theory and Self-Categorization Theory: A Historical Review." *Social and Personality Psychology Compass* 2 (1): 204–222.

Horowitz, Donald L. 1985. *Ethnic Groups in Conflict*. Berkeley: University of California Press.

Huddy, Leonie. 2001. "From Social to Political Identity: A Critical Examination of Social Identity Theory." *Political Psychology* 22 (1): 127–156.

Jorde, Lynn B., and Stephen P. Wooding. 2004. "Genetic Variation, Classification and 'Race'." *Nature Genetics* 36 (11 Supp.): S28–S33.

Kaufmann, Chaim. 2005. "Rational Choice and Progress in the Study of Ethnic Conflict: A Review Essay." *Security Studies* 14 (1): 178–207.

Kertzer, David I., and Dominique Arel, eds. 2002. *Census and Identity: The Politics of Race, Ethnicity, and Language in National Census*. Cambridge: Cambridge University Press.

Lane, Tom. 2016. "Discrimination in the Laboratory: A Meta-Analysis of Economics Experiments." *European Economic Review* 90: 375–402.

Lebens, Samuel. 2012. "Jews Are Not a Race, but a Nation." *Haaretz*, June 14.

Lijphart, Arend. 1968. *The Politics of Accommodation: Pluralism and Democracy in the Netherlands*. Berkeley: University of California Press.

Lipset, Seymour Martin. 1960. *Political Man: The Social Bases of Politics*. Garden City, NY: Doubleday.

Morning, Ann. 2008. "Ethnic Classification in Global Perspective: A Cross-National Survey of the 2000 Census Round." *Population Research and Policy Review* 27 (2): 239–272.

Ostrer, Harry. 2012. *Legacy: A Genetic History of the Jewish People*. New York: Oxford University Press.

Posner, Daniel N. 2004. "The Political Salience of Cultural Difference: Why Chewas and Tumbukas Are Allies in Zambia and Adversaries in Malawi." *American Political Science Review* 98 (4): 529–545.

Posner, Daniel N. 2005. *Institutions and Ethnic Politics in Africa.* Cambridge: Cambridge University Press.

Prewitt, Kenneth. 2013. *What is Your Race? The Census and Our Flawed Efforts to Classify Americans.* Princeton, NJ: Princeton University Press.

Rosecrance, Richard N., and Arthur A. Stein, eds. 2006a. *No More States? Globalization, National Self-Determination, and Terrorism.* Lanham, MD: Rowman & Littlefield Publishers.

Rosecrance, Richard N., and Arthur A. Stein. 2006b. "The Dilemma of Devolution and Federalism: Secessionary Nationalism and the Case of Scotland." In *No More States?: Globalization, National Self-Determination, and Terrorism,* edited by Richard N. Rosecrance, and Arthur A. Stein, 235–245. Lanham, MD: Rowman & Littlefield Publishers.

Roshwald, Aviel. 2006. *The Endurance of Nationalism: Ancient Roots and Modern Dilemmas.* Cambridge: Cambridge University Press.

Sen, Amartya. 2006. *Identity and Violence: The Illusion of Destiny.* New York, NY: W. W. Norton & Co.

Sesardic, Neven. 2010. "Race: A Social Destruction of a Biological Concept." *Biology & Philosophy* 25 (2): 143–162.

Smaje, Chris. 1997. "Not Just a Social Construct: Theorising Race and Ethnicity." *Sociology* 31 (2): 307–327.

Smedley, Audrey, and Brian D. Smedley. 2005. "Race as Biology is Fiction, Racism as a Social Problem is Real: Anthropological and Historical Perspectives on the Social Construction of Race." *American Psychologist* 60 (1): 16–26.

Smith, Anthony D. 1986. *The Ethnic Origins of Nations.* London: Blackwell Publishing.

Smith, Anthony D. 1989. "The Origins of Nations." *Ethnic and Racial Studies* 12 (3): 340–367.

Smith, Anthony D. 1991. *National Identity.* London: Penguin Books.

Smith, Anthony D. 1994. "The Problem of National Identity: Ancient, Medieval and Modern." *Ethnic and Racial Studies* 17 (3): 375–399.

Smith, Anthony D. 2004. *The Antiquity of Nations.* Cambridge: Polity.

Stopler, Gila. 2007. "Contextualizing Multiculturalism: A Three Dimensional Examination of Multicultural Claims." *Journal of Law and Ethics of Human Rights* 1 (1): 309–353.

Tajfel, Henri, ed. 1978. *Differentiation Between Social Groups: Studies in the Social Psychology of Intergroup Relations.* London: Academic Press.

Turner, John C., Michael A. Hogg, J. Oakes Penelope, Stephen D. Reicher, and Margaret S. Wetherell. 1987. *Rediscovering the Social Group: Self-Categorization Theory.* New York: B. Blackwell.

Turner, John C., and Katherine J. Reynolds. 2012. "Self-Categorization Theory." In *Handbook of Theories of Social Psychology,* edited by Paul A. M. Van Lange, Arie W. Kruglanski, and E. Tory Higgins, vol. 2, 399–417. Los Angeles: SAGE Publications.

Varshney, Ashutosh. 2003. "Nationalism, Ethnic Conflict, and Rationality." *Perspectives on Politics* 1 (1): 85–99.

Varshney, Ashutosh. 2007. "Ethnicity and Ethnic Conflict." In *The Oxford Handbook of Comparative Politics,* edited by Carles Boix and Susan Carol Stokes, 274–294. Oxford: Oxford University Press.

Weiss, Michael J. 1988. *The Clustering of America.* New York, NY: Harper & Row.

Weiss, Michael J. 2000. *The Clustered World: How We Live, What We Buy, and What it All Means About Who We Are*. Boston, MA: Little, Brown.

Wimmer, Andreas. 2008. "The Making and Unmaking of Ethnic Boundaries: A Multilevel Process Theory." *American Journal of Sociology* 113 (4): 970–1022.

Yinger, J. Milton. 1985. "Ethnicity." *Annual Review of Sociology* 11: 151–180.

Yudell, Michael, Dorothy Roberts, Rob DeSalle, and Sarah Tishkoff. 2016. "Taking Race Out of Human Genetics." *Science* 351 (6273): 564–565.

When and why do some social cleavages become politically salient rather than others?

Daniel N. Posner

ABSTRACT

Building on Posner (Posner, Daniel N. 2005. *Institutions and Ethnic Politics in Africa*. New York: Cambridge University Press), this article describes a framework for organizing the information about a community's social cleavage structure so as to identify the incentives that individuals face to adopt particular social identities. The framework is parsimonious but powerful: it generates predictions about the social cleavages that will emerge as salient in politics, the lobbying we can expect to see regarding the social categories with which community members should identify, and the attempts that will be made to assimilate or engage in "identity entrepreneurship" to fashion entirely new social identities. The framework also clarifies why partition is unlikely to be a remedy for intractable ethnic conflicts.

Conflicts and controversies can arise out of a great variety of relationships in the social structure, but only a few of these tend to polarize the politics of any given system. There is a hierarchy of cleavage bases in each system and these orders of political primacy not only vary among polities, but also tend to undergo changes over time. Such differences and changes in the political weight of sociocultural cleavages set fundamental problems for comparative research: When is religion, language or ethnicity most likely to prove polarizing? When will class take the primacy and when will denominational commitments and religious identities prove equally important cleavage bases? … Questions such as these will be on the agenda of comparative political sociology for years to come. There is no dearth of hypotheses, but so far very little in the way of systematic analysis.
– Lipset and Rokkan, Cleavage Structures, Party Systems and Voter Alignments (1967)

Individuals possess multiple social identities, and societies can accordingly be divided in terms of multiple bases of social cleavage. This raises a critical question: Under what circumstances do political competition and social conflict come to be organized along the lines of one cleavage rather than another? When does politics revolve around religion rather than language? When is a society's fundamental basis of social division rooted in differences of race rather than country of origin? When does conflict manifest itself along lines of tribe rather than sub-tribe or clan?

Lipset and Rokkan (1967) posed this question nearly fifty years ago and, as they predicted, it remains central to the agenda of comparative political sociology to this day. Some who have tackled the question have located their answers, as Lipset and Rokkan did, in the gyre of history. For these authors, the salience of particular social cleavages depends on the stage of historical development in which the political system happens to be located at the time (e.g. Kronenberg and Wimmer 2012). Others have pointed to the impact of colonial institutions in reifying particular social cleavages over others (e.g. Laitin 1986). Still others have emphasized the emotions attached to particular social cleavages that render them stable (Petersen 2012) or the innate characteristics of particular groups that make attachments to them particularly strong (Horowitz 1985) or that make cross-group differences particularly salient (Sambanis and Shayo 2013). A large number of scholars have, following Schattschneider (1960) and the foundational work of Tajfel et al. (1971), located their answers in the competition inherent in politics. These authors emphasize how the struggle for political power and public resources generates incentives for political actors to embrace or discard particular social distinctions in order to win elections (e.g. Bates 1983; Brass 1991; Chandra 2004; van der Veen and Laitin 2012).

The approach outlined here, which draws on and expands upon the discussion in Posner (2005), adopts this expressly instrumentalist and political orientation. Where it goes beyond other work in this vein – and where it distinguishes itself sharply from primordialist and constructivist approaches to identity politics – is by expressly laying out the implications of the insight that communal groups can be thought of as political coalitions mobilized to secure political power and public resources (Bates 1983).[1] The characterization of communal groups as political coalitions is usually deployed as a metaphor to underscore the tendency for social identities to be politicized. The contribution here is to take this approach literally and to trace the implications for both individual-level actions and society-level outcomes of viewing social identities in this manner. The result is an analysis that goes beyond the constructivist recognition that social identities can change to identify the conditions under which they will, the forms they will take, and the actors who will support and oppose these changes.

To do this, I employ a tool called a social identity matrix to organize the available information about a polity's social cleavage structure. As I show, the tool can be used to identify the incentives individuals face to adopt particular identities and to generate predictions about the social cleavages that will emerge as salient. The power of the framework is that it also provides insights into the lobbying we can expect to observe for the adoption or rejection of particular identities, as well as who is most likely to be engaged in such lobbying. It also generates predictions about the types of individuals who will be most likely to engage in "identity entrepreneurship" – attempts to create novel attachments, and novel social divisions, that might organize the polity in new ways. By pinpointing who stands to lose from the identity-based conflict, the approach also helps us to identify individuals who will have incentives to change their group memberships and hence generates predictions about the social boundaries that are likely to become contested.[2]

Generating these predictions requires accepting certain assumptions about what individuals value and how the political system is structured. However, these assumptions are consistent with considerable empirical evidence and accurately describe the real-world settings in which many individuals find themselves. Moreover, accepting these assumptions generates substantial payoffs for our understanding of identity politics. The objective is not to suggest that the framework described here provides the only way to think about why some social identities or cleavages become salient rather than others. The goal is to provide a simple, parsimonious way of thinking about social identity that, notwithstanding it spare foundations, provides powerful insights into the dynamics of identity politics.

A particular benefit of the approach is the illumination it provides regarding the (likely un-) usefulness of partition as a solution to ethnic conflict. By clarifying how changing the boundaries of the political arena alters the kinds of identities that become socially and politically salient, the social identity matrix shows how dividing a socially diverse polity into homogeneous new states is not likely to solve the problem of communal conflict. The approach makes it clear that as soon as the boundaries of the political arena change, actors' incentives change too, and this will give rise to new cleavages in the post-partitioned states. All that partition will do is shift the locus of competition and conflict from one dimension of social cleavage to another. Whether this alters the intensity of the conflict depends on the nature of the intergroup competition on each cleavage dimension, but partition itself will do nothing to change the inevitability of group competition itself.

Some preliminaries

The framework outlined in this article is built around a conceptualization of social identity as fluid and situation-bound. It assumes that individuals possess repertoires of identities whose relevance depends on the context in which the individuals find themselves. It assumes further that social identities are not just situational but instrumental: context affects not just how individuals understand who they are; it also affects the strategic calculations they make about which identity, if adopted, will generate the highest payoffs.[3]

What, then, determines the payoffs for a given identity choice? Although the rewards of membership in particular groups run the spectrum from material benefits such as access to jobs to non-material advantages such as prestige, social acceptance, or protection against shunning, the approach adopted here focuses on just one factor: the size of the group that the identity defines. The framework assumes that individuals will choose the identity that conveys membership in the group that, by virtue of its size vis-à-vis other groups, puts them in a minimum winning political coalition – and thus in a position to maximize their consumption of state resources. In sharp contrast to accounts that explain identity choices by invoking the deep attachments individuals have to particular social categories, the account here emphasizes the usefulness of the political coalition that the group defines – a usefulness determined exclusively by its size relative to other potentially mobilizable political coalitions (Posner 2004). Indeed, a key implication of the analysis is that "depth of attachment" may be more productively viewed as a *product* of identity mobilization rather than as a prior, innate condition that can be treated as an input to the identity choices we observe.

This is a quite radical way of thinking about the sources of social attachments. It strips them of their affect. Group labels become simply conveyors of information about the coalition to which a person belongs, and group memberships become simply admission tickets to political coalitions (as well as a source of information about the coalitions to which others belong). Symbols, history, customs, and traditions – the usual stuff of identity politics – still matter, but as *post hoc* explanations for why people should embrace particular social groupings rather than as first-order sources of the salience of those groupings.

Let me be clear: in adopting this approach, I am not claiming that this is the only reasonable way to think about social identity or that this is the most appropriate approach for every question. Indeed, for questions relating to why individuals are sometimes willing to kill in the name of their group, it is almost certainly not the right approach. I am simply trying to be clear about the assumptions that underlie the framework that I develop in this article, which should be judged based on the insights it provides into the processes of identity politics and the power of the predictions it generates about the social cleavages that are likely to animate politics in a given setting.

Social cleavages

A useful way to think about social cleavages and the relationship between cleavages, groups, and identity repertoires is to distinguish between what Sacks (1992) calls "identity categories" and "category sets".[4] Identity categories are the labels that people use to describe themselves. They include classifications such as "Serbian", "Hindu", "Xhosa", "Northerner", "Latino", and "English-speaker". These categories, in turn, can be sorted into category sets: broad axes of social division such as race, religion, language, or nationality. Sacks (1992) calls them "'which'-type sets" because they provide answers to the question "which, for some set, are you?" – for example, to which race do you belong? which religion do you practice? So, if language, religion, and country of origin are bases of social division in a given society, then every-one in that society should have a linguistic identity, a religious affiliation, and a national ancestry, and nobody should have more than one of each.

To illustrate, take the example of a hypothetical neighbourhood in London whose population can be classified on the basis of race, religion, and immi-grant status into ten distinct groups (with obviously overlapping member-ships): South Asians, African/Afro-Caribbeans, Chinese, whites, Christians, Muslims, Hindus, Buddhists, foreign-born, and British-born. In this example, race, religion, and immigrant status are the category sets and South Asian, African/Afro-Caribbean, Hindus, and so on are the identity categories. These ten identity categories constitute the complete universe of social units into which community members might be sorted. Each individual community member, however, can only assign herself (or be assigned) to one of these cat-egories for each set; that is, one racial category, one religious category, and one place-of-birth category. The community's social cleavage structure can be depicted as (R, F, and B), where R = race, F = faith (religion), and B = birth status (foreign-born or British-born), and

R = $\{r_1, r_2, r_3, r_4\}$, where r_1 = South Asian; r_2 = African/Afro-Caribbean; r_3 = Chinese; and r_4 = white

F = $\{f_1, f_2, f_3, f_4\}$, where f_1 = Christian; f_2 = Muslin; f_3 = Hindu; and f_4 = Buddhist

B = $\{b_1, b_2\}$, where b_1 = foreign-born and b_2 = British-born

In this example, race, faith (religion), and place-of-birth (R, F, and B) are the *cleavages* and r_1, r_2, r_3, r_4, f_1, f_2, f_3, f_4, b_1, and b_2 are the *groups*. Together, the number of cleavage dimensions that the community contains (in this case, three) and the number and relative sizes of the groups on each cleavage dimension define its *social cleavage structure*. Finally, *identity repertoires* are the inventory of group memberships that individuals possess – one from each cleavage dimension. In our example, we can depict them as (r_i, f_j, and b_k), where *i* and *j* are numbers from 1 to 4, and *k* is either 1 or 2. Thus, Karthik, a South Asian Hindu who migrated from Gujarat as a child, has an identity repertoire (r_1, f_3, and b_1) and Adebisi, a British-born Christian whose parents came from Nigeria, has an identity repertoire (r_2, f_1, b_2). Note that indi-viduals have as many identities in their repertoires as the cleavage structure has cleavage dimensions.

The social identity matrix

We can organize the information about a community's cleavage structure using a social identity matrix like the one depicted in Figure 1. In this example, A and B are the social cleavages and $a_1, b_1, a_2, b_2, \ldots, a_n,$ and b_m are the groups located on each cleavage dimension.[5] By convention, we list them in order of decreasing size, so that $a_1 > a_2 > a_3 > \ldots > a_n$ and $b_1 > b_2 > b_3 > \ldots > b_m$. Every individual in the community can be placed in one of the cells in the figure (note that some of the cells may be empty). Each therefore has a column identity (an a_j) and a row identity (a b_k). The question is: which will they use to identify themselves?

To answer this question, we need some assumptions. The first is that individuals will choose the social identity that will maximize their access to resources. Although this is, of course, not the only motivation for choosing one identity over another, a large literature suggests the plausibility of this assumption for many circumstances. Second, assume that resources are made available through a distributive process in which a single power-holder shares resources only with, but equally among, members of his own social group. Evidence for such an assumption, and for the organization of politics in this way, is also ubiquitous (Horowitz 1985; Chabal and Daloz 1999; Posner 2005). Assume further that the power-holder is elected under plurality rules. Finally, assume that all individuals have information about at least the relative sizes of all groups (i.e. they know the ordering of the rows and columns in the matrix, though not necessarily the values in each cell).

These assumptions have a number of important implications. They imply that coalitions across group lines (i.e. across rows or across columns) will be very difficult to form, since individuals will be willing to support only those leaders who will share resources with them and they believe that only leaders from their own groups will do so. In addition, the condition that resources will be shared equally among group members means that sub-divisions of the group will not take place after power has been won. For the purposes of the model, groups are taken to be unitary blocks: uncombinable and internally undifferentiable.[6] Instances in which two or more groups might be

$a_1 > a_2 > a_3 > \ldots > a_n$ and $b_1 > b_2 > b_3 > \ldots > b_m$

Figure 1. A social identity matrix.

combined under a single umbrella label – for example, Bisa and Bemba in Zambia as "Bemba-speakers", Puerto Ricans and Dominicans in New York as "Latinos", and Episcopalians and Presbyterians in Ireland as "Protestants" – can be accommodated in the framework not by allowing them to form a coalition but by adding another cleavage dimension (Bemba-speakers/Tonga-speakers, Latino/non-Latino, and Protestant/Catholic).

Four different categories of people can be identified, each with a different optimal strategy. I depict them in Figure 2 as w, x, y, and z.

Individuals located in the dark-shaded cell, w, are members of both the largest A group (a_1) and the largest B group (b_1). They will therefore be included in the winning coalition irrespective of whether power is held by the a_1s or the b_1s (the set-up of the matrix is such that, given plurality rules, power has to be held by one of them). They are the pivot. Their choice will determine which coalition wins. If they choose to identify themselves and to vote as a_1s, then a_1s will win power; if they choose to identify themselves and to vote as b_1s, then b_1s will hold power.

Individuals in the unshaded cells, x and y, are the possible co-power-holders with w. Individuals in x will always do best by identifying in terms of their row identity, a_1, whereas individuals in y will always do best by identifying in terms of their column identity, b_1. However, whether or not they are ultimately part of the winning coalition depends on what w chooses. Individuals located in the light-shaded cells, marked z, are members of neither a_1 nor b_1, so they will never be part of the winning coalition. In many situations, they will outnumber w, x, and y combined. But because of their inherent internal divisions – the people in z are a collection of discrete communities grouped together only for analytical purposes – they will, for the reasons described above regarding the challenges of building coalitions across columns or rows, have great difficulty banding together to wrest power from the a_1s or b_1s.

Which identity will individuals in w choose? Although they stand to win either way, they will maximize the resources they receive if they select the identity that puts them in the *smaller* of the two possible winning coalitions, since this will require them to share the spoils of power with fewer other

		B				
		b_1	b_2	b_3	...	b_m
	a_1	w		x		
	a_2					
A	a_3	y		z		
	...					
	a_n					

Figure 2. Four categories of actors.

people. Their choice will therefore depend on the relative sizes of x and y. When $x > y$, they will prefer to build a coalition with y by identifying themselves as b_1s. When $y > x$, they will prefer to ally with x by identifying themselves as a_1s. Only when $x > w + y$ or $y > w + x$ (i.e. when x or y are so large that they beat the minimum winning coalition of $w + y$ or $w + x$) will individuals in w not necessarily do best by choosing the identity that puts them in the smaller winning coalition. In such a situation, whether the winning coalition is made up of a_1s or b_1s will be out of their control, so choosing membership in the smaller group is not necessarily advantageous.

What about the individuals in x and y? Since their fate will depend on w's choice, they will devote their political energy to lobbying w. People in y will insist that politics is really about cleavage B and that b_1s need to stick together against the b_2s, b_3s, and so on. People in x, meanwhile, will argue that A is the more important axis of political division and that the social cleavage that really matters is the one that separates a_1s from the other a_js.

Individuals in z are an interesting case, since they have no way of ever being in the winning coalition under the present cleavage structure. Their best strategy will therefore be to engage in "identity entrepreneurship" – that is, to try to change the game by pushing for the introduction of a new cleavage dimension (as, for example, members of scheduled castes did in India by invoking a common label as "poor" (Chandra 2004) or as Jewish intellectuals did in early twentieth-century Europe by attempting to mobilize people along class lines).[7] Their plea will be that politics is not about either A or B but about some different cleavage, C. In theory, they should try to invoke a cleavage that defines them as members of a new minimum winning coalition. But they cannot choose – and expect people to mobilize in terms of – just any principle of social division. For the strategy to be effective, the cleavage they propose must be an axis of social difference that others will recognize as at least potentially politically salient, and not all bases of social division will resonate.[8] So, a big part of their energy will be put towards making the case – by invoking history and symbols and traditions – for the salience of the new cleavage they are pushing.

An alternative strategy for individuals in z (or in the larger of x or y) is to attempt to assimilate into the winning category – a sort of identity entrepreneurship aimed at themselves rather than at others in society. However, this strategy requires investments in language competency, religious observances, and other cultural practices that may take a generation to master (Laitin 1998). Furthermore, insofar as membership in the winning category provides access to scarce resources, attempts to claim membership in that category are likely to generate resistance from its members, who face the prospect of sharing the spoils with a larger number of people. So, while theoretically possible, the assimilationist path is rarely a practical option, at least in the short-term.

The social identity matrix helps to account for the identities individuals embrace, the lobbying they undertake, and the efforts they make to create wholly new identity categories. How do these individual choices then aggregate to shape the social divisions that animate the political system more broadly? The answer lies in the fact that, once w chooses x or y as its coalition partner (and thus a_1 or b_1 as its identity), the social landscape is transformed. As soon as w makes its choice (or as soon as other players figure out what choice w will make), the distinctions among members of a_1, a_2, and a_3 or among members of b_1, b_2, and b_3 disappear and a new division emerges between those that are in power (the "ins") and those that are not (the "outs"). Whatever dimension of cleavage that defines the difference between the "ins" and "outs" becomes the axis of conflict in the political system. Note that the "outs" will still not be able to do anything to overturn the situation, since cross-group coalitions are not feasible. But they will come to share the perception that political conflict is about what makes the "ins" different from everybody else.

An illustration

To illustrate how the approach might be applied to an actual case, consider the hypothetical London neighbourhood described earlier. Recall that this neighbourhood was divided by three different ethnic cleavages: race, religion, and foreign/native birth status. Leaving this last basis of social division aside for the moment to keep things simpler, we can represent the community's social cleavage structure in the matrix depicted in Figure 3. As in Figure 2, the w and z coalitions are shaded and the groups on each cleavage dimension are ordered from largest to smallest. To make the incentives facing people clear, the share of the population contained in each cell, row, and column is provided.

South Asian Christians are the pivot. They will be in the plurality coalition irrespective of whether it is formed based on religion or race. Note that they are the pivot even though they are a minority in both coalitions: more Christians are from other, non-South Asian racial groups and more South Asians are Muslim or Hindu than Chrisitian.

In terms of which group membership will they choose to identify themselves? South Asian politicians and community members will urge them to

		Religion				
		Christian	Muslim	Hindu	Buddhist	
Race	South Asian	5	20	15	0	40
	African/Afro-Caribbean	25	10	0	0	35
	Chinese	7	0	0	8	15
	White	10	0	0	0	10
		47	30	15	8	

Figure 3. A social identity matrix for a hypothetical London community.

turn their backs on their fellow Christians and ally with other South Asians. Christian politicians and community members will campaign equally strongly for them to ally with their fellow Christians and to reject the appeals from their non-Christian South Asian brothers and sisters. Indeed, we can imagine people standing at the end of each row and the top of each column urging their fellow row- and column-members to join forces with others who share their group membership as Muslims, Chinese, Hindus, and so on.

If maximizing their access to state resources is their goal, then South Asian Christians should ally with the smaller of the two groups in which they might claim membership. Since non-Christian South Asians make up 35 per cent of the population and non-South Asian Christians comprise 42 per cent, South Asian Christians should choose their racial identity and build a coalition with their fellow South Asians. African/Afro-Caribbean, Chinese, and white Christians will urge them to choose otherwise, insisting that religion is the cleavage that really matters and that they should embrace their shared Christian faith to ally against the Muslims, Hindus, and Buddhists. But if what matters most is controlling the greatest share of resources that one can, then the lobbying of fellow Christians will go unheeded.

Once South Asian Christians have chosen to identify themselves in terms of their race, we should see the politics of the community polarized along racial lines. As the plurality group, South Asians can be expected to use their numerical strength to elevate one of their own as the community's leader. Once they have done this, whether that leader is Christian, Muslim, or Hindu will be immaterial to non-South Asians. In their eyes, all that will matter is that the leader is a South Asian, that he took advantage of racial loyalties to get elected, and that he can be expected to be beholden to the interests of the South Asian sub-community. Grievances about how resources are distributed within the community will thus be framed in terms of why South Asians are getting more than their fair share.

The key point – and the fundamental way in which the framework differs from traditional approaches to the study of identity politics – is that race becomes the basis of political division in the community not because racial identities are inherently or historically stronger than religious attachments and not because the politicians who mobilize supporters in terms of racial differences are somehow more skilful than those emphasizing religion. Race becomes politically salient because of the relative sizes of the community's racial and religious groups and, in this specific example, because the coalition of South Asians is smaller (and thus more politically valuable to the pivot) than the coalition of Christians. Group size is what determines the individual-level identity choices and, through them, the social cleavage that comes to organize political conflict.

Changing boundaries; changing outcomes

One of the most powerful aspects of the social identity matrix framework is that it helps to clarify how the identity choices individuals make – and the society-level outcomes that follow – are sensitive to changes in the boundaries of the political community. To see why this is so, imagine that London is redistricted and that our hypothetical neighbourhood is divided into two separate electoral districts: "east" and "west". If racial and religious groups were evenly distributed in the original neighbourhood, then this division would have no effect on people's coalition-building strategies, since the distribution of groups in the two new neighbourhoods would be identical. But suppose that groups were residentially segregated and that the redistricting created a new district that was homogeneously South Asian. With no other racial group in the new district (i.e. with $y = 0$), the only cleavage that would matter would be the one that divides Christians, Muslims, and Hindus. Religion would thus become the primary basis of social division, and political coalition building and conflict would take place along religious lines.

But suppose that the redistricting created new districts that were more racially mixed. Suppose that most (but not all) of the South Asian population from the original neighbourhood wound up in the new "east" district and that all of the African/Afro-Caribbean population wound up in the new "west". The population distributions for each new community might look something like the matrices in Figures 4 and 5.

The relative sizes of the racial and religious groups are dramatically changed in the two new districts, both vis-à-vis the original district and each other, and these changes bring corresponding alterations in the coalition-building strategies that actors will find it advantageous to pursue. In the new "east" district, the shift in relative size between Christians and Muslims changes the pivot. Whereas South Asian Christians were the pivot in the original community, South Asian Muslims play this role in new one. South Asian Christians still do best by identifying themselves in racial terms, but this time whether or not they will share power is out of their hands. Meanwhile, whereas South Asian Muslims did best in the pre-redistricting situation by lobbying fellow South Asians to join them in a coalition along racial lines, they do best in the post-redistricting context by identifying themselves in

		Religion				
		Muslim	Christian	Hindu	Buddhist	
Race	South Asian	35	5	25	0	65
	Chinese	0	10	0	10	20
	White	0	15	0	0	15
	African/Afro-Caribbean	0	0	0	0	0
		35	30	25	10	

Figure 4. A social identity matrix for the new "east" district.

		Christian	Muslim	Buddhist	Hindu	
	African/Afro-Caribbean	50	20	0	0	70
Race	South Asian	5	5	0	5	15
	Chinese	4	0	6	0	10
	White	5	0	0	0	5
		64	25	6	5	

Figure 5. A social identity matrix for the new "west" district.

religious terms and turning their backs on their Christian and Hindu South Asian brothers and sisters. This is because the coalition of fellow Muslims is smaller than the coalition of fellow South Asians. Whereas politics in the old neighbourhood was about race, in the new "east" it will be about religion.

Residents of the new "west" district will also experience changes in their optimal strategies. African/Afro-Caribbean Christians still do best by identifying themselves in religious terms. This time, however, they are the pivot and wind up in the winning coalition. Meanwhile, South Asian Christians, who in the original community did best by allying with their fellow South Asians, now have the best chance of capturing power and resources by identifying themselves as Christians. For both of these groups, as for both the South Asian Christians and Muslims in the new "east", changing the boundaries of the political arena either changes their incentives for identifying themselves in terms of a particular identity or, because of the altered behaviour of others, changes the payoffs they will receive for having done so.

In addition to altering the choices that these actors make about which identities to emphasize, some actors (especially those in z) will have strong incentives to try to change the contents of their identity repertoires. Just as Russian speakers had incentives to learn the titular languages in the newly independent countries in which they found themselves in the aftermath of the break-up of the Soviet Union (Laitin 1998), Chinese Christians and Buddhists and white Christians in the new "east" may have incentives to adopt Islam and Chinese Buddhists and South Asian Hindus and Muslims in the new "west" may have incentives to convert to Christianity.

Implications for partition as a solution to ethnic conflict

In the example just discussed, the original multi-ethnic community was divided into two new communities that were also multi-ethnic. Sometimes, however, such divisions are made with an eye towards transforming a multi-ethnic space – especially one marked by seemingly intractable intergroup violence – into two or more homogeneous ones. The rationale, articulated most forcefully by Kaufmann (1996, 1998; see also Tullberg and Tullberg 1997), is that stable resolutions of ethnic conflicts are possible only when the opposing groups are segregated into separate polities. Advocates of decentralization and ethnic federalism (Horowitz 1985; Hechter 2000; Selassie 2003) make similar arguments. Assertions about the desirability of such remedies have been criticized by a number of researchers on several grounds (e.g. Sambanis and Schulhofer-Wohl 2009). The social identity matrix framework makes clear another deficiency, which is that partition or the creation of federal states is highly unlikely to generate ethnically homogeneous units – at least not permanently. Even if groups are sufficiently segregated to make the messy post-partition transfer of people who wind up on the wrong side of the new border non-issue – an assumption that history shows almost never to be met – the idea that the populations in the new units will be homogeneous is a fantasy.

To see why, consider Figure 6, which provides a social identity matrix for a different hypothetical community in London facing deep conflicts along racial lines between a South Asian majority and African/Afro-Caribbean minority. The problem with simply partitioning the community into two separate units, one for South Asians and one for African/Afro-Caribbeans, is that, as the matrix makes clear, these racial groups are internally divided by country of origin. The fact that some South Asians come from India, others from Pakistan, others from Bangladesh, and still others from Sri Lanka might be totally irrelevant in the context of a heated conflict between South Asians and African/Afro-Caribbeans (who themselves are divided into Nigerians, Jamaicans and Kenyans). But as soon as the community is partitioned, the homogeneity would give way to diversity (along a different cleavage dimension) as political actors in the new setting scrambled to create new minimum winning coalitions along country-of-origin lines. As Figure 7 illustrates, the ostensibly homogeneous South Asian and African/Afro-Caribbean blocks would immediately fragment. In the South Asian district, Indians would ban together against Pakistani, Bangladeshi, and Sri Lankans; in the African/Afro-Caribbean district, Nigerians would ban together against Jamaicans and Kenyans. By changing the boundaries, one dimension of social cleavage

		Race		
		South Asian	African/Afro-Caribbean	
Country of Origin	India	30	0	30
	Pakistan	20	0	20
	Nigeria	0	18	18
	Bangladesh	12	0	12
	Jamaica	0	10	10
	Kenya	0	8	8
	Sri Lanka	2	0	2
		64	36	

Figure 6. Another hypothetical London community with (what looks like) two groups.

		Race		
		South Asian	African/Afro-Caribbean	
Country of Origin	India	47	0	47
	Pakistan	31	0	31
	Bangladesh	19	0	19
	Sri Lanka	3	0	3
		100	0	

		Race		
		African/Afro-Caribbean	South Asian	
	Nigeria	50	0	50
	Jamaica	28	0	28
	Kenya	22	0	22
		100	0	

Figure 7. Homogeneity gives way to diversity post-partition.

would simply be displaced by another. The *depth* of conflict might be lessened (if for some reason racial conflict was more disruptive than national origin conflict), but the *fact* of conflict along group lines will remain, as long as there is a competition for who will control access to resources.

Figure 8 makes this point again in a different context. Here, the setting is Nakuru, a multi-ethnic district in Kenya that has witnessed significant inter-group violence in recent years (Gettleman 2008). The figure provides a social identity matrix for a hypothetical community that, for simplicity, is comprised of just two groups: Kikuyu and Kalenjin (Nakuru also contains significant numbers of Luo and Luhya). Would partitioning the community along tribal lines solve the problem? Perhaps. But as Figure 8 makes clear, the internal sub-tribe and clan divisions present within each seemingly monolithic

Pre-Partition

		Tribe		
		Kikuyu	Kalenjin	
Sub-tribe/clan	Nyeri Kikuyu	40	0	40
	Kipsigi	0	23	23
	Kiambu Kikuyu	15	0	15
	Tugen	0	12	12
	Turkana	0	5	5
	Nandi	0	3	3
	Keiyo	0	2	2
		55	45	

Post-Partition:
A New Kikuyuland

		Tribe		
		Kikuyu	Kalenjin	
Clan	Nyeri Kikuyu	73	0	73
	Kiambu Kikuyu	27	0	27
		100	0	

Post-Partition:
A New Kalenjinland

		Tribe		
		Kalenjin	Kikuyu	
Sub-tribe	Kipsigi	51	0	51
	Tugen	27	0	27
	Turkana	11	0	11
	Nandi	7	0	7
	Keiyo	4	0	4
		100	0	

Figure 8. A community in Nakuru, Kenya.

tribal block would emerge as salient in each of the post-partition units. In the new "Kikuyuland", divisions between Kikuyu from Nyeri and Kikuyu from Kiambu – a cleavage that has animated Kikuyu politics for a generation (Throup and Hornsby 1998) – would almost certainly become salient. In the new "Kalenjinland", divisions among the several Kalenjin sub-tribes that live in Nakuru, previously subsumed beneath the broader conflict between Kikuyu and Kalenjin, would emerge as bases of social differentiation.[9] Again, the partition would simply shift the locus of competition and conflict from one dimension of social identity to another. The displacement of the North–South conflict in Sudan by the conflict between Dinka and Nuer ethnic groups in post-independence South Sudan offers a clear – and tragic – real-world example of this phenomenon (Human Rights Watch 2014).

The social identity matrix framework even offers insight into the most famous example of partition in modern history: the partition of India in 1947. Born from a desire to separate Hindus and Muslims, the partition was

Before Partition

		Religion		
		Hindu	Muslim	
Language Group	Hindi	34	0	34
	Bengali	6	10	16
	Punjabi	1	6	7
	Telugu	6	0	6
	Marathi	6	0	6
	Tamil	5	0	5
	Urdu	1	4	5
	Gujarati	4	0	4
	Kannada	3	0	3
	Malayalam	2	0	2
	Pashto	0	1	1
	Sindhi	0	1	1
	Saraiki	0	1	1
		68	23	

A New Hindustan

		Religion		
		Hindu	Muslim	
Language Group	Hindi	50	0	50
	Bengali	9	0	9
	Telugu	9	0	9
	Marathi	9	0	9
	Tamil	7	0	7
	Gujarati	6	0	6
	Kannada	4	0	4
	Malayalam	3	0	2
	Punjabi	1.5	0	1.5
	Urdu	1.5	0	1.5
		100	0	

A New Islamistan

		Religion		
		Muslim	Hindu	
Language Group	Bengali	44	0	44
	Punjabi	27	0	27
	Urdu	17	0	17
	Pashto	4	0	4
	Sindhi	4	0	4
	Saraiki	4	0	4
		100	0	

Figure 9. The partition of India.

anything but neat (Pandey 2002; Wolpert 2006). As many as a million civilians died in the reshuffling of peoples that ensued following the drawing of the new borders of India and Pakistan. Figure 9 depicts an idealized version of partition in which, as was intended by its architects, Hindus and Muslims were somehow able to separate themselves into separate, religiously homogeneous states.

The matrix at the top of the figure divides pre-partition India along two dimensions: religion and language.[10] The two at the bottom depict how a "new Hindustan" and "new Islamistan" would look. Both are homogeneous with respect to religion, but are now divided by language group differences. Indeed, this is what actually happened in both India and Pakistan after 1947. As Horowitz (1975, 135) writes:

> hardly had the Indio-Pakistani subcontinent been partitioned along what were thought to be hard-and-fast Hindu-Muslim lines when, in 1948, Mohammed Ali Jinnah, who had done so much to foster subnational identities in undivided India, ironically found it necessary to warn against the 'curse of provincialism' in undivided Pakistan.

The separation of Pakistan and India led simply to the replacement of one basis of social division by another. As in the other examples, partition does not do away with ethnic conflict; it just shifts it to a different dimension of social cleavage. Indeed, in Pakistan, these new divisions led to a second partition in 1971 and the formation of an independent Bangladesh.

Conclusion

This article has described a simple framework for understanding the politics of socially heterogeneous societies. Rooted in a set of strong assumptions about the instrumentality of social identities and the role of communal groups as "coalitions which have been formed as part of rational efforts to secure benefits" (Bates 1983, 152), the approach generates predictions that are consistent with key features of the world we observe. It offers explanations for why certain cleavages emerge as socially salient rather than others, the kinds of identity-based appeals that different types of individuals are likely to make, and even the kinds of individuals we would expect to see undertake new identity-building projects. The framework also demonstrates how these outcomes and behaviours will change when the boundaries of the political arena are altered, and it traces the implications of these insights for the usefulness of partition as a remedy for ethnic conflict. Traditional approaches to identity politics that locate their explanations in historical trends or in the "depth of attachment" that people naturally feel towards some social identities provide useful accounts. But they cannot illuminate as broad a range of outcomes and processes as the framework described here.

Notes

1. The analysis most closely resembles Fearon (1999).
2. Chandra (2012) provides a similar treatment, but her focus is more narrowly on the identities that individuals choose.
3. A key question that I do not address in this article is what determines the roster of social identities that are potentially available for an individual to adopt. For a discussion of this issue, see Posner (2005).
4. Chandra (2012) makes a similar distinction, although she adds a third component, *attributes*, which refers to the observable characteristics – skin colour, education, surname, dietary practices, dress, and so on – that allow people to sort others, and gain entry themselves, into social categories. This is an important additional issue, but I leave it aside here.
5. While the example contains only two cleavages, the logic of the model extends to cleavage structures with three or more cleavages.
6. Such undifferentiability is emphasized by Ernest Renan in his famous 1882 lecture "What is a Nation?" in which he highlights that a key ingredient of a nation is the ability to forget. His point is that to constitute a nation (or presumably any social group), we need to forget the complexity of who we are, including our within-group divisions. In the terms of the model discussed here, it implies that thinking of oneself in terms of one's row or column identity means forgetting about the others, as well as about the divisions within the row or column.
7. Only in one special situation can people in z affect w's choice: when there exists within z a sub-coalition of a_js or b_ks that is greater than w plus the smaller of x and y – that is, greater than the winning coalition that would otherwise form. If this is the case, then w will have no choice but to identify itself as a_1 (b_1) and ally with x (y). The existence of this sub-coalition within z, while altering w's choice, will not affect the fate of anyone in z: as soon as w joins with y (x), everyone in z will still be shut out of power. Situations of this sort frequently occur when the A and B cleavages are organized such that groups from one cleavage dimension nest inside groups from another (as, for instance, when the regions of a country each contain distinct sets of region-specific tribes, when a tribe is divided into clans, or when a linguistic community is divided into speakers of multiple dialects).
8. Just how encompassing that roster of potentially relevant cleavages might be is a matter of some debate. Chandra (2012) takes the position that any combination of descent-based attributes serves as a potential basis of social mobilization, whereas Ferree (2012) and Petersen (2012) stress that many of these theoretically possible combinations are not viable in practice.
9. For an excellent treatment of the internal divisions within the Kalenjin block, and the artificiality of the "Kalenjin" category more generally, see Lynch (2011).
10. For the sake of space, I include only the thirteen largest language groups; hence, the column totals do not sum to 100.

Acknowledgments

The author thanks the Sol Leshin Program for BGU-UCLA Academic Cooperation for its support.

Disclosure statement

No potential conflict of interest was reported by the author.

References

Bates, Robert. 1983. "Modernization, Ethnic Competition and the Rationality of Politics in Contemporary Africa." In *State Versus Ethnic Claims*, edited by Donald Rothchild and Victor A. Olorunsola, 152–171. Boulder, CO: Westview.

Brass, Paul. 1991. *Ethnicity and Nationalism*. New Delhi: Sage.

Chabal, Patrick, and Jean-Pascal Daloz. 1999. *Africa Works: Disorder as Political Instrument*. Oxford: James Currey.

Chandra, Kanchan. 2004. *Why Ethnic Parties Succeed*. New York: Cambridge University Press.

Chandra, Kanchan. 2012. *Constructivist Theories of Ethnic Politics*. New York: Oxford University Press.

Fearon, James D. 1999. "Why Ethnic Politics and 'Pork' Tend to Go Together." Unpublished paper.

Ferree, Karen E. 2012. "How Fluid is Fluid? The Mutability of Ethnic Identities and Electoral Volatility in Africa." In *Constructivist Theories of Ethnic Politics*, edited by Kanchan Chandra, 312–340. New York: Oxford University Press.

Gettleman, Jeffrey. 2008. "Ethnic Violence in Rift Valley is Tearing Kenya Apart." *New York Times*, January 27.

Hechter, Michael. 2000. *Containing Nationalism*. Oxford: Oxford University Press.

Horowitz, Donald. 1975. "Ethnic Identity." In *Ethnicity: Theory and Experience*, edited by Nathan Glazer and Daniel P. Moynihan, 111–140. Cambridge, MA: Harvard University Press.

Horowitz, Donald. 1985. *Ethnic Groups in Conflict*. Berkeley: University of California Press.

Kaufmann, Chaim. 1996. "Possible and Impossible Solutions to Ethnic Civil Wars." *International Security* 20 (4): 136–175.

Kaufmann, Chaim. 1998. "When All Else Fails: Ethnic Population Transfers and Partitions in the Twentieth Century." *International Security* 23 (2): 129–156.

Kronenberg, Clemens, and Andreas Wimmer. 2012. "Struggling Over the Boundaries of Belonging: A Formal Model of Nation Building, Ethnic Closure, and Populism." *American Journal of Sociology* 118 (1): 176–230.

Laitin, David D. 1986. *Hegemony and Culture*. Chicago, IL: University of Chicago Press.

Laitin, David D. 1998. *Identity in Formation*. Ithaca, NY: Cornell University Press.

Lipset, Seymour M., and Stein Rokkan. 1967. "Cleavage Structures, Party Systems and Voter Alignments." In *Party Systems and Voter Alignments*, edited by Seymour M. Lipset and Stein Rokkan, 1–64. New York: Free Press.

Lynch, Gabrielle. 2011. *I Say to You: Ethnic Politics and the Kalenjin in Kenya*. Chicago, IL: University of Chicago Press.

Pandey, Gyanerndra. 2002. *Remembering Partition: Violence, Nationalism and History in India*. New York: Cambridge University Press.

Petersen, Roger. 2012. "Identity, Rationality, and Emotion in the Processes of State Disintegration and Reconstruction." In *Constructivist Theories of Ethnic Politics*, edited by Kanchan Chandra, 387–421. New York: Oxford University Press.

Posner, Daniel N. 2004. "The Political Salience of Cultural Difference: Why Chewas and Tumbukas are Allies in Zambia and Adversaries in Malawi." *American Political Science Review* 98 (4): 529–545.

Posner, Daniel N. 2005. *Institutions and Ethnic Politics in Africa*. New York: Cambridge University Press.

Sacks, Harvey. 1992. *Lectures on Conversation*. Oxford: Blackwell.

Sambanis, Nicholas, and Moses Shayo. 2013. "Social Identification and Ethnic Conflict." *American Political Science Review* 107 (2): 294–325.

Sambanis, Nicholas, and Johan Schulhofer-Wohl. 2009. "What's in a Line? Is Partition a Solution to Civil War?" *International Security* 34 (2): 82–118.

Schattschneider, E. E. 1960. *The Semisovereign People*. New York: Holt, Rinehart and Winston.

Selassie, Alemante. 2003. "Ethnic Federalism: Its Promise and Pitfalls for Africa." College of William & Mary Faculty Publications, Paper No. 88.

"South Sudan: Ethnic Targeting, Widespread Killings." 2014. *Human Rights Watch*, January 16. https://www.hrw.org/news/2014/01/16/south-sudan-ethnic-targeting-widespread-killings.

Tajfel, Henri, M. G. Billig, R. P. Bundy, and Claude Flament. 1971. "Social Categorization and Intergroup Behaviour." *European Journal of Social Psychology* 1 (2): 149–178.

Throup, David, and Charles Hornsby. 1998. *Multi-Party Politics in Kenya*. Oxford: James Currey.

Tullberg, Jan, and Birgitta S. Tullberg. 1997. "Separation or Unity? A Model for Solving Ethnic Conflicts." *Politics and the Life Sciences* 16 (2): 237–248.

van der Veen, A. Maurits, and David D. Laitin. 2012. "Modeling the Evolution of Ethnic Demography." In *Constructivist Theories of Ethnic Politics*, edited by Kanchan Chandra, 277–311. New York: Oxford University Press.

Wolpert, Stanley. 2006. *Shameful Fight: The Last Years of the British Empire in India*. New York: Oxford University Press.

Ethnicity, extraterritoriality, and international conflict

Arthur A. Stein ⓘ

ABSTRACT

The world has more ethnic groups than states and many ethnic groups are split across two or more states. One implication is that many ethnic conflicts are international phenomena in which transborder ethnic kin are involved. States concerned with co-ethnics or co-religionists in neighbouring countries are pursuing interests not included in our standard models of international politics. States that pursue such extraterritorial interests define national security and national survival in terms broader than merely maintaining the physical and territorial integrity of the state. Threats to their ethnic and religious brethren are seen as threats to them. And because such threats are seen as particularistic they also affect foreign policy alignments and the functioning of the balance of power.

Introduction

How selfish soever man may be supposed, there are evidently some principles in his nature, which interest him in the fortune of others, and render their happiness necessary to him, though he derives nothing from it except the pleasure of seeing it. (Adam Smith)

If lives and health of our compatriots are in danger, we won't stay aside. (Leonid Slutsky, head of a Russian parliamentary committee in charge of relations with ex-Soviet republics, speaking at a meeting in Crimea, Ukraine, Feb. 25, 2014)

Ethnic conflict is a major element of modern politics. The once hoped for decline in ethnic differences as a key element of social differentiation, predicted by theories of modernization and development did not occur and brought renewed interest in ethnicity (Esman 1977; Hechter and Levi 1979; Smith 1981).[1] The end of the Cold War constituted a shift in the strategic landscape that resulted in ethnic conflict becoming a major focus of inter-state relations.[2]

Most political violence in the current global political and economic setting occurs within countries and comes in the form of inter-communal conflict that endangers internal and international stability. Disparate literatures study inter-communal conflict – on secession, civil war, rebellion, and ethnic conflict – and in each there is a predisposition to treat such conflict as a feature of domestic politics to be explained by internal characteristics alone. Writing about internal conflict in general, Kalyvas (2010, xii) notes that "comparative politics scholars have tended to downgrade transnational and international factors affecting domestic political conflict". Scholars of civil war decry the predominant emphasis on a "closed polity" model (Gleditsch 2007) and note the inclination "to treat civil wars as purely domestic phenomena" with a consequent neglect of "transborder linkages and processes" (Cederman, Girardin, and Gleditsch 2009, 404). Writing about ethnic conflict in particular, Angstrom (2001, 60) notes as "a problem with some studies" being "the tendency to treat it as something uniquely internal".[3] Yet as argued below, ethnic conflicts sometimes originate abroad and are often sustained from abroad. This requires a focus on diffusion and on the international dimensions of ethnic conflict.[4]

Ethnic conflict has drawn the attention of international relations scholars who argue that their traditional approaches provide a theoretical framework for explaining such conflict in a manner similar to that used to explain interstate war.[5] Since "the collapse of imperial regimes" in the Soviet Union and Yugoslavia could be seen as resulting in "an emerging anarchy", the standard tools of realism could be applied and most specifically that the security dilemma could be used to explain ethnic conflict (Posen 1993, 27). Alternatively, ethnic conflict is simply treated as one of a class of conflicts, that include war, that are explainable by the same set of characteristics. These are costly conflicts and are explicable by one or more of the features that explain costly conflicts, and ethnic conflicts in particular result from a commitment problem (Fearon 1998).[6]

Much the same is true for religious conflict. It has received renewed attention as a source of conflict and is typically treated as an internal matter. Here, too, there is a debate about whether our standard perspectives on international politics can explain religious conflict.[7]

This paper argues, however, that ethnicity, as well as religion and ideology, constitutes an extraterritorial interest, and, as such, represents an important phenomenon that requires some modification of our core assumptions about the nature of international politics. More specifically, this paper argues that core state interests include extraterritorial elements of identity. This makes possible the incorporation of ethnic, religious, and nationalist interests in state behaviour and an assessment of their impact on international relations. This reconceptualization of state interests generates important modifications in standard propositions and arguments about the requisites for international stability. And it is this reconceptualization that constitutes an important element in our understanding of ethnic conflicts and their development.

Ethnic groups and ethnic conflict

The world has many more ethnic and ethno-linguistic groups than states. Estimates of the number of ethno-linguistic groups range from 5,000 to 6,800 (Gellner 1983; Carment 1993), whereas the UN has 193 member states (Growth in United Nations membership 1945–present, http://www.un.org/en/members/growth.shtml). Using a criterion requiring an ethnic group to make up 1 per cent of a country's population, Fearon (2003) finds 822 ethnic groups in 160 countries as of the early 1990s. In only about one-fifth of countries did one group constitute more than 90 per cent of the population, but one group did constitute a majority in 71 per cent of countries. That disjuncture drives many features of domestic and international politics and political science scholarship in comparative politics and international relations.

One implication is that few states are homogenous and many if not most countries must be multiethnic and thus embody, even if not tolerate, a multiplicity of cultures, languages, and religions. Irrespective of competing definitions of ethnic homogeneity or mono-nationality, only a minority of states fit the description.[8] Nearly two-thirds of 227 communal groups have kindred in another country (Gurr 1993); and 42 per cent of major ethnic groups are split among two or more states (Nielsson 1985).[9] It also implies that they contain the possibility of ethnic competition if not conflict. Scholars thus debate the viability of polycultural or multinational states and which distributions of ethnicities and which institutional arrangements are more or less conducive to ethnic cooperation. They also debate whether the system of nation-states is bound to experience continued fragmentation and new state formation (Rosecrance and Stein 2006).

Given the process by which state boundaries were created as well as the movement of people, a second implication is that many ethnic and religious groups have co-ethnic and co-religionists in neighbouring countries. When ethnic populations are not circumscribed territorially within states but exist across state borders, such linkages can affect both domestic and international conflict.

The substantial empirical work addressing ethnic conflict can be found in disparate literatures devoted to secession, irredentism, civil war, nationalism, as well as ethnic conflict, and although there are scholars who treat these as discrete domestic phenomena largely unaffected by international factors, others note the role of international politics in inter-communal conflict.[10] Disparate data sets, conceptualizations, specifications, and time periods generate somewhat different results about the extent of internationalization. For example, using a relatively small minimum casualty figure for characterizing civil wars, only 5 per cent are considered internationalized, whereas a data set using a higher threshold finds 25 per cent with foreign interventions (Gleditsch 2007, 295). In another study of armed internal conflicts, approximately one in eight had interventions by neighbouring states, constituting 2/3 of the cases with external interventions (Harbom and Wallensteen 2005).[11]

But external involvement need not involve intervention. Support can come in the form of financial and military assistance and the provision of sanctuary for fighters as well intervention. The empirical data make clear that many internal conflicts experience some form of external involvement (among others, Gleditsch 2007; Salehyan 2009; Salehyan, Gleditsch, and Cunningham 2011). In one study of armed internal conflicts, about half had forms of external assistance short of intervention (Harbom and Wallensteen 2005).

The evidence from a variety of studies using different data sets, conceptualizations, and specifications is that ethnic groups often receive support by ethnic kin in neighbouring countries. Scholars use a variety of terms for the situation: transborder ethnic affinities (Horowitz 1985), transnational ethnic alliances (Davis and Moore 1997), ethnonationalist triads (Cederman, Girardin, and Gleditsch 2009), transborder ethnic kin (Cederman et al. 2013), and even foreign constituencies (Salehyan, Gleditsch, and Cunningham 2011).

There is substantial evidence of a link between ethnic ties and conflict. In general, certain ethnic distributions are associated with inter-state conflict (Huibregtse 2010, 2011), and cross-national ethnic kin increase the likelihood of international conflict (Davis and Moore 1997; Trumbore 2003; Gartzke and Gleditsch 2006) and the contagion of intrastate armed conflict (Brown 1996; Lake and Rothchild 1998; Lobell and Mauceri 2004; Gleditsch 2007; Cederman, Girardin, and Gleditsch 2009; Forsberg and Karlén 2013). Transnational ethnic kin is a determinant of external support (Saideman 2002; Salehyan, Gleditsch, and Cunningham 2011). Recognition of the role of ethnic kin is such that it is included as a control in any attempt to assess other factors affecting the international spread of civil war, as for example in Salehyan and Gleditsch (2006).

Quantitative studies often articulate hypotheses about likelihood of support or intervention in a conflict under different conditions without articulating an analytic logic. Most studies, explicitly or implicitly, emphasize instrumental material factors. Yet the very fact that we observe ethnic kin in neighbouring countries to be the basis for both intra-state and inter-state conflict leads to a recognition of the impact of affective factors.[12] Not only do states support ethnic kin in neighbouring states, but they do so even when they themselves have ethnic minorities and thus vulnerable to secessionist movements themselves (Heraclides 1990; Saideman 1997, 2001).

The evolution of the literature has entailed finer distinctions in the situations which give rise to the internationalization of ethnic conflict. Discrimination against one's co-ethnics or their rebellion brings the issue of external support or involvement to the fore. An important survey finds 275 communal groups in 116 countries that are disadvantaged and characterized as "minorities at risk" (Gurr 2000, 12). The relative power of groups and the ability to affect an outcome play a role. Scholars focus on situations in which a discriminated against ethnic minority has ethnic kin that control a neighbouring state as the case most likely to generate external support and intervention (Davis and Moore 1997; Woodwell 2004; Saideman and Ayres 2008).[13]

That governments are concerned with ethnic kin in neighbouring countries, with their treatment and conditions, requires a modification of our conventional conceptions of state interests.

International relations theory and the territorial state

The study of international relations is a conflict riddled landscape of competing levels and units of analysis and warring isms. A review of the scholarly debates, grand and not so grand, is beyond the purview of this paper, but suffice it to say that everyone recognizes the centrality of the state and of interests in the explanation of both foreign policy and international politics. The state is the dominant actor in international relations and other actors, whether individuals, interest groups, non-state actors, or international institutions (which are really intergovernmental institutions), matter to the extent that they affect states and their policies.

Whether scholars emphasize the structural constraints of an anarchic system, or provide place for the domestic requisites of regime survival, or highlight the socially constructed aspects of nationality and sovereignty, their explanations of state behaviour begin with a focus on interests and the presumed primacy of security and survival.[14] The national interest is thus a touchstone concept and the compelling core of the scholarly understanding of international relations is that states pursue their interests in order to assure their continued existence and counter external threats. Even assertive, aggressive, and offensive actions are typically undertaken to assure security.[15] The maintenance of the physical and territorial integrity of the state is the core national interest (Krasner 1978).

The preeminent *raison d'état* is to assure survival against foreign threats. States act to ensure their own survival in the knowledge that no supranational institution or governing authority will protect them and that they cannot rely on other states to assist them even if they share a common ideology, political form, or ethnos.[16] Other countries are assessed for their threat potential, which derives from their foreign policy intentions and their relative power. Any state's concern is with others' foreign and defence policies, and only those domestic practices that affect these. Otherwise, there is presumed to be no concern with the domestic policies of other countries. Structural realists find all domestic politics irrelevant, whereas liberal institutionalists argue that political systems matter because they affect the relative ability to mobilize resources from their societies and because democracies and autocracies have different aggressive propensities. The point is that the domestic politics of other countries matters only in so much as it affects foreign and defence policy.

Such a view of the defining character of international politics is consistent with the absence of intervention in the domestic affairs of other states. After all, the purpose of having one's own country is to be able to establish communal institutions and practices apart from those of others. Having a state makes possible the pursuit of ways of life – political, social, and economic – apart from others. States are concerned with their autonomy, their ability to make independent decisions.

Yet states have historically demonstrated extraterritorial interests even while espousing a view of sovereignty that makes states the sole arbiters of their internal arrangements. Even when they do not have external consequences, states regularly display a concern with one another's internal arrangements and domestic affairs that are incomprehensible within a narrow self-interest framework. A preeminent concern with national security should generate no interest in extraterritorial ones.

The extraterritorial concerns of states include an interest in ethnicity and religion, yet our standard models include no sense of the role these play in the interests and interactions of states. Concern with ethnic kin and involvement in neighbouring states with ethnic kin cannot be explained in our standard model. Indeed, the same point can be made about the role of religion and ideology.

Extraterritoriality and an alternative formulation of state survival and security

The argument developed here, however, is that a reconceptualization of what constitutes national security and state survival is required. Assessing the impact of ethnicity and other extraterritorial interests requires a reconceptualization of the core interest of states.

Most important, the key assumption that states preeminently value survival is itself in need of more precise specification. Although typically treated as the territorial survival of the state, the full meaning of survival is never specifically elucidated and is presumed to be consistent over time and space.

My own argument is that for many states, survival also includes a political (ideological), or cultural (ethnic, religious, and national) component, or both. It is often argued that nationalism is not a long standing and deeply rooted phenomenon but a thoroughly modern and constructed one (Seton-Watson 1977; Anderson 1983; Gellner 1983; Hobsbawm 1990). But this is often said as if the force can be readily ignored or transcended. Not only is nationality a human artefact, so are states, ethnic groups, religions, ideologies, etc. That they are constructed does not mean that they can be reconstructed at will. All of these human creations are exclusive rather than inclusive, have great resiliency, and have become elements of individual identity.[17] Thus, just as international relations theorists take the existence of states as given, so an analysis of religion and nationality and ethnicity can take their existence as given.

For many states, survival has more than a purely territorial connotation; it encompasses political, cultural, and ethnic considerations.[18] And the international environment poses threats that are more than physical and territorial. After all, territory is not destroyed by warfare or conquest and factories and farms are typically reconstituted. And with the exception of genocide, only a relative minority is ever threatened physically. Rather, political and cultural autonomy are endangered. States define survival as encompassing an entire way of life.[19] States are interested in guarding a people and preserving a way of life. States therefore respond not just to threats posed by military power but to cultural and political threats as well.[20]

For those who root state interests in human nature, the case for an expansive conception of survival is straightforward.[21] History is replete with examples of people voluntarily giving their lives for causes and ideas. Physical survival has hardly been the preeminent motive force for all human beings all the time.[22] Were individual survival the preeminent consideration, mass armies would be more difficult to create and sustain, and individuals would not voluntarily swamp induction offices at the start of wars. It can be argued that it is the knowledge of their mortality and eventual death that is the basis of individuals' interests in the survival of more transcendent phenomena embodied in their offspring and kin. Human beings are distinguished as the animal that would fight and die on behalf of others with whom they do not share genetic material. Individuals care about passing on their cultural values, or memes. In short, a typology of state interests that is rooted in individual interests would necessarily require a more expansive notion of what individuals are willing to die for and how states define survival.[23]

Moreover, even a conceptualization that begins with the irreducibility of states confronts the problem that states are more than territorially bounded entities. They are institutions that embody different principles, including notions of legitimacy and mechanisms for arriving at a social choice. States in which sovereignty resides in a dynasty embody different conceptions of survival than states in which popular sovereignty reigns. The implications of the social choice mechanism are the basis for arguments about the different war propensities of representative governments from monarchical ones. Not surprisingly the survival of the state encompasses more than physical and territorial integrity.

In many if not most states, citizens and elites see the state as more than simply an entity controlling a particular land mass.[24] "Better dead than red", for example, captures a US conceptualization of survival that extends beyond the maintenance of territorial integrity and includes the political character of the state. In other countries, citizens and elites alike see the state as embodying other ideational features, not typically characterized as ideological, but as ethnic, national, and cultural. The emergence of nationalism in nineteenth-century Europe caught the imagination of many, including Jews who had managed to survive for almost two centuries as minorities in states dominated by other religions and peoples (Ben-Israel 2003). Zionism was a political means for assuring the survival of Judaism by providing a homeland free of persecution. Israel was constructed as a Jewish state and the survival of the Israeli state means the survival of Zionism and of a place for the in-gathering of Jews from around the world. Palestinians have, at times, proposed the creation of a secular state in Palestine in which Jews and Arabs could live freely. Such a proposal would not constitute a threat to Israel's survival if survival was defined purely in terms of the physical and territorial integrity of the state. The Israeli view of proposals for a binational secular state as tantamount to the liquidation of Israel, however, constitutes a more expansive view of survival. Indeed, our conventional models have no ability to explain the importance of concerns about diaspora Jews to Israeli foreign policy, or that of ethnic Germans to German foreign policy, or that of ethnic Russians to Russian foreign policy.[25]

The centrality of such concerns can also be seen in the domestic actions states take during wars. If states were solely concerned with the provision of the collective good of security against outside attack they would not treat many insiders as outsiders. Ironically, even as states often extend their protective concerns to those physically outside the state (citizens as well as ethnic and religious kin), they also exclude from such protection those inside the state who are deemed outsiders. It has not been unusual to see states expel people from within their borders when they come under attack. Even the US sequestered US citizens of Japanese descent during the Second World War. Ethnocracies sometimes force migrations of ethnic minorities in the hope of creating monoethnic states.[26] Obviously, the central state concern with providing protection against outside attack does not extend equally to all those within the territorial boundaries of the state and does not necessarily exclude those outside the territorial limits. In effect, there is some consideration of identity and belonging which extends beyond territorial location.[27]

The very conception of citizenship, regardless how conferred, captures the point that a state's concern extends to classes of individuals regardless of location. Expatriate citizens constitute state interests in a way that resident aliens do not. And the fact that some states automatically extend citizenship to individuals with certain characteristics (Israel and its law of return, which grants automatic citizenship to any Jew, and Germany's basing citizenship on bloodlines) amplifies the point about the extraterritorial concerns of certain states.[28]

Extraterritoriality and international politics

The alternative perspective offered here suggests an international system composed of states that are heterogenous rather than undifferentiated. Some are pure territorial states that are functionally equivalent. Others reflect extraterritorial concerns, including religion, ethnicity, and ideology. The latter define their survival in terms of specific extraterritorial interests.

A heterogenous system embodies more sources of conflict than a homogenous one. A homogeneous system of purely territorial states would see border and boundary disputes but would make it possible for states to ignore one another's internal policies and practices. Further, as boundaries become accepted and fixed (Zacher 2001) and as territory declines in relative economic importance (Rosecrance 1986), one would expect fewer international disputes. In fact, an inductive historical survey of issues that give rise to wars finds a

Table 1. Salience of issues as a source of wars, 1648–1989[a].

Issues	1648–1714	1714–1814	1815–1914	1918–1941	1945–1989
Territory and boundary	55	68	42	47	31
Strategic territory	23	17	13	30	21
Maintain integrity of state/empire	–	8	55	30	28
State/regime survival	23	17	6	37	22
Autonomy	–	–	6	7	7
Nation-state creation	4	8	55	13	52
National liberation	4	8	29	13	28
National unification/consolidation	–	–	26	–	17
Secession/state creation	–	–	–	–	7
Ideology	–	15	23	27	45
Government composition	–	14	13	17	28
Ideological liberation	–	1	10	10	14
Protect ideological confreres	–	–	–	–	3
Human sympathy	14	11	32	24	21
Protect religious confreres	14	11	10	–	–
Protect ethnic confreres	–	–	16	7	9
Ethnic/religious unification/irredenta	–	–	6	17	12

[a] Frequency of issues as percent of wars, that is, percentage that a particular issue contributed to the origin of wars in the period.
Source: Constructed from Holsti (1991, 280, 282, 308).

constant concern with strategic territory and a declining role for territorial disputes that exclude strategic territories (Holsti 1991, presented in Table 1).

In contrast, a heterogeneous international system generates additional sources of conflict. States with extraterritorial concerns of ideology, ethnicity, nationality, and religion come to blows over one another's internal political arrangements and their international implications.[29] Those with ethnic, national, and religious counterparts in other nations are affected by the repression of their brethren elsewhere.

States come to support separatist movements and alternative territorial arrangements as a way of resolving such conflicts. Their extraterritorial concerns can lead to irredentism, an irredentism focused less on the recovery of ancestral homelands than on the incorporation of a region in which one's ethnos is concentrated (even if rooted only in a recent migration).[30] In such cases, it is the extraterritoriality of ethnos or nation that generates territorial disputes absent geopolitical and strategic considerations. Thus, in Holsti's (1991) analysis of the conflict-producing issues that have been sources of war, issues of ideology, religion, and ethnicity rise in importance even as purely territorial issues decline (see Table 1). The confluence implies that not all wars in which territory is an issue are disputes that would have occurred absent ethnic, religious, and nationality considerations.

States that are either ethnically homogenous or ethnocracies dominated by one ethnic group and that find some of their members living in significant concentrations abroad tend to pursue foreign policies that reflect this concern for the ethnos. Concern with the status of group members abroad generates an extraterritorial dimension to foreign policy and a concern with the domestic politics of other states – concerns that become magnified when those other nations do not assure the protection of minority rights.[31] Such states' foreign policies are not wholly driven by considerations of relative power. Threats to an ethnic minority in another nation become important security concerns that reflect more than mere territoriality.[32]

Such ethnic interests can also constrain the extent of hostility (absent an expectation of victory in war). That is, extraterritorial concerns can mute and dampen traditional balancing behaviour for fear of jeopardizing group members living abroad. In such cases, extraterritoriality makes possible deterrence by way of holding hostages.

States are also concerned that changes in the internal politics of their neighbours will affect their own internal politics. Changes in the dominant ethnic, religious, or ideological faction in one's neighbours can have tremendous consequences for oneself (Nelson 2014).

The historical data make clear the elements of continuity and change that have characterized extraterritoriality. In earlier eras in the inter-state system, religious conflicts were regular occurrences, whereas ethnicity and nationality had yet to exist as salient political factors. In the years between the end of the

First World War and the end of the Cold War, religious conflicts disappeared as causes of war and the ethnic concerns that only emerged after the Congress of Vienna continued and grew in importance (Holsti 1991, presented in Table 1).[33] In the post-Cold War world, ethnicity and religion have played a larger and growing role in intrastate conflicts (on religion: Ellingsen 2005; Toft 2006; Fox 2007).

Extraterritoriality, threat, and the balance of power

In a heterogeneous international system in which some states pursue extraterritorial interests, the bases of threat are expanded. The traditional realist argument is that states view adverse changes in the distribution of power as inherently threatening and respond, either by internal mobilization or external alignment, in ways that reestablish a balance of power. Yet, states find other changes threatening as well.

States can find internal political changes in others threatening (or less threatening) even absent changes in relative power. The rise to power of a totalitarian universalistic ideology, even in a relatively minor power, is recognized immediately as a threat by other countries. The universalistic aspirations, especially when combined with its totalitarianism, generate immediate concern among other states, not even necessarily neighbouring ones.[34]

Monoethnic and monoreligious states, or states clearly dominated by one religion (theocracies) and ethnicity (ethnocracies), and nationalistic states have all generated concerns among their neighbours in those cases in which ethnic, national, and religious lines did not match territorial ones. A nationalistic Germany in the 1930s immediately created fear among neighbours with substantial populations of ethnic Germans.[35]

Extraterritoriality affects not only threat perception but also foreign policy alignments and, as a consequence, the prospects for the functioning of the balance of power. Extraterritorial interests not only can form the basis of conflicts of interest separate from geopolitical calculations but also determine the nature of threat assessment and response. Ironically, even realists, such as Walt (1987), who emphasize that states balance against threats rather than power, downplay precisely those factors – ideology, religion, and ethnicity – that are the basis of threat assessments separate from power.

Expansive foreign policies dominated by particularistic (non-universalistic) extraterritorial concerns do not generate the balancing behaviour traditionally described by international relations theorists. Territorial expansion driven by ethnic interests does not generate balancing responses on the part of other great powers because the threats posed by such states are seen as circumscribed by their extraterritorial concerns. A Germany interested in the incorporation of ethnic Germans need not pose any threat to one without ethnic Germans. A Russia concerned with the reincorporation of ethnic Russians poses a threat to some but not all of its neighbours. Thus, whereas alliances built on perceptions of common threat might be created by certain changes in the balance of power are not constructed when there is an asymmetric sense of threat posed by expansive extraterritorial concerns. The relative growth of German power in the late 1930s was quite clear, but the nature of its aspirations was not. As long as it was seen as a racist state bent on bringing together ethnic Germans, its territorial ambitions were seen as directed primarily eastward. Further, German racialism could be seen as more hostile to Slavs than to fellow Anglo-Saxons (indeed, the basis for periodic German references to a British–German arrangement for Europe). Thus, the coalition constructed to oppose Hitler awaited German aggression clearly not aimed at reuniting ethnic Germans.[36]

Inter-state wars rooted in ethnicity thus typically attract only states with populations of the relevant nationals and do not generate standard balancing behaviour in response to aggression. It is the local distribution of power (between states in the region) that interacts with the territorial distribution of ethnic groups (how they are divided across borders), and with the nature of domestic political arrangements (ethnocracy or not) to shape and constrain state policies and determine regional stability.[37]

In contrast, the emergence of a universalistic ideology in another state is quite quickly and immediately seen as a challenge and threat and generates countercoalitions even absent major changes in the balance of power. The threat posed by a Communist Soviet Union was felt in many countries, including those quite far from the military reaches of the Soviet Union. And there was an immediate coalition formed to contain the spread of Communism even when the USSR was weak. Something similar occurred in the Arab world with the emergence of a fundamentalist Islamic regime in Iran. The arrival of the ayatollahs in Teheran, although immediately weakening Iran economically and militarily, also generated fears throughout the Arab and Muslim world (Nelson 2014). Indeed, Iran pursued policies similar to those of the Soviet Union, encouraging and supporting revolutionary fundamentalists elsewhere.[38] And those states responded in concert and out of all proportion to actual Iranian military might. Such states are seen as expansive and threatening even when they are not in a position militarily to export their revolutionary ideas.

Conclusion

The prospects for international order and stability are profoundly affected by the pursuit of extraterritorial interests by the states that compose the international system. In our conventional model of international politics, the balance of power preserves order and maintains stability. But that model presumes that a preeminent state concern with security and survival is primarily about the maintenance of the physical and territorial integrity of the state.

States, their elites and citizens, have an abiding interest in security and survival which also encompasses political ideals, nationality, ethnicity, and religion. These elements of identity constitute affective interests and are reflected in threat perceptions and international responses. Thus, changes in domestic political arrangements absent any change in the international balance of power can be seen as threatening. And because such threats are seen as particularistic they also affect foreign policy alignments and the functioning of the balance of power. Nation-states encompass some territory with a set of residents and extant resources and capabilities, but given that their borders do not circumscribe their affective concerns, they have extraterritorial interests that transform domestic practices in one state into international concerns of others.[39] Ethnicity and ethnic conflict embody this extraterritoriality.

Notes

1. The same point can be made about the predictions of secularization theory about the declining importance of religion (Fox 2012).
2. For the impact of the end of the Cold War on regional conflicts, see Stein and Lobell (1997), and for the impact on civil wars, see Kalyvas and Balcells (2010).
3. Cross-national studies of ethnic conflict find mixed results using a variety of measures of both ethnic fractionalization and concentration as well as mixed results attempting to reduce such conflict to economic inequality. A particular problem of closed polity approaches that focus on purely material considerations is that they point to determinants of ethnic conflict that would preclude any basis for external involvement by co-ethnics. For an example of one such model, see Caselli and Coleman (2013).
4. One can compile a long list of references discussing in one form or another the neglected international dimension of ethnic conflict stretching from Ryan (1988) to Carment, James, and Taydas (2006).
5. Ethnic conflict resurfaced in the 1990s as a major topic in the study of international relations, as once again, real-world events drive the interests of scholars and set an agenda for the field.
6. For a characterization of the factors that explain costly conflict, see Fearon (1995).
7. On religion and conflict, see, among others, Fox (1998), Ellingsen (2005), Gorski and Türkmen-Dervişoğlu (2013), and Brubaker (2015). On the link between religion and ethnicity and other factors for conflict, see, among others, Fox (2000, 2003, 2004). On religion and international relations theory, see Fox (2001), Fox and Sandler (2004), Snyder (2011), and Sandal and Fox (2013).
8. Connor (1972) finds the percentage under ten, Nielsson (1985) finds it just slightly more than 25 per cent.
9. The breakup of multinational empires in the last century has affected the geopolitical distribution of different ethnic groups. For the impact of the breakup of the Soviet Union, see Harris (1993).

10. The paper references a small proportion of the relevant empirical literature. Scholars with multiple contributions, only some of which are referenced, include Carment, Cederman, Davis and Moore, Gleditsch, Regan, and Saideman.
11. For a discussion of the internationalization of communal conflicts since 1945, see Gurr (1993). Also see Checkel (2013).
12. This distinction was originally made by Suhrke and Noble (1977) and developed by Heraclides (1990) and Carment (1993). Others who point to emotional attachments and affinities include Regan (2000) and Carment, James, and Taydas (2006).
13. It should be noted that states also intervene on behalf of ethnic groups for strategic and not just affective reasons (Biddle, Friedman, and Long 2012).
14. The key assumption of neorealism is that in a self-help system, "states seek to ensure their survival" (Waltz 1979, 91, 105). Comparably, Wendt's (1999, 198) constructivism defines the national interest as consisting of four needs of which two are physical survival and autonomy.
15. A core assumption of John Mearsheimer's (2001, 31) "offensive realism" is that security is the most important objective of states and "that survival is the primary goal of great powers".
16. Williams (1994) uses the term "ethnies" for ethnic collectivities.
17. For an argument that identity need not be defined versus an other, see Lebow (2008).
18. This perspective contrasts sharply with those in which states pursue ontological security by actions intended to secure moral, humanitarian, and honour-driven self-identity needs (Steele 2008).
19. In this sense, ethnic fear is something that is embedded in different identities and political competition and does not require the construction of "aggressive social identities", as argued by Arfi (1998).
20. The argument can also be put in terms of the interests of governing elites. Elites are interested in retaining their positions of power. And certainly, they take their political survival very seriously. But even their survival entails broader issues. Kings, for example, were not only interested in their own personal survival but in the maintenance of the monarchy.
21. Morgenthau, a classical realist, as for example, roots his view of realism in a conception of human nature.
22. More recently, the survival argument for individuals is made at the level of the gene. Individuals have an interest in the survival and success of their genes and thus sacrifice on behalf of offspring and kin.
23. Note that individuals vary. There are those who chose to die rather than convert to another religion. Others chose conversion, and still others pretended to convert and continued to practice their religion covertly. Presumably, survival was at issue for each of these types, but that they weighed different aspects of survival differently or assessed the probability of successful covert practice differently, etc.
24. Saideman and Ayres (2008) argue that domestic politics can drive irredentism.
25. On diasporas and international politics, see Shain and Barth (2003) and Shain and Sherman (1998).
26. On forced migrations in central European history, see Stola (1992); and on the migrations that follow the collapse of empire, see Brubaker (1995a).
27. Ironically, most jurisprudence is territorially demarcated and has had great difficulty with incorporating extraterritorial constructs (Note 1990).

28. On German citizenship, see Brubaker (1992a) and Klusmeyer (1993). For a discussion of citizenship issues in the Soviet successor states, see Brubaker (1992b).
29. Nationalism as used in this essay refers to a concern with co-nationals living outside the state. It can also refer to the idea that national groups should live in or be represented by a state.
30. Horowitz (1992) discusses the neglected connection between irrendentas and secessions. On the pattern of relationships between national minorities, nationalizing states, and external national homelands in the new Europe, see Brubaker (1995b). Rothschild (1981) argues that state-supported secessionist movements are the form of politicized ethnicity most problematic for international politics (in contrast to ethnicities partitioned among other states, and in contrast to pan movements and diasporas). A reading of the contributions to Chazan (1991) reveals some scholarly disagreement about the cases to which the label irredentism would apply.
31. Even with the assurance of minority rights in representative political systems, the resilience of ethnicity and the continuing role of diasporas suggest a continuing identification that forms the basis of interests and calculations.
32. Carment and James (1995) find that crises characterized by an irredentist setting are more likely to have a high level of perceived threat.
33. Although of peripheral concern in this paper, the extraterritorial concern of ideology has also grown in importance.
34. It can be argued that other universal ideologies have been seen as a threat to elites, but as long as they are not totalitarian and acceptant of pluralism, they are not seen as threats to societies.
35. Nationalistic is used here to refer to a concern with nationality. Nationalists are those who struggle for statehood. But once statehood is achieved, nationalists press for the in-gathering of nationals from foreign lands, sometimes through expansion.
36. See Pfaff's (1993) argument of Nazism as a totalitarian universalistic ideology. For a discussion of the impact of nationalistic aggression on international politics, see Williams (1994).
37. Note that the same would be said of theocracies, unless they were proselytizing ones.
38. See Nelson (2014) for an excellent delineation of the extraterritorial impact of revolutions in international politics.
39. The lack of overlap is the basis for Connor's (1978) argument about the modern nation-state and for the clever title of his article.

Acknowledgements

Thanks to Alan Kessler for research assistance. For comments thanks to anonymous reviewers for the journal as well as Henry Nau and panel participants at the annual meeting of the American Political Science Association, Chicago, September 1995, and to Rebecca Kook and conference participants at Ben-Gurion University, March 2014.

Disclosure statement

No potential conflict of interest was reported by the authors.

Funding

The author thanks the Sol Leshin Program for Ben-Gurion University of the Negev-UCLA Academic Cooperation for financial support. This work was also supported by the University of California's Institute on Global Conflict and Cooperation (IGCC) and UCLA's Academic Senate.

ORCID

Arthur A. Stein ⓘ http://orcid.org/0000-0002-1955-2898

References

Anderson, Benedict R. 1983. *Imagined Communities*. London: Verso.

Angstrom, Jan. 2001. "The International Dimensions of Ethnic Conflict." *Studies in Conflict & Terrorism* 24: 59–69.

Arfi, Badredine. 1998. "Ethnic Fear." *Security Studies* 8: 151–203.

Ben-Israel, Hedva. 2003. "Zionism and European Nationalisms." *Israel Studies* 8 (1): 91–104.

Biddle, Stephen, Jeffrey A. Friedman, and Stephen Long. 2012. "Civil War Intervention and the Problem of Iraq." *International Studies Quarterly* 56: 85–98.

Brown, Michael E., ed. 1996. *The International Dimensions of Internal Conflict*. Cambridge, MA: MIT Press.

Brubaker, Rogers. 1992a. *Citizenship and Nationhood in France and Germany*. Cambridge, MA: Harvard University Press.

Brubaker, Rogers. 1992b. "Citizenship Struggles in Soviet Successor States." *International Migration Review* 26 (2): 269–291.

Brubaker, Rogers. 1995a. "Aftermaths of Empire and the Unmixing of Peoples." *Ethnic and Racial Studies* 18: 189–218.

Brubaker, Rogers. 1995b. "National Minorities, Nationalizing States, and External National Homelands in the New Europe." *Daedalus* 124 (2): 107–132.

Brubaker, Rogers. 2015. "Religious Dimensions of Political Conflict and Violence." *Sociological Theory* 33 (1): 1–19.

Carment, David. 1993. "The International Dimensions of Ethnic Conflict." *Journal of Peace Research* 30: 137–150.

Carment, David, and Patrick James. 1995. "Internal Constraints and Interstate Ethnic Conflict." *Journal of Conflict Resolution* 39: 82–109.

Carment, David, Patrick James, and Zeynep Taydas. 2006. *Who Intervenes?* Columbus: Ohio State University Press.

Caselli, Francesco, and Wilbur John Coleman. 2013. "On the Theory of Ethnic Conflict." *Journal of the European Economic Association* 11 (s1): 161–192.

Cederman, Lars-Erik, Luc Girardin, and Kristian Skrede Gleditsch. 2009. "Ethnonationalist Triads." *World Politics* 61: 403–437.

Cederman, Lars-Erik, Kristian Skrede Gleditsch, Idean Salehyan, and Julian Wucherpfennig. 2013. "Transborder Ethnic Kin and Civil War." *International Organization* 67: 389–410.

Chazan, Naomi, ed. 1991. *Irredentism and International Politics*. Boulder, CO: Lynne Rienner.

Checkel, Jeffrey T., ed. 2013. *Transnational Dynamics of Civil War*. Cambridge: Cambridge University Press.

Connor, Walker. 1972. "Nation-Building or Nation-Destroying?" *World Politics* 24: 319–355.

Connor, Walker. 1978. "A Nation Is a Nation, Is a State, Is an Ethnic Group Is a ... ." *Ethnic and Racial Studies* 1: 377–400.

Davis, David R., and Will H. Moore. 1997. "Ethnicity Matters." *International Studies Quarterly* 41: 171–184.

Ellingsen, Tanja. 2005. "Toward a Revival of Religion and Religious Clashes." *Terrorism and Political Violence* 17 (3): 305–332.

Esman, Milton J., ed. 1977. *Ethnic Conflict in the Western World.* Ithaca, NY: Cornell University Press.

Fearon, James D. 1995. "Rationalist Explanations for War." *International Organization* 49: 379–414.

Fearon, James D. 1998. "Commitment Problems and the Spread of Ethnic Conflict." In *The International Spread of Ethnic Conflict,* edited by David Lake and Donald Rothchild, 107–126. Princeton, NJ: Princeton University Press.

Fearon, James D. 2003. "Ethnic and Cultural Diversity by Country." *Journal of Economic Growth* 8 (2): 195–222.

Forsberg, Erika, and Niklas Karlén. 2013. "Bombs to Brethren, Cannons to Comrades." Paper prepared for the International Studies Association, San Francisco, CA, April 3–6.

Fox, Jonathan. 1998. "The Effects of Religion on Domestic Conflicts." *Terrorism and Political Violence* 10 (4): 43–63.

Fox, Jonathan. 2000. "The Ethnic-Religious Nexus." *Civil Wars* 3 (3): 1–22.

Fox, Jonathan. 2001. "Religion as an Overlooked Element of International Relations." *International Studies Review* 3 (3): 53–73.

Fox, Jonathan. 2003. "Counting the Causes and Dynamics of Ethnoreligious Violence." *Totalitarian Movements and Political Religions* 4 (3): 119–144.

Fox, Jonathan. 2004. "The Rise of Religious Nationalism and Conflict: Ethnic Conflict and Revolutionary Wars, 1945–2001." *Journal of Peace Research* 41: 715–731.

Fox, Jonathan. 2007. "The Increasing Role of Religion in State Failure: 1960–2004." *Terrorism and Political Violence* 19 (3): 395–414.

Fox, Jonathan. 2012. "The Religious Wave: Religion and Domestic Conflict from 1960 to 2009." *Civil Wars* 14 (2): 141–158.

Fox, Jonathan, and Shmuel Sandler. 2004. *Bringing Religion into International Relations.* New York: Palgrave Macmillan.

Gartzke, Erik, and Kristian Skrede Gleditsch. 2006. "Identity and Conflict." *European Journal of International Relations* 12 (1): 53–87.

Gellner, Ernest. 1983. *Nations and Nationalism.* Ithaca, NY: Cornell University Press.

Gleditsch, Kristian Skrede. 2007. "Transnational Dimensions of Civil War." *Journal of Peace Research* 44: 293–309.

Gorski, Philip S., and Gülay Türkmen-Dervişoğlu. 2013. "Religion, Nationalism, and Violence." *Annual Review of Sociology* 39: 193–210.

Gurr, Ted Robert. 1993. *Minorities at Risk.* Washington, DC: US Institute of Peace.

Gurr, Ted Robert. 2000. *Peoples versus States.* Washington, DC: US Institute of Peace.

Harbom, Lotta, and Peter Wallensteen. 2005. "Armed Conflict and Its International Dimensions, 1946–2004." *Journal of Peace Research* 42: 623–635.

Harris, Chauncy D. 1993. "New European Countries and Their Minorities." *Geographical Review* 83: 301–320.

Hechter, Michael, and Margaret Levi. 1979. "The Comparative Analysis of Ethnoregional Movements." *Ethnic and Racial Studies* 2 (3): 260–274.

Heraclides, Alexis. 1990. "Secessionist Minorities and External Involvement." *International Organization* 44: 341–378.

Hobsbawm, E. J. 1990. *Nations and Nationalism since 1780*. Cambridge: Cambridge University Press.

Holsti, Kalevi J. 1991. *Peace and War: Armed Conflicts and International Order, 1648–1989*. Cambridge: Cambridge University Press.

Horowitz, Donald L. 1985. *Ethnic Groups in Conflict*. Berkeley: University of California Press.

Horowitz, Donald L. 1992. "Irredentas and Secessions." *International Journal of Comparative Sociology* 33 (1–2): 118–130.

Huibregtse, Ada. 2010. "External Intervention in Ethnic Conflict." *International Interactions* 36 (3): 265–293.

Huibregtse, Ada. 2011. "Interstate Conflict and Ethnicity." *Civil Wars* 13 (1): 40–60.

Kalyvas, Stathis N. 2010. "Internal Conflict and Political Violence." In *Rethinking Violence*, edited by Erica Chenoweth and Adria Lawrence, xi–xiii. Cambridge, MA: MIT Press.

Kalyvas, Stathis N., and Laia Balcells. 2010. "International System and Technologies of Rebellion." *American Political Science Review* 104: 415–429.

Klusmeyer, Douglas B. 1993. "Aliens, Immigrants, and Citizens: The Politics of Inclusion in the Federal Republic of Germany." *Daedalus* 122 (3): 81–114.

Krasner, Stephen D. 1978. *Defending the National Interest*. Princeton, NJ: Princeton University Press.

Lake, David A., and Donald Rothchild, eds. 1998. *The International Spread of Ethnic Conflict*. Princeton, NJ: Princeton University Press.

Lebow, Richard Ned. 2008. "Identity and International Relations." *International Relations* 22: 473–492.

Lobell, Steven E., and Philip Mauceri, eds. 2004. *Ethnic Conflict and International Politics*. New York: Palgrave Macmillan.

Mearsheimer, John J. 2001. *The Tragedy of Great Power Politics*. New York: Norton.

Nelson, Chad E. 2014. "Revolutionary Waves." PhD diss., UCLA.

Nielsson, Gunnar P. 1985. "States and 'Nation-Groups'." In *New Nationalisms of the Developed West*, edited by Edward A. Tiryakian and Ronald Rogowski, 27–56. Boston, MA: Allen & Unwin.

Note. 1990. "Constructing the State Extraterritorially." *Harvard Law Review* 103: 1273–1305.

Pfaff, William. 1993. *The Wrath of Nations*. New York: Simon and Schuster.

Posen, Barry R. 1993. "The Security Dilemma and Ethnic Conflict." *Survival* 35 (1): 27–47.

Regan, Patrick M. 2000. *Civil Wars and Foreign Powers*. Ann Arbor: University of Michigan Press.

Rosecrance, Richard N. 1986. *The Rise of the Trading State*. New York: Basic Books.

Rosecrance, Richard N., and Arthur A. Stein, eds. 2006. *No More States?: Globalization, National Self-Determination, and Terrorism*. Lanham, MD: Rowman & Littlefield.

Rothschild, Joseph. 1981. *Ethnopolitics*. New York: Columbia University Press.

Ryan, S. 1988. "Explaining Ethnic Conflict: The Neglected International Dimension." *Review of International Studies* 14: 161–177.

Saideman, Stephen M. 1997. "Explaining the International Relations of Secessionist Conflicts." *International Organization* 51: 721–753.

Saideman, Stephen M. 2001. *The Ties That Divide*. New York: Columbia University Press.

Saideman, Stephen M. 2002. "Discrimination in International Relations." *Journal of Peace Research* 39: 27–50.

Saideman, Stephen M., and R. William Ayres. 2008. *For Kin or Country*. New York: Columbia University Press.

Salehyan, Idean. 2009. *Rebels Without Borders*. Ithaca, NY: Cornell University Press.

Salehyan, Idean, and Kristian Skrede Gleditsch. 2006. "Refugees and the Spread of Civil War." *International Organization* 60: 335–366.

Salehyan, Idean, Kristian Skrede Gleditsch, and David E. Cunningham. 2011. "Explaining External Support for Insurgent Groups." *International Organization* 65: 709–744.

Sandal, Nukhet A., and Jonathan Fox. 2013. *Religion in International Relations Theory*. London: Routledge.

Seton-Watson, Hugh. 1977. *Nations and States*. Boulder, CO: Westview Press.

Shain, Yossi, and Aharon Barth. 2003. "Diasporas and International Relations Theory." *International Organization* 57: 449–479.

Shain, Yossi, and Martin Sherman. 1998. "Dynamics of Disintegration: Diaspora, Secession and the Paradox of Nation-States." *Nations and Nationalism* 4: 321–346.

Smith, Anthony D. 1981. *The Ethnic Revival*. Cambridge: Cambridge University Press.

Snyder, Jack L., ed. 2011. *Religion and International Relations Theory*. New York: Columbia University Press.

Steele, Brent J. 2008. *Ontological Security in International Relations*. London: Routledge.

Stein, Arthur A., and Steven E. Lobell. 1997. "Geostructuralism and International Politics." In *Regional Orders*, edited by David A. Lake and Patrick M. Morgan, 101–122. University Park: Penn State University Press.

Stola, Dariusz. 1992. "Forced Migrations in Central European History." *International Migration Review* 26: 324–341.

Suhrke, Astri, and Lela Garner Noble, eds. 1977. *Ethnic Conflict in International Relations*. New York: Praeger.

Toft, Monica Duffy. 2006. "Religion, Civil War, and International Order." BCSIA Discussion Paper 2006–03, Kennedy School of Government, Harvard University, July.

Trumbore, Peter F. 2003. "Victims or Aggressors?" *International Studies Quarterly* 47: 183–201.

Walt, Stephen M. 1987. *The Origins of Alliances*. Ithaca, NY: Cornell University Press.

Waltz, Kenneth N. 1979. *Theory of International Politics*. Menlo Park, CA: Addison-Wesley.

Wendt, Alexander. 1999. *Social Theory of International Politics*. Cambridge: Cambridge University Press.

Williams, Robin M., Jr. 1994. "The Sociology of Ethnic Conflicts." *Annual Review of Sociology* 20: 49–79.

Woodwell, Douglas. 2004. "Unwelcome Neighbors." *International Studies Quarterly* 48: 197–223.

Zacher, Mark W. 2001. "The Territorial Integrity Norm." *International Organization* 55: 215–250.

Representation, minorities and electoral reform: the case of the Palestinian minority in Israel

Rebecca Kook

ABSTRACT

The article examines the impact of the recent change in the electoral threshold in Israel, from 2 per cent to 3.25 per cent, on the political representation of the Palestinian minority in Israel in the 2015 national election. I argue that the change in the threshold had a direct impact on Palestinian electoral representation and that this change provided incentives to Palestinian leadership to broaden their appeal and become more inclusive in their agenda. Following recent scholarship on ethnic minorities and employing the concept of "representational claims", I suggest that through the provision of electoral incentives, institutional design can influence not only the degree of representation, but its substantive claims as well.

Introduction

Modern democracy is defined, largely, by the claim of the democratic state to represent its citizens. While historically, representation and democracy were often at odds, today, the ultimate reference for democratic state power is electoral representation (Urbinati and Warren 2008). Hence, issues concerning representation drive to the heart of democracy; the legitimacy of the democratic regime lies in its ability to represent, adequately and fundamentally, the interests of its citizens.

Despite this *promise* of democracy, many democracies include minorities who feel that their interests are far from adequately represented; minorities with histories of exclusion, whose voice and interests have been and continue to be systematically excluded from the centres of power, and who are marginalized within the societies in which they live. More often than not, these minorities define themselves in terms of ethnicity, race or religion.

Prompted largely by the models proposed by Arendt Lijphart starting in the early 1970s (Lijphart 1969, 1975, 1984), and the growing discourse on identity politics and group rights (Gutmann 1992; Kymlicka 1995), contemporary literature on ethnic minorities in democracies is driven by three main assumptions (Nordlinger 1982; Diamond and Plattner 1994; Norris 2008; Lublin 2014). First, that electoral systems can play a central role in promoting legitimacy; second, that legitimacy can be enhanced by ethnic political representation; and finally, that representation needs to incorporate a dimension of proportionality so that the groups themselves feel that their identity is directly present within the political institutions. Therefore, from amongst the different types of electoral systems, the *proportional* ones are better equipped, or, in the words of Pippa Norris "kinder and more gentle" to the demands of marginalized minority representation (Norris 2008).

Underlying this set of assumptions is a specific conception of representation which corresponds to the widely accepted distinction between substantive and descriptive representation. Most of the literature on ethnic minorities implicitly assumes that descriptive representation is best suited to ethnic and other so-called "identity" minorities.[1] In other words, it is assumed that members of the same identity group are best suited to represent the interests of the group itself.

Hence, an essential paradox has emerged within much of the relevant literature. On the one hand, an essentially *constructivist* position that argues for the capacity of institutions to impact on and structure the nature of majority–minority relations, coupled with a basically *essentialist* position that assumes that interests are derived from identity and are "given". The paradox lies in the idea that while the nature of minority–majority *relations* can be constituted by institutions and is therefore subject to change, the nature of the representation itself, or – *what it is* that is represented – is so deeply rooted in *identity* that it is presumably immutable. Following recent scholarship on ethnic minorities (Chandra 2004; Posner 2004; Lublin 2014), I challenge this assumption and suggest that institutional design can do more than just bring about electoral realignment; that institutional design informs electoral incentives which in turn have a direct impact on the type of representation, or on "what it is" that is represented. Furthermore, employing Michael Saward's insight that political parties "do not so much represent or fail to represent, but rather *claim* to represent" (2006, 298), I suggest that what minority leaders claim to represent is influenced by the very electoral rules that inform the structure of political parties. Seen this way, it is possible to recognize that no specific form of representation is appropriate or inappropriate for minorities, but rather that claims of representation take on a variety of forms that are subject to a variety of influences and are essentially dynamic.

I explore this theoretical issue within the context of the relationship between Israel and its ethnic Palestinian-citizen minority[2]. In January 2013, the Israeli parliament voted to raise the electoral threshold from 2 per cent to 3.25 per cent. It was clear that the raising of the threshold would have immediate consequences for the political participation of the Palestinian minority in Israel whose representative political parties had, over the past twenty years, garnered enough votes to pass the previous threshold but would be hard pushed to pass the new one (Sheferman 2013). Indeed, the immediate result was that the existing four Palestinian political lists[3] united to form The Joint List (JL), and went on to win thirteen seats in the parliament in the elections in March 2015, making them the third largest party in the parliament. Palestinian representation rose from eleven parliament members in the nineteenth Knesset, to thirteen in the twentieth. Thus, far from minimizing Palestinian representation in the Israeli parliament (which was the fear), the reform actually strengthened their potential political power. In addition, Palestinian voting rates rose from 56.5 per cent in the elections to the nineteenth Knesset to 63.5 per cent in the elections to the twentieth (Rudnitzky 2015).

In this paper, I argue that the rise in the electoral threshold had an impact on two dimensions of Palestinian representation: the first was on the representational *form*, and the second was on its *claims*. In terms of form, the rise in the threshold prompted unification and the creation of a larger minority party. However, I argue that the act of unification was not merely technical, it also changed the *claims of representation* making them more inclusive and hence of appeal to a much larger segment of Palestinian society in Israel. Ultimately, the higher threshold benefited the Palestinian minority.

The paper is composed of two parts. In the first, I discuss theoretical notions of minority representation. In the second, I examine the case of the representation of the Palestinian minority in Israel. I end with a summary and discussion of the case and the theory.

Democracy, ethnic minorities and representation

Questions about democracy, ethnic divisions and minority representation raise significant and enduring intellectual puzzles and have engendered a rich and wide scholarly literature. Much of the literature focuses on the idea of power-sharing regimes as the basis for moderating ethnic conflict (Lijphart 1984; Norris 2004, 2008). The basis for this debate is the observation that within democratic regimes characterized by deep ethnic or other cultural cleavages, minorities are often excluded from the loci of power, as their interests are highjacked by those of the ruling majorities. Within these types of multiethnic societies, power-sharing regimes (also referred to as "consociational" or "consensus", Norris 2008, 3) through a series of institutional arrangements and procedures, "turn political opponents into cooperative partners", by providing ethnic leaders with "a guaranteed stake" in the democratic process (Lublin 2014).

The most common institutional mechanisms for maximizing "stakeholders" are the Proportional Representation (PR) multi-party system and low electoral thresholds. Electoral thresholds exist in many parliamentary democracies. They determine a pre-set minimum number of votes necessary to enter parliament. Since minority groups and minority parties have relatively limited voting power, PR systems with *low* thresholds are considered more amenable to minority representation. As proportional electoral systems lower the hurdles for smaller parties, the inclusion of ethnic parties into the legislature and ultimately into coalition governments is seen as more likely. And hence, within these systems, potential ethnic conflict is presumably moderated by leaders whose stake in the decision-making processes provides them with incentives to cooperate with other leaders, thereby promoting the legitimacy of the political system in the eyes of their constituents (Elkins and Sides 2007).

Central to the logic of power-sharing, therefore, is the treatment of leadership and representation. But while representation is, in itself, a complex and varied political concept, the type of representation that underlies the logic of power-sharing, however, is left under-theorized (Hazan and Rahat 2000).

Representation and representational claims

The literature on representation has generated a number of influential distinctions. Most important is that between ideological and identity-based representation or as it is commonly known, between substantive and descriptive representation (Pitkin 1972; Runciman 2007; Squires 2008; Urbinati and Warren 2008). The ideological approach to representation implies that voters elect parties on the basis of their position on major issues facing the country, while the identity-based approach to representation implies that representatives reflect the social composition of the electorate in terms of descriptive qualities (Norris and Marsh 1997). According to the "ideological" model, a parliament is representative when it adequately reflects the spectrum of positions held by the population; and according to the "identity" model, a parliament is representative when it includes the same proportion of each relevant subgroup as the population from which it is drawn. In the former, legitimacy is derived from its policy outcomes, while in the latter, it derives less from its decisions, and more from its composition. These two types of representation imply different types of relationships between constituencies and candidates.

Most power-sharing approaches to ethnic conflict assume that ethnic groups go hand in hand with identity-based or "descriptive" representation – presumably, since the nature of the cleavage is rooted in the distinguishing characteristics of the group (Harff and Gurr 2004; Olzak 2004; Smith 2013). Accordingly, we have come to expect that ethnic parties should (if they wish to truly "represent" their groups' interests) focus on particularistic agendas and dedicate themselves to promoting interests that are seen as derived from the identity of the group. Hence, identity-based representation has built-in incentives to maintain the boundaries of the group constant.

However, it is precisely on this point that theories of power-sharing have attracted the most criticism. One of the first scholars to voice this criticism was Donald Horowitz. In a series of articles, he argued that these types of power-sharing regimes often serve to institutionalize ethnic cleavages rather than moderate them (Horowitz 2003, 2014). PR systems and lower thresholds provide ethnic leaders with incentives to maintain exclusive agendas and to promote particularist interests. Since PR electoral systems and low thresholds allow ethnic leaders to maintain narrow, particular agendas, they lack incentives to try to appeal to wider constituencies and tend to maintain static definitions of group boundaries (Cohen 1997; Selway and Templeman 2012; Horowitz 2014; Lublin 2014).

A number of recent studies of ethnic parties and ethnic conflict have adopted this criticism, looking at the impact of a wide array of such institutional arrangements, such as regime type and political boundaries on the *structure* of the cleavage itself. Chandra, in her research of Indian ethnic politics (Chandra 2004), looks at how ethnicity fluctuates across federal and state levels demonstrating that the strength of the same cleavages differs in different levels of government; Posner, in his study of ethnicity in Africa (Posner 2004, 2005), demonstrates the impact of group size relative to the larger population on the politicization of the cleavage and the way in which the change in regime type changes the focus from constituency to national level in the significance of the ethnic cleavage. Lublin (2014) proposes a "renewed" institutional approach that builds on the insights of Posner and Chandra in terms of the "flexibility of identities" and the ability of political institutions – particularly democratic institutions – to "alter the relevant identity" (2014, 18).

What these studies share is their insight that electoral and other institutional design can impact on the nature of ethnic cleavages, and hence the salience of ethnic divisions. Therefore contrary to the logic of descriptive representation, *what it is that is represented* in ethnic (i.e. descriptive) representation is not "given". Once we acknowledge the ability of institutions to impact on the interests of the group, and hence that interests are not immutably derived from identity, the logic of descriptive representation, that is, that interests of identity groups are inherent in the identity itself, and that representatives – as members of the same group – can, and do, represent those very same interests, loses much of its potency.

Following in the path of these recent studies, I suggest in the following analysis that changes in electoral rules can impact not merely on the ability of ethnic parties to garner more or less seats, but that they influence the nature of their relationship with their constituency. To best understand this relationship, I adopt Michael Saward's notion of "representative claims" and suggest that given the weakness of the notion of descriptive representation noted above, the critical question is no longer what representatives succeed or fail in representing, but rather, what they *claim* to represent (Saward 2006, 2010). Thinking in terms of representative "claims" allows us, on the one hand, to acknowledge that there is always a gap between what leaders claim to represent, and what is actually represented, and on the other hand, to see that the relationship between leaders/candidates and constituencies is fluid and dynamic. The concept of representative claims offers a way to think of representation that corresponds to the types of fluidities suggested by Posner, Chandra and Lublin discussed above.

In the following part, I examine how raising the threshold in Israel impacted on the incentives of the Israeli Palestinian leadership and affected the nature of their relationship to their constituency and hence the nature of their representation.

Electoral design in Israel

Israel is a parliamentary democracy, with a multi-party PR political system (Hazan and Rahat 2000). Over the years, the electoral system has become increasingly fragmented with up to thirty-two political parties at times competing amongst themselves for seats in the Israeli parliament. No government has ever managed to establish a majority government on its own and therefore all thirty-four Israeli governments have been coalition governments (Knesset 2016).

Amongst the differences between Israel's PR system and others, two stand out. The first is that the entire country constitutes one single voting district (with 120 members), and the second is that it is very easy to compete in the elections: garnering 100 signatures, 2256 NIS (approximately $580) and then, on election day – to pass the pre-determined electoral threshold is sufficient to guarantee representation in the Israeli parliament.

The relatively loose barriers to entry, coupled with Israel's plural and polar society, have rendered the political system increasingly fragmented. (Bueno de Mesquita 2000; Hazan and Rahat 2000; Rahat 2004). Indeed, Israel has been struggling with the issue of political fragmentation since its establishment, and the debate surrounding the level of the threshold has been a relatively constant feature of public discourse. In addition to the deep rift between the ideological left and right wings, the identity-based divisions are national, ethnic and religious: between the Jewish majority and Arab-Palestinian minority; and within the Jewish majority, divisions between a largely secular majority and a large minority of orthodox Jews and between Jews of European descent, and those of middle eastern and north African descent (Shafir and Peled 2002). Both the Palestinians and the orthodox

Jews have parties "of their own", while others are loosely associated with different ascriptive identities. Growing polarization has produced a parliament that is highly fragmented. Representation has become more and more identity-based, with political ideology overlapping rather than cross cutting differences in cultural, ethnic and religious identity. For example, the right-wing party established by Avigdor Leiberman, *Yisrael Beiteinu* is identified largely with both a right-wing ideology, and voters of Russian descent, while the left-wing Meretz is identified almost exclusively with Ashkenazi Jewish voters. These overlapping cleavages have rendered Israeli society more and more polarized (Kimmerling 2005; Shafir and Peled 2002). Efforts to combat fragmentation have resulted in the gradual raising of the electoral threshold: to 1 per cent in 1951; to 1.5 per cent in 1992 and to 2 per cent in 2004. The recent reform, adopted in January 2015, raised it to 3.5 per cent (Kenig 2015).

The 2015 electoral reform

The Israeli parliament passed the Governance Law on 14 March 2014, with a majority of 67 votes, thereby raising the electoral threshold from 2 per cent to 3.25 per cent – the rough equivalent of four parliamentary seats (*Haaretz* March 14, 2014).

The Governance Law was promoted by the coalition as a reform of the system: a reform aimed at producing a strong executive and legislature that would be capable of passing laws and promoting difficult (controversial) political policy by cutting down on fragmented coalitions (*Haaretz* February 2, 2013). Nonetheless, opposition to the law was widespread. The raising of the threshold had potentially complicated implications for all political parties that hovered over the four-seat mark in the nineteenth parliament. These included the four Palestinian parties, the Jewish ultra-orthodox parties, the left-wing Meretz party, "Ha'Tnua" centre-party led by Tzippi Livni and some smaller parties that had already combined forces such as the right-wing Moledet party with the Jewish Home. However, the moment the law was passed, public and political discourse surrounding the proposed law was dominated by a single issue: while all the parties mentioned above were theoretically challenged by the reform, the Palestinian parties clearly had the most to lose. The reason was self-evident: at four seats each – the scenario whereby none of the parties would pass the 3.25 per cent threshold was a realistic one. Since the representation of Palestinian interests was seen as the exclusive role of Palestinian-ethnic parties, the disappearance of the Palestinian parties would in effect mean the disappearance of Palestinian representation. On January 20, then-Labor chairman Herzog called the move "a danger to pluralism and the lifeblood of democracy." The same day, Meretz chairwoman Zehava Galon stated that the government was trying to "throw out of the political arena populations that are already discriminated against" and to "mortally harm Israeli democracy". And Ahmad Tibi – head of the Raam-Taal alliance – called the move "anti-democratic", describing it as "a right-wing initiative" aimed at Arab parties and other minorities (quoted in Green 2015). Almost in a blink of an eye, the entire discourse on stability and governability was dismissed, and the reform was perceived exclusively as a blatant attempt to eliminate Palestinian representation in the Israeli parliament.

The Palestinian minority in Israel

The Palestinian citizens of Israel, including 80 per cent Muslims and 20 per cent Christians, constitute a minority of 18 per cent in a predominantly Jewish state (Waxman 2012). Given the fact that Israel is a self-defined Jewish State that recognizes no distinction either between religion and state or between religion and nationality, the Palestinian minority in Israel is both a religious and a national minority. In addition, they are Arabic speakers, and are also a linguistic minority in a predominantly Hebrew-speaking society. Hence, the Palestinian minority embodies three overlapping cleavage lines (Ghanem and Rouhana 2001; Kook 2002).

Despite their official citizenship status, the relationship between the state and the Palestinian minority has been an unresolved source of tension and conflict. For many of Israel's Jewish citizens, as for its leaders, it is difficult to disentangle the identity and interests of this citizen minority, from those of the larger Palestinian nation, with whom Israel has been involved in an often violent ethno-national conflict over sovereignty and territory since its establishment. Hence, the relationship between this minority and the state is ambivalent and ambiguous: in their identity straddling between being equal bearers of democratic rights in a non-liberal democratic state, and being members of a shunned and discriminated minority (Ghanem and Rouhana 2001; Frisch 2011; Haklai 2011; Waxman 2012).

While the Palestinian citizens of Israel are eligible for the rights and legal protections provided for by the democratic system in Israel, there are many ways in which they are treated unequally. Some of that inequality is a function of their identity as non-Jews in a Jewish state. Eligibility for land ownership and property rights in large portions of the territory of the state, alongside "homeland" immigration rights, for example, are the exclusive rights of Jews (Kook 2002). In addition, there exists deep inequality in government budget allocation in most areas – including education, welfare and health (Waxman 2012). Finally, the Palestinian citizens are largely segregated from the mainstay of Jewish Israeli society as they reside largely in exclusively Palestinian villages, study in Arabic language schools, and are employed in a limited number of labour sectors (Ghanem and Rouhana 2001; Haklai 2011). All of this results in the fact that despite changes over the years, the Palestinian minority in Israel is considered both a marginalized and discriminated minority.

The issue of political participation is particularly important, as it constitutes one of the main rights ascribed to the minority (Peretz and Gideon 1997). The reality, however, is complex. Following two decades of Military Rule, it took until the early 1980s for independent Palestinian political parties to develop, and by the early 1990s, a number of distinct political lists existed which reflected a varied ideological and religious landscape (Jamal 2006, 2011; Frisch 2011). A crucial turning point in terms of Palestinian voting patterns occurred in 2000 with the second Intifada. At that point, following the death of thirteen citizens in protests by the police, a sharp decline in Palestinian support of Jewish-Zionist parties began. If in 1996, 62.4 per cent supported Palestinian and joint parties, and 37.6 per cent supported Jewish-Zionist parties, this changed to 69.2 per cent and 30.8 per cent, respectively, in 2003, and then to 77.2 per cent and 22.8 per cent, respectively, in 2013 (Rudnitzky 2015). This trend was accompanied by a gradual decline in Palestinian voting rates – from 77 per cent in 1996, to 62 per cent in 2003 to 53.4 per cent in 2009 and 56.5 per cent in 2013 (Rudnitzky 2015). Since 2003, Palestinian political representation has stabilized with four to five local Palestinian political parties represented in each parliament. These include Balad, established in 1996 by Palestinian intellectual Azmi Bishara, which has run on an Arab nationalist ticket and is considered the most radical amongst the Palestinian parties, as it supports the establishment of a democratic secular state in the entire area of Palestine; Ra'am, that represents what is known as the southern faction of the Islamic movement which runs on an Islamist ticket, Ta'al – The Arab Movement for Renewal, and Ma'da – the Arab Democratic List (Jamal 2006). Amongst the Palestinian parties, only Hadash – the communist party – is a joint Arab-Jewish political list. Table 1 illustrates the breakdown of seats garnered by each party over the past four electoral campaigns.

It is important nonetheless to point out that despite the gradual increase in the number of parliament seats gained by Palestinian representatives, they are still not proportionally represented in the Israeli parliament. For example, in the elections to the nineteenth Knesset in 2013, out of the 5,656,705 total voters in Israel – 800,000 were Palestinian citizens – 14 per

Table 1. Breakdown of seats won by Arab-Palestinian political parties during elections to the sixteenth, seventeenth, eighteenth and nineteenth parliaments.

	16th Knesset (2003)	17th Knesset	18th Knesset	19th Knesset
Ra'am Ma'da	1–Mada	1–Mada	1–Mada	3–Raam
Ta'al	1–Ra'am	2–Raam	2–raam	1–taal
		1–Taal	1–taal	
Balad	3	3	3	3
Hadash	3	3	4	4
Total	8	10	11	11

Note: Data taken from Israeli Knesset website (www.knesset.gov.il).

cent of the electorate. However, only 56 per cent of the eligible Palestinian voters voted (as opposed to 68 per cent of the Jewish electorate). In the Knesset, there were a total of twelve Palestinian members (if we include a Palestinian MK from the Likud party). The low voting rates and the consequent low degrees of representation constitute an important context to the emergence of the JL.

The establishment of The Joint List

On 8 December 2014, then Prime Minister Netanyahu called a press conference at which he announced that he was dismantling the government and calling for elections. The following day, the Knesset approved the act with a majority of ninety-three votes. The elections were called for 17 March 2015 (*Haaretz* December 10, 2014). Less than one month later, after numerous appeals submitted to the Supreme Court were rejected, the Governance law was finalized and made into law.

The raising of the threshold caused a realignment of the party system. The first change was the merger of the Labor Party with "Ha'Tnua" led by Tzippi Livni, and the creation of a new party entitled "The Zionist Camp." Others, between smaller Jewish parties, followed. The most dramatic and significant was the unification of the four separate Palestinian lists and the creation of the JL.

On 23 January, the leaders of the four Palestinian political parties convened a press conference in Nazareth at which they announced their decision to unite and form the JL (Purat 2015). The four parties included all four that had parliament representatives: Hadash, Balad, Ta'al, and Ra'am. Ayman Odeh, newly elected chair of the Hadash list, was placed at the head. The first fourteen places (which were considered realistic slots on the list) were allocated proportionally to the electoral power of each separate list: five candidates from Hadash, four from Balad, three from Ra'am and two from Ta'al. These fourteen included representatives of all religions – Christian, Muslim and Druze – and two women who were placed in realistic positions – Aida Toma Sleiman from Hadash and Hanin Zuabi from Balad. Hence, the list claimed to be representative both politically (of the existing political parties) and in terms of gender and religion.

The raising of the threshold seemed to provide a tailwind to long-standing efforts by groups of Palestinian intellectuals to promote a political unification. During the 2013 elections for the nineteenth parliament, there were preliminary negotiations between the political parties led by then leaders of Hadash, Balad and Ta'al. Months earlier, a position paper was written by three leading intellectuals recommending the raising of threshold, arguing that it would provide a positive incentive for the Palestinians to unite and in this way augment their influence within the parliament (Smooha, Ghanem, and Ali

2013). The paper was presented to the constitution and law committee of the Knesset during the debates over the Governance Law. However, despite long debates and efforts, the Palestinian leadership was unable to reach an agreement to unite (Ali 2015).

The passing of the Governance Law provided the necessary incentive. While many expressed scepticism that given the ideological and political diversity of the four component parties – particularly the deep differences between the Islamists and the Communists – real unification was unlikely, support for the unification was widespread and pervasive. Unification was widely seen as a survival mechanism which, despite its possible shortcomings, was the only means to ensure Palestinian representation faced with the growing strength of the radical right wing, the increase in anti-pluralist legislation passed in the parliament, and the deep sense of emergency evoked by these political processes (Ali 2015; Watad 2015).

For others, however, unification was perceived as more than a survival mechanism and was heralded as a political opportunity. Declining voting rates indicated two things: first declining levels of belief in the ability of an increasingly right-wing Israeli political system to genuinely address the minority's needs, and secondly, a reflection of the growing disappointment from the established national political leadership. Survey results comparing positions from 2003 to 2012 are available on a number of relevant issues. For example, in response to the question – "Despite its flaws Israel is democratic towards its Arab citizens", support went from 63.1 per cent in 2003 to 54.2 per cent in 2012. In a series of questions regarding the effectiveness of Israel's democratic institutions, in response to the statement "The Arab citizens can improve their lot through voting, persuasion and political pressure", 81.4 per cent responded positively in 2003, compared to only 65.6 per cent in 2012. Over 80 per cent believed that Israel was not established in 1948 on the basis of justice, and 81 per cent believed that Israel is a democracy only for Jews (Smooha 2013).

The same survey provides evidence as to the declining belief in political leadership as well. In response to the statement, "The leaders of the Arab political parties are effective and authentic representatives of Palestinian society" – 61.1 per cent supported it in 2003, and in 2012, it fell to 53.1 per cent. In 2012, 63.2 per cent of the respondents said that they did not feel that their political leaders were helpful in promoting their daily interests, and 76 per cent responded that there needed to be a change in the agenda promoted by the leadership. Similarly, the percentage of respondents who supported illegal demonstrations rose from 9.9 per cent in 2003 to 25.8 per cent in 2012, and those that voiced support for all forms of opposition including violence, rose from 5.4 per cent in 2003 to 16.6 per cent in 2012 (Smooha 2013). Finally, in a survey taken by the Palestinian research institute Mada El Carmel in December 2012, 76 per cent of the respondents replied that they would support a unification, and this went up to 88 per cent in December 2014 (quoted in Sheindlin 2014).

Discussion

Ultimately, in the elections on 17 March, the JL garnered thirteen seats – which constituted two more than the total number of seats gained by the four component parties in the previous election. The voting rate of the Palestinians rose from 56.5 per cent in the 2013 elections, to 63.5 per cent in the 2015 elections. Moreover, 83.2 per cent of the Palestinian vote went to the JL with only 16.8 per cent voting for Jewish lists (a 6 per cent decline from the 2013 elections) (Rudnitzky 2015). This dramatic change would not have occurred without the previous change in electoral design.

The results of the election positioned the JL as the third largest party in the Israeli parliament – in itself an unprecedented achievement for the Palestinian minority in Israel. If, at any point, the second largest party – The Zionist Camp – were to join the ruling coalition, the JL would be head of the opposition – a significant role that carries with it much symbolic – and political – potential. As it is, as third largest party, they qualify for an average of two representatives on all parliament sub-committees. One of the members serves as chair of a sub-committee. This too is an unprecedented achievement for the Palestinians who in previous parliaments qualified at most for one seat on a smaller number of committees (Knesset 2016). Hence, both symbolically, and in terms of potential influence, the electoral achievement of the JL is significant and unprecedented. The shift in electoral design which brought about the unification of the Palestinian lists resulted in higher rates of political representation, higher voting rates and higher levels of political visibility and participation in the Israeli parliament.

Hence, the first part of the argument – that higher thresholds can improve the electoral performance of minorities – has been demonstrated. This leaves us with the second puzzle or question: can we identify the impact of the electoral change on the *nature* of the representational claims. There seem to be three representative claims made by the JL that are significantly different from the claims previously made by the separate Palestinian lists.

The claim to represent the entire Palestinian society

The first change is that while each separate Palestinian list – up until the unification – claimed to represent different sub-identities within the larger Palestinian society, the JL claims to represent all of the dominant sub-identities within Palestinian society. While this might be self-evident, it is nonetheless central: the JL claimed and continues to claim to represent both nationalists and socialists; women and men and secularists and Islamists. In this sense, there is no question that the representational claims have become more inclusive.

During the first year of the JL's term, there were many provocative challenges to this inclusive claim. The most significant challenge came from the friction caused by the rhetorical differences between two of the factions – Hadash and Balad. During the first year in Parliament, elected members of Balad made provocative statements and actions that clearly went beyond the moderate line presented by the JL leader Ayman Odeh and which gave rise to behind-the-scenes talk of a break-up of the party (Benbaji 2016).

However, and this is an interesting and unacknowledged dimension of Palestinian party politics, the ideological differences are not at all reflected in the parliamentary activity of the JL, in which all members of the party initiate, and support *exactly the same legislation and issues*. This leads us to the second change in claims.

The claim to represent the domestic (civic) interests of the Palestinian citizens of Israel rather than interests embedded in the larger Palestinian–Israeli conflict

The second shift marks less of a shift in the political practices of the Palestinian lists, and more of a shift in their claims. Over the years, one of the main criticisms made against the different Palestinian lists was that they "don't care about their constituency but spend most of their time fighting the Occupation." (Azoulai 2012, 1; see also Shizaf 2014). Curiously, while this was never supported by empirical data, and in fact data reveal that, over the years, the Palestinian Lists *consistently focused almost entirely on domestic issues* – including issues of building permits, education, employment and welfare benefits (Knesset 2016) – they themselves did not take issue with the accusations and did little to counter them.

The JL, on the other hand, from its inception, has taken issue with this accusation and one of the main representational claims made by them has been that they will act as trustees of the local Palestinian population and promote issues of relevance to their daily lives (Kaminer 2015). Thus, during their first year alone, members of the JL submitted over 400 proposed pieces of legislation covering a wide range of civic issues including, but not limited to, the funding of Christian schools, raising minimum wage for university students, facilitating the process of obtaining building permits, the rights of Beduoin women, and many many more (Knesset 2016). This is true of all members of the JL from all four political factions.

Combatting the image of a nationalist-Palestinian party has been particularly emphasized by Ayman Odeh, leader of the JL and member of Hadash. Indeed, repeatedly, both in pre- and post-electoral interviews, Odeh emphasized that while as a Palestinian he will fight for a solution to the Israeli–

Palestinian conflict, he sees promoting the local interests of the Palestinian citizens of Israel as primary on his agenda. In a symbolic and demonstrative action, the JL's first actions were to protest the government plan for Beduoin resettlement in the Negev region in the south of Israel and to bring to fruition a multi-million finance programme aimed at decreasing the economic gaps between the Arab and Jewish towns in Israel (Huri and Seidler 2015). It appeared that with these major issues, the JL sought to set the tone for their leadership.

Claiming to represent the "democratic" elements within Israeli society

Finally, it would appear that to a certain extent, the JL is claiming to represent not merely the interests of the Palestinian minority, but the interests of "democratic elements" within Israeli society at large. In a speech made at a conference in June 2016, Odeh was quoted as saying: "We are emerging as the democratic alternative within the Israeli political system. Jews and Arabs, those who fear for democracy in Israel should support us as their representatives" (Odeh 2016). The more inclusive reach of the JL is evidenced by claims made (mainly) by members of the Hadash party to represent the interests of other disadvantaged groups within Israeli societies such as the African refugees, and the marginalized lower class Israelis (Matar 2015). Furthermore, analysis of proposed legislation during their first year in Parliament reveals that around one quarter of proposals offered by members of the JL focused on issues of relevance to Israelis in general – relating to democratic issues of freedom of speech, of political opposition, of wage inequality and so on (Knesset 2016). Related to this issue is the possibility that the JL is more open to dialogue and cooperation with the Israeli–Zionist parties. In an interview in late February on Israel's TV Channel 1, commenting indirectly on the heretofore taboo question of potentially joining the government, Odeh declared, "We really truly want to influence. … If we find a partner who will agree to our demands of peace and of equality between Jews and Arabs, we will be able to support them" (cited in (Green 2015)).

Indeed, it has been Ayman Odeh, who has attracted most media and political attention and whose name is singularly identified with the list and what it represents. The electoral campaign of the JL, under the guidance of Odeh, was very clearly geared not only at the Palestinian voters, but at the Jewish voters as well. Odeh's Hebrew is fluent, and his public persona is moderate and aimed at cooperation between Jews and Arabs. While the JL declined the Jewish left-wing Meretz's offer to sign an after-election agreement, it was widely known that Odeh himself supported the move (reference). In his opening address to the Israeli parliament, Odeh, in a speech that was clearly reminiscent of Martin Luther

King, emphasized Jewish and Arab cooperation and spoke of his vision of a truly equitable and just state that would incorporate both majority and minority on equal terms.

Conclusion

In this article, I make three basic arguments. The first concerns the potential impacts of electoral design. I argue that raising the electoral threshold in Israel resulted in a unification of small minority lists into one larger party, and that this change in the form of the lists was translated into a change in the claims of the representation – claims that became more inclusive. I argue that the merger of four separate lists provided incentives for the joint leadership to claim to be representative of a more inclusive, broadly based constituency.

The second argument is about the potential benefits of higher electoral thresholds for minorities in deeply divided societies. Based on the success of the JL in the 2015 elections, I suggest that higher thresholds, given their impact on the leadership incentives to become more inclusive, have the potential to improve the electoral power of minority parties.

The third and final argument concerns the theoretically pervasive assumption that ethnic minorities fare best with descriptive representation. I suggest that the example of the JL highlights the fact that "representation" is not a given artefact – either descriptive or substantive. Political leaders and elected officials will make representative claims that are dynamic – shifting between the substantive and descriptive, between the inclusive and the exclusive. Claims to representation involve a dynamic relationship between leaders and constituencies and are constituted by multiple influences, some of which, as this case demonstrated, are structural and institutional such as electoral design. The point is that while making representative claims, leaders and candidates are actively engaged in constituting changing and dynamic images of their constituents – which are always selective, always partial and always subjective. As Saward notes, the common categorization – substantive/descriptive – "assume a fixed, knowable set of interests for the represented" (2006, 301) – but in fact, these very interests are a product of the process of claim making that constitutes representation. Indeed, the same Palestinian citizens constituted separate, particularist constituencies up until 2015 with a presumed "fixed set of knowable interests". In 2015, they became constituted as a unified constituency, with a set of diverse, yet also shared interests.

Israel's relationship with its Palestinian minority looms over its political history as a long-standing source of discontent and an immediate threat to its democratic nature. It is a relationship besieged by mutual distrust and suspicion. Hence, the long history that Israel has had with PR, low voter threshold

73

and semi-autonomous culture and language institutions has failed to produce legitimacy and support for the political system on the part of its Palestinian minority – as prescribed by proponents of power-sharing. Both official and unofficial long-term discrimination and continued exclusion from any of the ruling coalitions have precluded this possibility. Over the years, as I mention above, not only has belief in the system declined, but the propensity to consider other than political means of opposition is on the rise.

While the evidence directly linking the declining belief in the legitimacy of the state, the effectiveness of their political leaders and the overall voting rates is perhaps inconclusive, the electoral success of the JL surely indicates that alongside a declining sense of legitimacy in Israel's democratic institutions, there is a rising demand for a new kind of leadership and a new kind of representation. The unification of the Palestinian lists was given overwhelming support amongst the Palestinian voters. This was evidenced both in pre-election surveys, and in the results themselves.

One year following the electoral success of the JL, it is too soon to assess its long-term impact. However, its proven ability to constitute the Palestinian constituency as more unified, and more inclusive, suggests strongly that future research and political thinking about minority representation in conflicted societies need to go beyond the traditional categorizations, and should encourage creative thinking about the different ways in which electoral design can impact on increased cohesion and legitimacy in these kinds of societies and the different ways in which representative claims can constitute constituencies.

Notes

1. While in this paper, I focus on ethnic minorities, the theoretical literature tends to collapse different identity minorities – religious, linguistic, cultural and racial – into the same theoretical category.
2. I refer here to the minority of Palestinians who are citizens of the state of Israel – otherwise referred to at times as Israeli Arabs. On the different labels of this minority, see Ghanem (2001).
3. Hadash the communist party; Balad the nationalist party; Ra'am the Islamic party and Ta'al the Arab Movement for Renewal.

Disclosure statement

No potential conflict of interest was reported by the author.

References

Ali, Nohad. 2015. "The Birth Pangs of the Joint Arab List and Arab Public Opinion." *Bayan; The Arabs in Israel*, no. 4 (February): 4–8.

Azoulai, Moran. 2012. "Arab MKs – Traitors." *Ynet*, February 26. http://www.ynet.co.il/articles/0,7340,L-4194869,00.html.

Benbaji, Ido. 2016. "The JL Promises not to fall apart." *Galei Zahal*, January 20. http://glz.co.il/1363-75382-HE/Galatz.aspx.

Bueno de Mesquita, Ethan. 2000. "Strategic and Nonpolicy Voting: A Coalitional Analysis of Israeli Electoral Reform." *Comparative Politics* 33 (1): 63–80.

Chandra, Kanchan. 2004. *Why Ethnic Parties Succeed? Patronage and Ethnic Head Counts in India*. Cambridge: Cambridge University Press.

Cohen, Frank S. 1997. "Proportional Versus Majoritarian Ethnic Conflict Management in Democracies." *Comparative Political Studies* 30 (5): 607–30.

Diamond, Larry Jay, and Marc F. Plattner. 1994. *Nationalism, Ethnic Conflict, and Democracy*. Baltimore, MD: Johns Hopkins University Press.

Elkins, Zachary, and John Sides. 2007. "Can Institutions Build Unity in Multiethnic States?" *American Political Science Review* 101 (04): 693–708.

Frisch, Hillel. 2011. *Israel's Security and its Arab Citizens*. Cambridge: Cambridge University Press.

Ghanem, As 'ad. 2001. *The Palestinian-Arab Minority in Israel, 1948–2000*. Albany, NY: Suny Press.

Ghanem, As 'ad, and Nadim N. Rouhana. 2001. "Citizenship and the Parliamentary Politics of Minorities in Ethnic States: The Palestinian Citizens of Israel." *Nationalism and Ethnic Politics* 7 (4): 66–86.

Green, David. 2015. "The Arab Joint List is Reshaping Israeli Politics." *Tablet Magazine*, March 12. http://www.tabletmag.com/jewish-news-and-politics/189554/arab-joint-list.

Gutmann, Amy. 1992. *Multiculturalism and the Politics of Recognition: An Essay*. Princeton, NJ: University of Princeton Press.

Haklai, Oded. 2011. *Palestinian Ethnonationalism in Israel*. Philadelphia: University of Pennsylvania Press.

Harff, Barbara, and Ted Robert Gurr. 2004. "Ethnic Conflict in World Politics." *Refugee Survey Quarterly* 23 (3): 310.

Hazan, Reuven Y., and Gideon Rahat. 2000. "Representation, Electoral Reform, and Democracy: Theoretical and Empirical Lessons from the 1996 Elections in Israel." *Comparative Political Studies* 33 (10): 1310–1336.

Horowitz, Donald L. 2003. "Electoral Systems: A Primer for Decision Makers." *Journal of Democracy* 14 (4): 115–127.

Horowitz, Donald L. 2014. "Ethnic Power Sharing: Three Big Problems." *Journal of Democracy* 25 (2): 5–20.

Huri, Jackie, and Shirli Seidler. 2015. "Odeh and Representative of Unrecognized Villages March." *Haaretz*, March 26. http://www.haaretz.co.il/news/local/.premium-1.2600249.

Jamal, Amal. 2006. "The Arab Leadership in Israel: Ascendance and Fragmentation." *Journal of Palestine Studies* 35 (2): 6–22. doi:10.1525/jps.2006.35.2.6.

Jamal, Amal. 2011. *Arab Minority Nationalism in Israel*. London: Routledge.

Kaminer, Matan. 2015. "The JL; Left and Social." *Siha Mekomit*, February 3. http://mekomit.co.il/%D7%A2%D7%9C-%D7%94%D7%98%D7%A2%D7%A0%D7%94-%D7%9C%D7%A4%D7%99%D7%94-%D7%97%D7%91%D7%A8%D7%99-%D7%9B%D7%A0%D7%A1%D7%AA-%D7%A2%D7%A8%D7%91%D7%99%D7%9D-%D7%9C%D7%90-%D7%93%D7%95%D7%90%D7%92%D7%99%D7%9D/.

Kenig, Ofer. 2015. *Electoral Threshold, Wasted Votes and the Proportionality of the System*. http://www.idi.org.il/ספרים-ומאמרים/מאמרים/electoral_threshold_and_wasted_votes/.

Kimmerling, Baruch. 2005. *The Invention and Decline of Israeliness: State, Society, and the Military*. Berkeley: University of California Press.

Knesset Website. 2016. http://main.knesset.gov.il/Pages/default.aspx.

Kook, Rebecca. 2002. *The Logic of Democratic Exclusion: African Americans in the United States and Palestinian Citizens in Israel*. Lanham: Lexington Books.

Kymlicka, Will. 1995. *The Rights of Minority Cultures*. Oxford: Oxford University Press.

Lijphart, Arend. 1969. "Consociational Democracy." *World Politics* 21 (02): 207–225. doi:10.2307/2009820.

Lijphart, Arend. 1975. *The Politics of Accommodation: PLuralism and Democracy in the Netherlands*. Berkeley: University of California Press.

Lijphart, Arend. 1984. *Democracies: Patterns of Majoritarian and Consensus Government in Twenty-One Countries*. New Haven, CT: Yale University Press.

Lublin, David. 2014. *Minority Rules; Electoral Systems, Decentralization and Ethnoregional Party Success*. Oxford: Oxford University Press.

Matar, Hagai. 2015. "Odeh Goes to Southern Tel Aviv with Mizrahi Activists." שיחה מקומית, September 9. http://mekomit.co.il/%d7%90%d7%99%d7%99%d7%9e%d7%9f-%d7%a2%d7%95%d7%93%d7%94-%d7%93%d7%a8%d7%95%d7%9d-%d7%aa%d7%9c-%d7%90%d7%91%d7%99%d7%91/.

Nordlinger, Eric A. 1982. *On the Autonomy of the Democratic State*. Cambridge, MA: Harvard University Press.

Norris, Pippa. 2004. *Electoral Engineering: Voting Rules and Political Behavior*. Cambridge: Cambridge University Press.

Norris, Pippa. 2008. *Driving Democracy: Do Power-Sharing Institutions Work?* Cambridge: Cambridge University Press.

Norris, Pippa, and Michael Marsh. 1997. "Political Representation in the European Parliament." *European Journal of Political Research* 32 (2): 152–164.

Odeh, Ayman. 2016. "One year later." Speech at conference in Tel Aviv University. June 9.

Olzak, Susan. 2004. "Ethnic and Nationalist Social Movements." In *The Blackwell Companion to Social Movements*, 666–693. Oxford: Blackwell Press.

Peretz, Don, and Doron Gideon. 1997. *The Government and Politics of Israel*. Boulder, CO: Westview Press.

Pitkin, Hanna Fenichel. 1972. *The Concept of Representation*. Berkeley: University of California Press.

Posner, Daniel N. 2004. "The Political Salience of Cultural Difference: Why Chewas and Tumbukas Are Allies in Zambia and Adversaries in Malawi." *American Political Science Review* 98 (04): 529–545.

Posner, Daniel N. 2005. *Institutions and Ethnic Politics in Africa*. Cambridge: Cambridge University Press.

Purat, Nassar. 2015. "Arab parties will run together." *Online 2*. January 22nd.

Rahat, Gideon. 2004. "The Study of the Politics of Electoral Reform in the 1990s: Theoretical and Methodological Lessons." *Comparative Politics* 36 (4): 461. doi:10.2307/4150171.

Rudnitzky, Arik. 2015. "An Analysis of the 20th Knesset Election Results in the Arab Sector." *Bayan; The Arabs in Israel*, no. 5 (June): 3–14.

Runciman, David. 2007. "The Paradox of Political Representation." *Journal of Political Philosophy* 15 (1): 93–114.

Saward, Michael. 2006. "The Representative Claim." *Contemporary Political Theory* 5 (3): 297–318.

Saward, Michael. 2010. *The Representative Claim*. Oxford: Oxford University Press.

Selway, Joel, and Kharis Templeman. 2012. "The Myth of Consociationalism? Conflict Reduction in Divided Societies." *Comparative Political Studies* 45 (12): 1542–1571.

Shafir, Gershon, and Yoav Peled. 2002. *Being Israeli; The Dynamics of Multiple Citizenship*. Cambridge: Cambridge University Press.

Sheferman, Karin Tamar. 2013. "Participation, Avoidance and Banning: Trends in the Participation of the Arab Citizens of Israel in the Elections to the Israeli Knesset." http://www.idi.org.il/-ספרים-ומאמרים/פרלמנט/גיליון-61/השתתפות,-הימנעות-והחרמה גליון-61-והחרמה-הימנעות-/מגמות-בהשתתפותם-של-הערבים-אזרחי-ישראל-בבחירות-לכנסת.

Sheindlin, Dahlia. 2014. "Exclusive Survey: A joint list will raise voting rates dramatically." *שיחה מקומית*, December 12. http://mekomit.co.il/%d7%a1%d7%a7%d7%a8-% d7%91%d7%9c%d7%a2%d7%93%d7%99-%d7%a8%d7%a9%d7%99%d7%9e% d7%94-%d7%9e%d7%a9%d7%95%d7%aa%d7%a4%d7%aa/.

Shizaf, Noam. 2014. "Do the Arab MK's really care about their public?" *Siha Mekomit*, June 27. http://mekomit.co.il/%D7%A2%D7%9C-%D7%94%D7%98%D7%A2%D7%A0%D7% 94-%D7%9C%D7%A4%D7%99%D7%94-%D7%97%D7%91%D7%A8%D7%99-%D7% 9B%D7%A0%D7%A1%D7%AA-%D7%A2%D7%A8%D7%91%D7%99%D7%9D-%D7% 9C%D7%90-%D7%93%D7%95%D7%90%D7%92%D7%99%D7%9D/.

Smith, Anthony. 2013. *Nationalism and Modernism*. London: Routledge.

Smooha, Sammy. 2013. "Still PLaying by the Rules: Inex of Arab-Jewish Relations in Israel 2012." http://www.idi.org.il/media/2519505/Lo%20Shovrim.pdf.

Smooha, Sammy, Asad Ghanem, and Nuhad Ali. 2013. "The Electoral Threshold, Remains Agreements and the Arab Population in Israel." Position paper presented to the Law Constitution and Legal Committee of the Israeli parliament.

Squires, Judith. 2008. "'From the Substantive Representation of Women to the Constitutive Representation of Gender: The Representative Process in WPA and GM.'" http://ecpr.eu/ Filestore/PaperProposal/072e1e41-0837-454e-aa05-8acf208a48af.pdf.

Urbinati, Nadia, and Mark E. Warren. 2008. "The Concept of Representation in Contemporary Democratic Theory." *Annual Review of Political Science* 11 (1): 387–412. doi:10.1146/annurev.polisci.11.053006.190533.

Watad, Muhamad. 2015. "Raising the Threshold – a Historical Opportunity for the Arab Parties." *NRG*, February 2. http://www.nrg.co.il/online/1/ART2/674/905.html.

Waxman, Dov. 2012. "A Dangerous Divide: The Deterioration of Jewish-Palestinian Relations in Israel." *The Middle East Journal* 66 (1): 11–29.

The paradox of power-sharing: stability and fragility in postwar Lebanon

Amanda Rizkallah

ABSTRACT

This article examines the consequences of civil war and power-sharing settlements for the development of sectarian networks of mobilization. While power-sharing presents a viable mechanism for ending civil war, it allows the participating militias-turned-parties access to state resources and leaves their population networks and organizations intact. This continuity reduces the militias-turned-parties' start-up costs for violent mobilization in the future, enabling them to mobilize more effectively than new parties with no combat experience. I exploit rich variation in the wartime legacies and settlement status of the major postwar parties in Lebanon to explain whether and how parties mobilized during the clashes of May 2008, the most serious internal violence to plague Lebanon since the end of its civil war in 1990.

Introduction

Divided societies recovering from protracted conflict are becoming more common in our world, as internal wars have increasingly been ended through negotiated power-sharing settlements (Hartzell and Hoddie 2003). These states and societies face the huge tasks of economic and social recovery. However, the success of these efforts hinges on preventing the recurrence of conflict. While a rich literature has done much to illuminate the national-level and institutional characteristics that make the recurrence of war more likely (Licklider 1995; Walter 1997; Luttwak 1999; Hartzell and Hoddie 2003, 2015; Walter 2004; Roeder and Rothchild 2005; Doyle and Sambanis 2006; Collier, Hoeffler, and Soderbom 2008; Collier 2010; Toft 2010), less attention has been paid to how civil war transforms associational life and creates networks that facilitate mobilization for violence.

In situations where outright victory is neither possible nor desirable, ending the war in a way that ensures that powerful players will have an incentive to cooperate often sows the seeds for recurrent violence. This article examines the consequences of civil war and power-sharing settlements for the mainten-ance, destruction, and development of sectarian networks of mobilization. I argue that the challenges of controlling territory during civil war force militias to develop networks within the population. If a war ends in power-sharing, this leaves the participating militias-turned-parties organizationally intact and allows them access to state resources. These advantages reduce parties' start-up costs for violent mobilization in the future and allow them to do so more effectively than both defeated militias and new groups with no combat experience. And yet, because of their organizational capacity, these parties are also able to restrain their members, preventing conflict when it is in their interest to do so.

Research objectives and contributions

This articles provides an analytic framework for thinking systematically about how wartime network-building and the terms of a settlement affect postwar parties' likelihood of participating in violence, and how suc-cessful their mobilization efforts are likely to be. In doing so, it proposes a possible mechanism underlying the propensity of post-conflict countries to revert to civil war and uses a case study of postwar Lebanon to demon-strate the validity of the mechanism. The study also underscores a key paradox inherent in power-sharing agreements. Although it is a viable res-olution to civil war, power-sharing retains the basis for conflict and instabil-ity. Such arrangements give a political role to and preserve the organizations of those who achieve power during a civil war. In doing so, power-sharing retains these organizations as bases of power and sites for mobilization in times of crisis. While this dilemma is particularly acute in fragile postwar contexts, such tensions between the devolution or dis-persal of power and the imperatives of state-building are ubiquitous (Stein and Rosecrance 2006).

The analysis below generates new insights into the factors contributing to Lebanon's simultaneous stability and fragility. In contrast to the policy-making and scholarly community's focus on foreign support for domestic groups as a primary explanation for patterns of conflict in Lebanon (i.e. Ellis 1999; Zahar 2005; Talbot and Harriman 2008; Hourani 2013), I emphasize the equally important role of outside powers in defeating or demobilizing other groups during the war or immediate postwar period. Moving beyond international and external explanations for Lebanon's instability, this research also high-lights the importance of domestic factors in their own right. Understanding how foreign support or repression interact with local organizational structures is critical to evaluating the potential for recurrent conflict in Lebanon and other post-conflict countries.

Methodology

I demonstrate the plausibility of the argument through a case study of postwar Lebanon, drawing on the secondary historical literature. I exploit rich variation in the wartime legacies and settlement status of Lebanon's major postwar parties to generate theoretical expectations for each group's ability to mobilize successfully during a moment of crisis. I then use this classification of political groups to explain patterns of mobilization in the clashes of May 2008, the most serious internal violence to plague Lebanon since the end of its civil war in 1990. The event study relies on a media analysis of the archive of *The Daily Star*, Lebanon's largest English language newspaper. I use a search for the keyword "clashes" in all articles written between 1 May and 31 May 2008, the month surrounding and including the weeklong crisis. The search generates twenty-eight articles.[1] I conduct a comprehensive analysis of these articles and supplement the data with accounts in the secondary literature.

Networks for high-risk mobilization

Several scholars have pointed to the importance of mobilization networks for explaining patterns of ethnic conflict. Networks and effective brokers who link different networks together are key for coherent mobilization (McAdam, Tarrow, and Tilly 2001). The reason that people mobilize along religious or ethnic lines is simply that their social networks are more likely to be within their own group (Kaufman 2011). In his investigation of ethnic riots in India, Varshney (2002) finds that towns with organizations that cross communal lines experience much less rioting than those in which networks exist primarily inside ethnic groups. Scacco (2010) finds that membership in local social networks makes an individual more likely to participate in a riot. These studies provide insight into the importance of networks in shaping individual decision-making and the geographic distribution of violence. However, less attention has been paid to why different ethnic or religious groups, within the same context, mobilize differently and with varying degrees of success. I ask why some groups participate in violent clashes while others do not. Furthermore, why are some more effective mobilizers than others?

I find that a party's previous experience as a civil war militia allows it to establish networks that are effective in mobilizing partisans for violence. This is one of the reasons why postwar countries can remain unstable after negotiated settlements, even years after the initial commitment problems (Walter 1997) have been solved and militias have disarmed. Several scholars have shown that networks are crucial to understanding organizational behaviour during conflict. Weinstein (2007) demonstrates that rebel organizations that rely on social networks exhibit more discipline than those that rely on economic endowments. Parkinson (2013) finds that high-risk mobilization during civil war involves extensive networks of support beyond the front lines and understands organizational resilience to stem from the overlap between formal and social networks. These new and transformed networks of mobilization rarely disappear with the termination of conflict and can leave enduring legacies (Wood 2008). One of them is the facilitation of mobilization for future violence.

Legacies of civil war militias

The development of militia organizations during civil war has long-term consequences for postwar stability. If the organizational structures and population networks of a militia remain intact after the conflict, they serve to significantly reduce the start-up costs of violent mobilization. If leaders are in favourable political positions after the war, they will use their organizations for electoral politics. However, if shifts in the political context or in the behaviour of other actors are perceived as threats to the sectarian group or its leadership, these networks can be used to mobilize the organization for violent confrontation. That said, these organizations are cohesive enough to be able to enforce restraint among their members when politically advantageous. For example, Hezbollah exhibited both of these behaviours during May 2008. It responded violently to a policy and personnel change that threatened its telecommunications networks and control over the Beirut airport. And yet, it also demonstrated an ability to restrain its militia members and prevent further escalation (Dakhlallah 2012). In contrast, militias defeated during the civil war and new parties with no experience during periods of conflict are likely to face higher start-up costs and are therefore less effective at mobilizing their group for violence. The rest of this section elaborates the logic of this argument.

Militia development

Most militias have a goal of consolidating control over territory during a civil war. Acquiring territory is advantageous for several reasons. It can provide access to natural resources, ports, and the control of drug traffic, while making it more feasible to use the population as a tax base, source of local information (Kalyvas 2006), and pool of recruits. Territory also provides groups with a military advantage by functioning as a safe haven. So great is the importance of controlling territory and the population that inhabits it that scholars and warlords alike consider territorial control to be the best proxy for a group's bargaining position vis-a-vis other players in negotiations. For example, Christia (2012) uses changes in territory as a crucial metric for understanding shifts in the balance of power during the Afghan Intra-Mujahedin War in 1992–98.

Despite its advantages, controlling territory can be a liability, as populations can turn against a militia and provide information to its opponents. Militias need populations to be cooperative or quiescent. In order to accomplish this, militias pursue a variety of strategies. They may change the composition of the population through forced displacement of perceived opponents. They may also work to attract displaced sympathetic populations, such as co-religionists, through the promise of safety from other groups' attacks (Steele 2009). Militias must also focus on turning the remaining population into an advantage, by co-opting local elites and providing safety and services in exchange for cooperation. They must also develop systems for detecting and punishing the uncooperative. To accomplish these goals, militias need to develop organized contact with the population. Over the course of the conflict, the repeated interactions with populations needed to consolidate territorial control allow militias to establish networks that can be mobilized for political participation.

Postwar migration of networks

Keeping a wartime network intact in the postwar era is not an automatic process. Militias need to gain postwar control over a consistent stream of resources to maintain networks and survive politically. They need to ensure that the war's settlement gives them a share of government power and resources. This may include everything from election quotas and integration into the state's armed forces to control over ministry budgets and reconstruction projects. Militias-turned-parties can then combine this access to the state with their wartime networks. This powerful mix gives settlement beneficiaries large advantages in mobilizing populations for costly and violent political participation.

Another closely related factor that contributes to militias' ability to migrate networks into the postwar era is foreign patronage. In fragile postwar contexts, where borders are still permeable and the central state weakened, foreign patrons are likely to continue funding groups that further their interests. In the Lebanese case, the foreign powers that shaped the terms of the war's ending settlement remained intimately involved in the country's politics by continuing to fund their domestic allies and clients.

In contrast to settlement beneficiaries, particularly those with foreign patrons, defeated militias are not able to maintain robust networks for mobilization. While they may have had significant organizational infrastructure at certain points during the conflict, defeated groups no longer have access to resources. Instead, their organizations are often dismantled through repression, or their networks simply atrophy.

Postwar parties with no civil war background may also emerge, particularly in situations where a vacuum of leadership exists in a sectarian community. New postwar parties may even have success in accessing resources and building their capacity for political mobilization. However, these parties are qualitatively different from the war-tested and cohesive militias-turned-parties (Lyons 2016). Deploying militants for violent confrontation is orders of magnitude costlier than peaceful political mobilization (Collier 2010) and requires an organization with the capacity to motivate its recruits for high-risk behaviour through significant material, social, or ideological investment (Weinstein 2007).

Former militias also have another, less tangible advantage over new parties. They have communal legitimacy as organizations that, despite their harsh methods, protected their co-religionists in times of great insecurity. New postwar parties cannot make such claims. In a fragile postwar context, this legacy of demonstrated ability to "protect" may be worth a great deal to core supporters – the type of persons most likely to participate in violence. Recent developments in the Lebanese case illustrate this dynamic. The conflict in neighbouring Syria has led most of the country's religious communities to rally around their respective militias-turned-parties. However, the major Sunni party, an organization with no history of militancy, has experienced a crisis of confidence. In their search for protectors in an unstable environment, some Sunnis have gravitated towards a variety of smaller but historically militant Islamist organizations that are willing to take more strident positions against the Syrian regime and Hezbollah (Lefèvre 2014).

The Lebanese civil war

Lebanon's civil war and postwar experience make it an ideal case for testing the plausibility of the argument. First, Lebanon's civil war led to the proliferation of sectarian militias and when it ended in a power-sharing settlement, many of them were able to maintain their wartime networks for mobilization. Others, however, were defeated or repressed, leading to the dismantling of their wartime organizations. Lebanon also has a prominent postwar party with no background as a civil war militia. This diversity of experience among the major postwar players allows for comparisons to be made while holding the national context fixed. Furthermore, the parties also have varying degrees of foreign support, allowing for an exploration of how this factor interacts with on-the-ground networks to produce different patterns of mobilization for violence. The rest of this section provides a brief background on the Lebanese civil war and postwar period. Based on this narrative, I place each of the six major postwar parties within the framework of the argument and outline the expectations for whether and how each group should mobilize for violence in a moment of crisis.

Background

Since independence in 1943, Lebanon's political system has been based on consociational power-sharing between elites from the country's many sectarian communities. The largest of these communities include Shia and Sunni Muslims, Druze, and Maronite and Orthodox Christians. This system enshrined strict sectarian quotas in all parts of government and administration, with the ratio fixed at five Muslims to every six Christians. In the pre-war era, political life was controlled by notables from landowning families, whose legitimacy derived from their ability to strike compromises and maintain a peaceful if fragile status quo. In the 1960s and 1970s, rapid social and economic changes, including rural migration to urban areas and growing inequality, created a sizeable disenfranchised population that became the constituencies for ideological and religious movements that sought an alternative to the consociational system (Hanf 1993).

In 1969, the watershed Cairo Agreement allowed Palestinian guerrillas resisting Israeli occupation to move their headquarters to Lebanon. The Lebanese population differed sharply on how to handle this new armed population. These differences were compounded by divisions over support for the consociational system. Christians and right-wing groups supported a status quo in which they held a privileged position. They also prioritized Lebanon's sovereignty and sought to detach it from the majority-Muslim Arab world surrounding it, which meant keeping a neutral stance in the Israeli–Palestinian conflict. Muslims sought a much greater connection to the rest of the Arab world, often espousing the ideology of pan-Arabism. This translated to supporting the Palestinians, even if that meant getting involved in a conflict with neighbouring Israel. They were joined by leftists who sought to overturn the sectarian system (Hanf 1993). In the early 1970s, tensions between the two coalitions rose as both sides acquired more weapons. In 1975, a massacre of a bus of Palestinian civilians became the spark that ignited the war.

Militias during the war

The Lebanese civil war began in 1975 and lasted fifteen years. The war ended largely because of the Taif Agreement, a power-sharing deal that was brokered by Saudi Arabia and enforced by a Syrian military occupation (Hanf 1993). The Lebanese civil war was a complex conflict, which, in its final years, resulted in the collapse of the state. There were a multitude of militias involved in the war, and although the fighting began as a two-sided conflict, the war quickly degenerated into a sectarian war of all against all. Much of the worst fighting was due to power struggles between rival militias competing to be the dominant representative of a single community (Hanf 1993; Cammett 2014). Several excellent studies exist detailing the developments of the war itself (Salibi 1988; Fisk 1991; Hanf 1993; Traboulsi 2007), but I will focus on the rise of militia organizations and networks, and the implications this had for postwar party development.

The outbreak of conflict in 1975 meant that power was now achieved through force of arms, giving a comparative advantage to those leaders who could mobilize militia fighters to effectively compete in the struggle for control over Lebanon's political future. As the war went on, "the established political and religious leaders gradually lost power to mercenary bosses" (Hanf 1993, 181). Pre-war elites were effectively marginalized by a new generation of wartime leaders (Hanf 1993). The rise of militias also had profound implications for the population living under their rule. To consolidate their control over territory, militias expelled populations whose denomination differed from their own. Territories became sharply defined by sect. A full third of the population was expelled or forced to flee with little possibility of return (Hanf 1993).

In order to finance their operations, militias taxed the population under their control. Protection rackets developed that required businesses and homeowners to pay a direct tax. Much of the militias' revenue came from customs duties on goods entering or exiting their territories and the cultivation and trade of drugs. These activities were made possible and profitable because several militias controlled access to Beirut's most important ports. Bank robberies, fraudulent banking practices, and outright thievery were also part of the militias' repertoires (Hanf 1993; Picard 2000; Zahar 2000; Makdisi and Sadaka 2003). Overall, Makdisi and Sadaka (2003) estimate that the militias were able to amass $15 billion from these various sources.

In order to extract most of the revenue, militias set up administrations, military and civilian police forces, and intelligence agencies. Doing so required the cooperation of the population as well as the rank and file of the militias. This was of particular concern because none of the main militias ever monopolized the political scene in their respective sectarian community and had to constantly fend off other militias looking to poach their supporters and fighters. This competition increased expenditures, making revenue and networks of civilian support critical (Picard 2000). The largest militias provided generously for militiamen and their families and established social welfare departments, and press and media outlets (Zahar 2000). Militias gained popular loyalty by providing security and relative order. However, the militias' financial success meant that substantial personal wealth was also accumulated by the leadership (Makdisi and Sadaka 2003), causing more popular resentment as the war dragged on (Zahar 2000). This was perhaps one of the reasons motivating most wartime leaders to accept the terms of the Taif Agreement.

By 1985, the Lebanese Forces (LF), Amal Movement, and Progressive Socialist Party (PSP) emerged as the three largest militias. All three became very similar in organization and behaviour. They controlled large territories where they had homogenized populations, co-opted local elites, gained control of ports, established civil administrations, and taken control of state facilities (Picard 2000). It is not an exaggeration to say that each operated as a state within a state (Hanf 1993). By the end of the war, these militias had a wealth of local information, networks of members that they selectively rewarded, and institutionalized contact with the population – all assets for future violent mobilization. This also became true of two other militias that emerged after the mid-1980s. These were Hezbollah (Shia), which contested Amal's control of Shia strongholds in the later years of the war, and the Aounist faction of the Lebanese Army (Christian), which gained control of heavily populated Christian areas in the last year of the war until its routing by the Syrian Army (Hanf 1993).

The Taif Agreement

The Taif Agreement was signed in 1989 by the surviving members of the pre-war parliament and provided the basis for a deal that would end the Lebanese civil war. It was signed in Taif, Saudi Arabia with the support and backing of Syria, which was to act as the guarantor of the agreement (Hudson 1999). The agreement reinstated Lebanon's sectarian power-sharing system but included provisions for restructuring the parliament's sectarian quotas, taking the proportion of Christians to Muslims from six to five to an equal five to five. The Christian president's powers were reduced and the powers of the Sunni prime minister and Shia speaker of the parliament were strengthened. This created a "troika" executive, where the president, prime minister, and speaker govern together in a more equal arrangement.

The Taif Agreement also included provisions for the disarmament of militias, which were enforced by the Syrian Army. Plans were made for the rehabilitation of militia men and many took positions in the Lebanese army, intelligence, police, and civil service. The government collected most weapons but gave up on small arms, which many believe the former militias still have hidden in Lebanon in case war should break out again (Hanf 1993). Hezbollah was allowed to keep its arms to resist Israeli occupation of the south (Hudson 1999).

By making Syria the enforcer of its provisions, Taif legalized the Syrian army's indefinite presence in Lebanon. The Christian camp, which was generally against Syrian involvement in Lebanon, split over whether to accept the terms of the agreement. This led to a bloody confrontation that further divided the Christian community and resulted in the defeat of General Aoun, the leader of the faction that did not accept the agreement, at the hands of the Syrian military (Hanf 1993). The Taif Agreement also increased the size of parliament. The number of deputies was a contentious issue particularly because the vacant and new seats were to be filled by appointees chosen by Damascus until elections could be organized (Hanf 1993; Wantchekon 2000). This gave the upper hand to warlords and militiamen, particularly those that were Syrian allies, and led to a severe underrepresentation of most Christian parties (Hanf 1993).

Postwar developments

When the civil war ended, militia leaders transformed their organizations into political machines that continued to provide services and mobilize their constituents for demonstrations and elections (Cammett 2014). However, the success of militia leaders in transforming their militias into parties depended heavily upon their relationship with a Syrian regime that virtually ruled over postwar Lebanon. Militias that were allies of the Syrian regime or were willing to cooperate with Syria were successful in transforming their military power into political power (El-Husseini 2012). In addition to Syrian influence, Iran, a close ally of the Syrian regime, had its own particularly close relationship with Hezbollah. This provided the group with unrivalled financial resources for maintaining and expanding its patronage networks and recruiting core supporters for high-risk activities.

The important militia leaders all received positions as ministers in the first postwar government and gained access to resources necessary for maintaining their wartime organizational capacity. Several gained control of agencies that were critical in the process of reconstruction, including the Ministry of the Displaced (PSP leader) and the Council of the South (Amal leader), which was tasked with region-specific reconstruction efforts. These positions provided militia leaders with great discretion in the distribution of state resources (El-Husseini 2012), and allowed them to maintain loyalty and further develop sectarian patronage networks in their regional strongholds. Postwar elections became a mechanism for monitoring constituent loyalty and reinforcing patron–client relationships. Corstange vividly describes this process:

> [The] parties insert themselves deeply into people's social networks by leaning on kinship and sectarian links, organizing machines of their own, collaborating with local notables, and subcontracting with "electoral keys" (roughly analogous to the old "ward bosses" or "precinct captains" of American city machines) to deliver political support in the latter's bailiwicks. (2012, 448)

However, not all militia leaders ended up with the freedom and resources to maintain their organizations. Syria's strong influence over the implementation of the Taif Agreement and military superiority allowed it to sideline anti-Syrian militias and their leaders (Hanf 1993; El-Khazen 1994; El-Husseini 2012; Cammett 2014). Aoun was militarily defeated by the Syrian army, as was previously mentioned. The LF, although formally a signatory of the agreement, was quickly repressed for its lack of cooperation. The organization was banned and its leader was imprisoned (El-Khazen 1994). While these two militias were significant wartime organizations, their networks and capacity were either destroyed or left to atrophy following the war.

The only major party that emerged as a new organization, without links to a civil war militia, was the Future Movement (FM) led by Rafik Hariri. This was made possible by the fact that the Sunni community ended the civil war with no clear militia leadership. The community's position in this regard was due to several historical reasons. At the beginning of the war, Lebanese Sunni militias were closely allied with and dependent on Palestinian militias that were a dominant player in the first half of the civil war. When Palestinian groups were defeated by the Israeli military in 1982, Sunni militias were significantly weakened and later defeated in conflict with other militias (Cammett 2014). This created a political and military vacuum within the Sunni-majority regions of Lebanon. Although religious figures and Islamist parties sought to fill this void, they were only moderately successful, partly due to Syrian interference to prevent a strong Sunni militia from emerging (El-Husseini 2012).

Hariri, an independently wealthy businessman, used this opening to establish networks among the population through a private charitable foundation. Although he had no military presence on the ground, Hariri's close relationship with Saudi Arabia led him to become that country's key representative in mediating the Taif Agreement. Saudi patronage and backing, as well as his substantial private wealth, facilitated Hariri's entrance into Lebanese politics. Much of Hariri's success in postwar politics can be traced back to his appointment as head of the Council for Development and Reconstruction, which became an important source of patronage for the FM (Cammett 2014).

In 2005, the assassination of Hariri prompted a popular protest movement against Syria's presence in Lebanon, as well as a counter protest supporting Syria. Under international pressure, Syrian troops withdrew from Lebanon. This shock to the political system granted greater freedom to Syria's traditional opponents. Geagea and Aoun, the marginalized leaders of the LF and Lebanese Army faction, respectively, quickly revived their militias as parties and contested the 2005 elections. Despite their legalization, the Christian parties had much rebuilding to do, as fifteen years of repression had significantly atrophied their networks and mobilization capacity. This is evident in the marked weakness of their service and patronage distribution systems as compared to other parties (Cammett 2014).

Postwar parties

Table 1 summarizes each organization's history of militia organization, whether the group was a settlement beneficiary, whether the group is still officially armed, and whether or not it has a consistent international patron. The PSP had a close relationship with Syria in the immediate postwar years, but

Table 1. Postwar parties in Lebanon.

Party	Civil war militia	Position in war Settlement	Still armed	Consistent international patron	Violent mobilization in crisis	Successful mobilization
Hezbollah	Yes	Beneficiary	Yes	Iran/Syria	Yes	Yes (most success)
Amal	Yes	Beneficiary	No	Syria	Yes	Yes (most success)
PSP	Yes	Beneficiary	No	—	Yes	Yes
FM	No	Beneficiary	No	Saudi Arabia	Yes	No
LF	Yes	Repressed (legalized in 2005)	No	—	No	—
FPM (Aounists)	Yes	Defeated (legalized in 2005)	No	—	No	—

this relationship was inconsistent and deteriorated markedly after 2000, ending with the party's support for Syria's withdrawal from Lebanon in 2005. Also, while no party besides Hezbollah is officially permitted to have a militia, frequent allegations are made that several other parties have access to light weapons and conduct training exercises in preparation for crises (Rowayheb 2011).

Based on the profile of each group, we should expect them to behave differently in a moment of crisis. Each of these key variables affects both the availability of networks for mobilization and how well those networks are supplied resources through foreign patronage. On the two extremes are Hezbollah and the Christian parties. Hezbollah is the actor most likely to mobilize and to do so successfully during an internal conflict. The organization has a standing militia and its networks are intact and well supplied. The Christian parties are the least likely to mobilize, despite the fact that they had cohesive militias during the civil war. The dismantling of their organizations in the postwar period and their lack of access to state resources and foreign patronage impede mobilization.

The interesting cases are Amal, the PSP, and the FM. Amal and the PSP have the advantage of being organizations that had mobilized for armed conflict in the past, but that have also been able to preserve those networks, if not their formal militias. Amal has the further advantage of foreign patronage. In a moment of crisis, the argument suggests that these parties would be able to effectively mobilize supporters for an armed conflict in a cohesive and disciplined way. However, Amal should be more successful than the PSP in this effort due to the resources its patron supplies. The FM, while it has other endowments, does not have experience as a civil war militia. In this sense, it is the opposite of the PSP, a group with military experience but no consistent foreign patron. We should expect that due to its resources and favourable position in the power-sharing agreement, the FM would be able to mobilize its supporters. However, since it is a group that only has experience winning votes and not battles, its networks are structured to meet those electoral goals. This is evident in the FM's pattern of service provision. They provide patronage to a wide but shallow network, incentivizing large numbers of supporters with smaller, more temporary goods and services. This is effective for winning votes, but not for high-risk mobilization (Cammett 2014). For this reason, the FM's mobilization efforts will be relatively unsuccessful, lacking the cohesion, discipline, and the effectiveness of other groups.

The May 2008 conflict

In this section, I examine the clashes that occurred in Lebanon in May 2008 with the aim of investigating whether the patterns of mobilization during the conflict accord with the theoretical expectations outlined above. This event is a good candidate for examining the plausibility of the argument, as it represents the most serious episode of internal conflict in Lebanon since the end of the civil war in 1990. With over sixty-five dead and 200 wounded, many observers feared that these clashes were the beginning of Lebanon's descent into another civil war (Dakhlallah 2012), making it a theoretically important instance of mobilization.

The clashes of May 2008 were the culmination of an eighteen-month stalemate that had its roots in the 2005 withdrawal of the Syrian army from Lebanon after the assassination of Hariri. The protests that ensued after the assassination split the country and the political landscape into two opposing coalitions, one for and the other against the Syrian military's continuing presence in Lebanon. These coalitions were named March 8 and March 14 for the respective dates on which their largest protests occurred. March 8 was mostly composed of Shia supporters of Hezbollah and Amal, whereas March 14 began as a mixed grassroots protest against Syrian occupation but was soon co-opted by the Druze and Sunni parties. Eventually, Syria withdrew from Lebanon under international pressure and the coalitions struck a bargain in anticipation of the 2005 elections. The LF and Aounists (now the Free Patriotic Movement [FPM]) were legalized and resurfaced as members of the March 14 coalition. After the elections, the FPM, frustrated by being shortchanged by its own partners, abandoned the March 14 coalition and signed a Memorandum of Understanding with Hezbollah (Mansour 2010), making it an official partner in the March 8 coalition.

The two coalitions soon reached a stalemate. Hezbollah demanded greater representation for its allies in the cabinet so that it could have a veto over government decisions. This occurred as the government was passing a law to create an international court to try the perpetrators of Hariri's assassination (Haddad 2009). To block the signing of the law, Hezbollah and Amal members resigned from the cabinet. When the remaining members passed the law, the president declared the cabinet unconstitutional for no longer having representatives from all of Lebanon's sects. March 14 refused to give March 8 veto power, so the opposition coalition retaliated with a massive sit-in protest in downtown Beirut that lasted for eighteen months (Knio 2008). In early May 2008, the government took two important decisions that Hezbollah interpreted as an attack on its militia apparatus and a de facto declaration of war. The Lebanese cabinet declared Hezbollah's telecommunications network "illegitimate, illegal and a violation of state sovereignty and public funds". The government also relieved Brigadier Shoucair of his post as head of airport security due to allegedly close ties to Hezbollah (Dakhlallah 2012). On 7 May, clashes erupted between Hezbollah and Sunni militias affiliated with the FM. Within 12 hours, Hezbollah and Amal controlled half of Beirut. Clashes began spreading to other cities and renewed civil war became a real possibility. It was averted by Hezbollah's decision to pull its men off the streets (Dakhlallah 2012) and international pressure convincing all parties to meet in Doha, Qatar to work out a comprehensive political agreement, which they did on 21 May (Haddad 2009). The following section details the roles and responses of the various Lebanese parties in the conflict.

Party mobilization

Despite being deeply involved in the political crisis and committed to their coalition partners, the FPM (March 8) and the LF (March 14) remained completely on the sidelines due to their military weakness and lack of weapons (*The Daily Star*, May 13, 2008). These two parties also have the experience of fighting against each other in the so-called war of elimination at the end of the civil war, when internecine conflict almost destroyed the Christian community from within (*The Daily Star*, May 13, 2008). Finding themselves on opposite sides during the crisis, LF and FPM leaders seemed eager to avoid such a situation, despite forcefully backing the political stances of their coalitions. These decisions align with the theoretical expectation that the two parties would be unable to mobilize effectively due to a variety of disadvantages. Also, mobilization against members of one's own sectarian community would be a higher cost activity, making the two Christian parties unwilling to mobilize.

The effective mobilization of Amal and Hezbollah fall at the other end of the spectrum. Amal and Hezbollah began their mobilization carefully and deliberately, timing it to correspond to a twenty-four-hour general strike and using civil disobedience to persuade the government to reverse its decisions (Quilty 2008). When the government did not back down, Hezbollah's leader Hassan Nasrallah announced that shutting down the party's telecommunication network was a serious threat to the party's resistance against Israel, stating that "we will cut off the hand that targets the weapons of the Resistance" (Quilty 2008). After the speech and the still resolute response from the FM,

Hezbollah and Amal almost immediately changed their tactics, launching a series of armed attacks in Beirut that quickly spread to other regions, most notably isolating and threatening the PSP's strongholds in southern Mount Lebanon (ICTJ 2013). The offensive is described as a "carefully calculated and coordinated operation" (Haddad 2009, 409). Within twelve hours, Hezbollah and Amal had taken over the better part of West Beirut, the epicentre of the FM, disarming the party's outposts and hundreds of its militants, and shutting down and vandalizing its media offices. The military defeat of the FM was swift and humiliating (Quilty 2008; Dakhlallah 2012). The victory in Beirut was so decisive that one security official stated on condition of anonymity that "there are no clashes anymore because no one is standing in the way of the opposition forces" *(The Daily Star*, May 9, 2008). And yet, Hezbollah and Amal's organizational capacity is also evident in the restraint and discipline demonstrated by their militias. Once they had taken over west Beirut, Hezbollah systematically turned each neighbourhood over to the army (Dakhlallah 2012), which had stayed out of the fighting for fear of dividing along sectarian lines. They disarmed pro-government militants instead of resorting to more violence to subdue them. Perhaps most interestingly, when Hezbollah and Amal surrounded and isolated West Beirut and parts of Mount Lebanon, the militants were careful to spare FM leader Hariri (the son) and PSP leader Jumblat's residences (Haddad 2009), potentially a signal of their amenability to a resolution.

And yet, Hezbollah and Amal's successes had their limits, particularly when encountering militants in PSP strongholds in Mount Lebanon. In contrast to the Sunni community, "the Druze combatants were able to resist and even repel the Hezbollah offensive against their regions" (Haddad 2009). Despite having disarmed after the civil war and having no formal militia, the PSP's ranks were united and cohesive. And yet, they were noticeably weaker in material terms. A young Druze youth describes the situations. "We only had our own personal weapons, they were shooting M-16s and rockets at us. All we had were guns" *(The Daily Star*, May 13, 2008). Their cohesiveness, coupled with the militants' familiarity with the terrain in their home region, terrain they had experience fighting on during the civil war, allowed them to put up a strong front and challenge Hezbollah's fighters. Even though the PSP had disarmed in 1990, its organization remained intact and its members still trained and were able to coordinate to defend their home region (Rowayheb 2011). This is perhaps surprising, given that the PSP has no consistent foreign patron. Yet, the preservation of networks and capacity built during the civil war explain the resilience of this organization. This is evident in its successful mobilization despite being faced with a much more militarily sophisticated opponent.

The PSP's pattern of mobilization stands in contrast to that of its ally, the FM (Rowayheb 2011). If anything is certain about the FM, it is that in 2008, their party was awash in resources stemming from the Hariri family's private wealth, its access to state coffers, and foreign patronage. Yet, this conflict clearly demonstrated that the party was in no way prepared to challenge Hezbollah militarily. Although FM partisans were armed, they were ill-trained and these arms were much fewer in quantity and lower in quality than Hezbollah's arsenal. In fact, FM militants only used violence against Hezbollah in a few small cases when it took over their Beirut neighbourhoods, but generally responded by surrendering (Rowayheb 2011). This stands in contrast to the PSP rank and file's reluctance to put down their weapons (*The Daily* Star, May 12, 2008) until urged by their leader to cooperate with army searches for heavy weapons (*The Daily Star*, May 16, 2008).

One explanation for the FM's inability to mobilize effectively centres on party leaders' lack of interest and investment in building a militia. When the Sunni community ended the civil war without a strong militia-turned-party, this provided an opportunity for a new class of business elites, including Hariri and other FM members, to emerge as the community's leaders. With significant investments to protect throughout the country, playing the electoral game and eschewing violent modes of contestation became the favoured strategy of this new elite (Cammett 2014). These elites also used patronage to create an election-based clientelist machine that siphoned Sunnis away from more militant Islamist groups (Rowayheb 2011).

While the FM's prioritization of an electoral politics is undeniable and crucial to understanding the leadership's strategy for party development, such accounts imply that the FM was simply unwilling to create a militia. However, the FM was also unable to create a militia. Journalists allege that the FM had been in the business of attempting to do so through the Secure Plus company, a private security firm with over 3,000 employees and unofficial associates on the payroll. The party militants' poor performance in the 2008 crisis is evidence of the failure of this experiment in military organization. When speaking about the reasons for failure in 2008, one expert in the field of private security stated, "You can't just spend millions of dollars to build an army in one year, they have to be motivated and believe in something. They have to be willing to die" (*Los Angeles Times*, May 12, 2008). This simple statement demonstrates that while material resources may be a very helpful asset in building a capacity for violence mobilization, they are not enough. When compared to militias-turned-parties, parties developed and built around the contestation of elections, which require the gathering of large and loose coalitions of supporters, have a distinct disadvantage in mobilizing a core of supporters for high-risk behaviour.

Conclusion

This article argues that civil wars, through their often profound impact on social networks, have the potential to leave enduring legacies on postwar political mobilization and modes of contestation. When power-sharing allows civil war militias to translate their organizations into political parties, they become able to use their networks to mobilize partisans for violent activity in a way that is cohesive, disciplined, and effective. This is in contrast to parties that developed in times of peace, building organizations that are designed for electoral and other peaceful forms of mobilization. The plausibility of this argument is examined through a study of the Lebanese case. An investigation into how sectarian militias and parties mobilized during the May 2008 conflict demonstrates that a party's history of organizational development is key to understanding its willingness and ability to mobilize for violent activity.

The analysis demonstrates that the media and scholarly community's focus on the importance of foreign funding in explaining patterns of conflict, particularly in Lebanon and other Middle Eastern cases, obscures important domestic factors. Understanding the processes and organizational structures through which foreign support is translated into local action is a crucial factor in evaluating the impact of foreign funding. It is this interaction between the international and the local that has the potential to produce war or peace in fragile and divided post-conflict countries.

Finally, this study examines the consequences of civil war and sectarian militia building for perpetuating violence in the postwar era. In doing so, it proposes a possible mechanism underlying the propensity of post-conflict countries to revert to civil war. This study also highlights one of the central dilemmas inherent in power-sharing agreements. By empowering wartime leaders and preserving their power bases, power-sharing stunts the process of state formation and postwar unification, and leaves intact their capabilities for inciting future conflict. Paradoxically, it is precisely this inclusion of wartime groups in a settlement and the preservation of their capacity for organizational discipline and restraint that allow for the possibility of enduring peace.

Note

1. List of articles and links available upon request.

Disclosure statement

No potential conflict of interest was reported by the author.

References

Cammett, Melani. 2014. *Compassionate Communalism*. Ithaca, NY: Cornell University Press.
Christia, Fotini. 2012. *Alliance Formation in Civil Wars*. Cambridge: Cambridge University Press.

Collier, Paul. 2010. *Wars, Guns, and Votes*. New York: Harper Perennial.

Collier, Paul, Anke Hoeffler, and Mans Soderbom. 2008. "Post-conflict Risks." *Journal of Peace Research* 45 (4): 461–478.

Corstange, Daniel. 2012. "Vote Trafficking In Lebanon." *International Journal of Middle East Studies* 44 (3): 483–505.

Dakhlallah, Farah. 2012. "The Arab League in Lebanon: 2005–2008." *Cambridge Review of International Affairs* 25 (1): 53–74.

Doyle, Michael W., and Nicholas Sambanis. 2006. *Making War and Building Peace*. Princeton: Princeton University Press.

El-Husseini, Rola. 2012. *Pax Syriana*. Syracuse, NY: Syracruse University Press.

El-Khazen, Farid. 1994. "Lebanon's First Postwar Parliamentary Election, 1992." Centre for Lebanese Studies.

Ellis, Kail C. 1999. "Lebanon: The Struggle of a Small Country in a Regional Context." *Arab Studies Quarterly* 21 (1): 5–25.

Fisk, Robert. 1991. *Pity the Nation*. Oxford: Oxford University Press.

Haddad, Simon. 2009. "Lebanon: From Consociationalism to Conciliation." *Nationalism and Ethnic Politics* 15 (3–4): 398–416.

Hanf, Theodor. 1993. *Coexistence in Wartime Lebanon*. London: Centre for Lebanese Studies and I.B. Tauris.

Hartzell, Caroline, and Matthew Hoddie. 2003. "Institutionalizing Peace." *American Journal of Political Science* 47 (2): 318–332.

Hartzell, Caroline, and Matthew Hoddie. 2015. "The Art of the Possible." *World Politics* 67 (1): 37–71.

Hourani, Najib B. 2013. "Lebanon: Hybrid Sovereignties and U.S. Foreign Policy." *Middle East Policy* 20 (1): 39–55.

Hudson, M. C. 1999. "Lebanon after Ta'if." *Arab studies Quarterly* 21 (1): 27–40.

ICTJ (International Center for Transitional Justice). 2013. "Lebanon's Legacy of Political Violence." Technical Report, International Center for Transitional Justice.

Kalyvas, Stathis N. 2006. *The Logic of Violence in Civil War*. Cambridge: Cambridge University Press.

Kaufman, Stuart J. 2011. "Ethnicity as a Generator of Conflict." In *Handbook of Ethnic Conflict*, 91–101. New York: Routledge.

Knio, Karim. 2008. "Is Political Stability Sustainable in Post-'Cedar Revolution' Lebanon?" *Mediterranean Politics* 13 (3): 445–451.

Lefèvre, Raphaël. 2014. "The Roots of Crisis in Northern Lebanon." Carnegie Middle East Center No.20, Beirut.

Licklider, Roy. 1995. "The Consequences of Negotiated Settlements in Civil Wars, 1945–1993." *American Political Science Review* 89 (3): 681–690.

Luttwak, Edward N. 1999. "Give War a Chance." *Foreign Affairs* 78 (4): 36–44.

Lyons, Terrence. 2016. "From Victorious Rebels to Strong Authoritarian Parties: Prospects For Post-War Democratization." *Democratization* 23 (6): 1026–1041.

Makdisi, Samir, and Richard Sadaka. 2003. "The Lebanese Civil War, 1975–1990." AUB Institute of Financial Economics Working Paper Series (3).

Mansour, Imad. 2010. "Washington and Hezbollah." *Middle East Policy* 17 (2): 82–104.

McAdam, Doug, Sidney Tarrow, and Charles Tilly. 2001. *Dynamics of Contention*. Cambridge: Cambridge University Press.

Parkinson, Sarah Elizabeth. 2013. "Organizing Rebellion." *American Political Science Review* 107 (3): 418–432.

Picard, Elizabeth. 2000. "The Political Economy of Civil War in Lebanon." In *War, Institutions, and Social Change in the Middle East*, edited by Steven Heydemann, Chap. 10, 372. Berkeley: University of California Press.

Quilty, Jim. 2008. "Lebanon's Brush with Civil War." Middle East Report Online. http://www.merip.org/mero/mero052008.

Roeder, Philip G., and Donald S. Rothchild. 2005. *Sustainable Peace*. Ithaca, NY: Cornell University Press.

Rowayheb, Marwan George. 2011. "Political Change and the Outbreak of Civil War." *Civil Wars* 13 (4): 414–436.

Salibi, Kamal. 1988. *A House of Many Mansions*. London: I.B. Tauris and Co.

Scacco, Alexandra. 2010. "Who Riots?" PhD diss., Columbia University.

Steele, A. 2009. "Seeking Safety." *Journal of Peace Research* 46 (3): 419–429.

Stein, Arthur, and Richard N. Rosecrance. 2006. "The Dilemma of Devolution and Federalism." In *No More States?* edited by Richard Rosecrance, and Arthur A. Stein, 235–245. Lanham, MD: Rowman & Littlefield.

Talbot, Brent J., and Heidi Harriman. 2008. "Disarming Hezbollah." *Mediterranean Quarterly* 19 (4): 29–53.

Toft, Monica Duffy. 2010. *Securing the Peace*. Princeton: Princeton University Press.

Traboulsi, Fawwaz. 2007. *A History of Modern Lebanon*. London: Pluto.

Varshney, Ashutosh. 2002. *Ethnic Conflict and Civil Life*. New Haven: Yale University Press.

Walter, Barbara F. 1997. "The Critical Barrier to Civil War Settlement." *International Organization* 51 (3): 335–364.

Walter, Barbara F. 2004. "Does Conflict Beget Conflict? Explaining Recurring Civil War." *Journal of Peace Research* 41 (3): 371–388.

Wantchekon, Leonard. 2000. "Credible Power-Sharing Agreements." *Constitutional Political Economy* 11: 339–352.

Weinstein, Jeremy M. 2007. *Inside Rebellion*. Cambridge: Cambridge University Press.

Wood, Elizabeth J. 2008. "The Social Processes of Civil War." *Annual Review of Political Science* 11: 539–561.

Zahar, Marie-Joëlle. 2000. "Is All the News Bad News for Peace?" *International Journal* 56 (1): 115–128.

Zahar, Marie-Joëlle. 2005. "Power Sharing in Lebanon: Foreign Protectors, Domestic Peace, and Democratic Failure." In *Sustainable Peace*, edited by Philip G. Roeder, and Donald S. Rothchild, 219–240. Ithaca, NY: Cornell University Press.

Changing Islam, changing the world: contrasting visions within political Islam

Nimrod Hurvitz and Eli Alshech

ABSTRACT
How do political Islamists, movements and thinkers view political change? To what extent do they promote violence as a means of bringing about change? Are they themselves willing to change and adapt to modern political systems? There is a wide array of movements in the Muslim world that grapple with these questions and as a consequence, numerous answers and disagreements. This paper will focus on three cardinal and contested issues: Is violence a legitimate means to bring about change? Is it legitimate to adopt Western political institutions? How should Muslim movements and regimes coexist with ancient political entities such as tribes and ethnic groups? By comparing and contrasting the political outlooks of the Muslim Brothers and the Salafi-Jihadis, the article highlights the ideological gaps between moderate and militant political Islam.

Introduction

Since the 1970s, Muslim movements have intensified their efforts to transform Muslim-majority states, be it through political participation or political violence. From the 1990s another dimension was added to this struggle, as a new strain of violent Muslim movements that challenged the contemporary global order struck at American and European targets. All of these movements can be described as "political Islam", since they aim to bring about political change and their agendas are inspired by their interpretations of Islam. However, it is essential to bear in mind that there are profound ideological differences between these movements, and that they resort to opposed courses of action (Mandaville 2007).

The ideological disagreements have generated dozens of movements that debate numerous issues and practical matters. Yet, despite this diversity, it is possible to identify among them two central political orientations: moderates and militants. The defining feature that distinguishes between these two trends is their position regarding how to bring about change. More specifically, is violence a legitimate or illegitimate means by which they can bring about social and political change. Moderate movements, such as al-Nahda in Tunisia, Muslim Brothers in Egypt and the AKP in Turkey, eschew political violence as a means to attain power. By contrast, militant movements, such as al-Qaeda, IS and their affiliates, espouse violence as a legitimate means of affecting change.

Another issue of contention that distinguishes between moderate and militant political Islamists is their attitude towards social and political organizations that did not originate in Muslim environments and have not been sanctioned by authoritative Muslim texts. These foreign institutions – modern states, political parties, the contemporary global order or pre-Islamic social entities such as tribes and ethnic groups – are powerful players in modern Muslim politics, and they eclipse the revered institution of the Caliphate. At present, most moderate political Islamists continue to pay lip-service to the Caliphate, yet concurrently they recognize the legitimacy of democratic states and the international world order. Furthermore, they maintain a modus vivendi with the tribes who live inside their states. Their political agenda is to operate with or within these institutions and through them reform Muslim-majority states.

By contrast, militant political Islamists reject the legitimacy of modern states and the international world order and turn to violence in order to bring back the Caliphate. Furthermore, due to their belligerent attitude towards any group or trend that differs from them, after they recruit tribes who live within their spheres of influence they force them to rescind their beliefs and norms and to follow the militants' religious vision. Their goal is to bring down any institution that was not part of the Caliphate and its institutions.

These two issues, violence as a means of affecting change and non-Muslim political institutions, are at the centre of this study because they are the core of the political Islamists' vision of politics. It is also interesting to note that there is a negative correlation between how each of the Islamist orientations answers these questions. Movements that reject violence are often more receptive to non-Muslim institutions; movements that accept and promote violence reject the legitimacy of non-Muslim institutions. This negative correlation will be examined and explained in this article.

The first part of the article will present how moderates and militants perceive political change. After presenting their contrasting outlooks, it will survey the moderates' efforts to join the political arena by establishing political parties. The second part will examine how moderates and militants think and write about Western political institutions such as nation-states and the international global order. The third part will explore tribes and ethnic groups, a social organization that predates Islam, and focus on the surprising alliances between the new global force, Muslim militant movements such as al-Qaeda and IS and the ancient social entities, such as tribes in various parts of the Muslim world.

Political violence or political participation

Muslim discussions about political violence are nearly as old as Islam itself and they have focused on whether or not believers who deviate from the religious norm are to be treated as Muslims or infidels. A few decades after the death of the Prophet, the question of deviants evolved into a major theologico-political controversy in which a puritan strand of thought, known pejoratively as the Khawarij (Secessionists) argued that Muslims who committed grave sins ought to be executed. Basing themselves on the notion of *takfir* (the accusation that a Muslim is in fact an apostate), the Khawarij attempted to cleanse Muslim societies of these supposed apostates by assassinating them (Watt 2002, 9–37). Their efforts to purify Muslim societies failed, though they often fragmented the Muslim community.

The failure of the Khawarij's homicidal crusade against their co-religionists was a result of their inability to mobilize widespread support for their cause. Most Muslims rejected the Khawarij and mainstream Islam ostracized them. Scholars articulated religious arguments against them, while rulers persecuted them until they were effectively eradicated. By the ninth century, nearly 300 years after their advent, the Khawarij sects were subdued, although their puritanical sentiments of cleansing Islam of all deviant tendencies continued into the twenty-first century. Throughout Islamic history these two trends, the *violent purifiers* and the *pacific unifiers*, contested each other, and for the most part, the unifiers gained the upper hand.

The historic dominance of mainstream moderates, who marginalized the violent militants, did not prevent twentieth-century militants from advocating the use of violence against their ideological adversaries. One such group came from the ranks of the Muslim Brothers, and in the 1930s it set off a debate within the movement, which led to its first split (Mitchell [1969] 1993, 17–19; Lia [1998] 2006, 250–251). The place of political violence in the Muslim Brothers' agenda continued to be a contested issue, and as a consequence, modern thinkers and political opponents accused them of being Khawarij (Mitchell [1969] 1993, 320; Kenney 2006, 89–116). Hence, although the historical Khawarij were destroyed during the first centuries of Islam, the term persisted and was levelled by the moderates at violent activists. The Muslim Brothers' internal controversy over the use of violence was carried into the 1950s and 1960s, and flared up again during the latter part of the 1960s, when thousands of them were incarcerated by the Nasser regime.

The major spokesmen in this debate were Sayyid Qutb, the radical ideologue of Islamic extremism (Calvert 2010), and Hasan Ismàil al-Hudaybi, the more moderate General Guide of the Muslim Brothers, both of whom were jailed in the 1960s. At its centre were two religio-political tracts, Qutb's *Milestones* and Hudaybi's *Preachers ... not Judges*, which articulated opposite views regarding the legitimacy of violence in religio-political reforms. In *Milestones*, Qutb outlined an ideology that was based on the premise that Muslims can accuse other believers of apostasy in the name of purifying Muslim society. His main argument was based on redefining the term Ignorance (*Jahiliyya*) which divides the world into two: Islam and Ignorance. According to Qutb, Ignorance is a situation in which people subject themselves to the law of other human beings rather than solely to Allah's law and sovereignty, which jeopardizes the moral fibre of Islam and threatens its existence (Qutb 2005, vol. 2, 904). Due to the moral and religious danger that Ignorance poses, Muslims must resist its onslaught, "[W]e must also free ourselves from the clutches of jahili society, jahili concepts ... " (Qutb, n.d., 14). The revolutionary component of this outlook was that self-styled Muslims are often sinners who do not qualify as Muslims. As a result, the notion of Ignorance enables Muslims to judge the behaviour of other Muslims and ex-communicate them on the basis of their opinions or conduct.

In *Preachers ... not Judges*, al-Hudaybi counters Qutb's assertion that one believer can pass judgment on another believer's faith merely on the basis of the latter's behaviour, and states "all the Sunnis agree that a perpetrator of a grave sin did not renege his faith to the extent that merits his removal from the (Sunni) community, as the Khawarij claim, ... " (Al-Hudaybi 1977, 58). In other words, as the title of al-Hudaybi's book suggests, Muslims are expected to preach true belief to others, but they cannot act as each other's judges. Although it is expected that once a person embraces Islam he will obey all its instructions, his disobedience does not nullify his status as a Muslim. Hence, according to al-Qaradawi, a leading contemporary moderate thinker held in esteem by the Muslim Brothers, although Islam has a long list of rules that regulate a believer's conduct, abiding by these rules is not a litmus test for one's status as a true believer (Al-Qaradawi 2007). And if one believer cannot judge another believer, then he certainly cannot perform acts of violence against him. Interestingly, al-Hudaybi labels his ideological rivals "Khawarij", thus suggesting that extremists such as Qutb (whom he never mentions by name) are in fact heretics themselves.

By the 1960s and 1970s, the chasm between the Muslim Brothers' militant and moderate trends of thought grew bigger, and they split into different organizations. When Qutb's followers were released from jail, they established illegal underground organizations. Once the militants parted ways from the moderates and established separate clandestine movements, the Muslim

Brothers were able to rehabilitate their image. As a consequence, Hudaybi's followers who aspired to change society by legal means continued their social and educational activities and even made attempts to enter the sphere of legitimate politics (Zollner 2009, 48–49).

However, from the earliest stages of the movement's existence, their focus on society and charitable work did not satisfy many of its members and they discussed whether they ought to enter politics by establishing a political party and participate in elections. The notion of "partyism" drew heavy criticism. Between the 1930s and 1950s, when Egypt was under British Occupation, it was often deemed a form of cooperation with the imperialists (Mitchell [1969] 1993, 218–220). However, once the British left, that attitude changed, though the debate continued.

A terse summary of this debate comes up in an exchange between Yusuf al-Qaradawi and an interlocutor (Al-Qaradawi 2004, 201). The interlocutor points out that the opponents of the "multi-party system" cite Hasan al-Banna, the founder of the Muslim Brothers, who feared that "partyism" would cause social and political strife. The wider context of this fear was the opinion that political fragmentation led to weakness and that Western imperialists introduced the party system in order to undermine Muslim unity and promote Western interests (Al-Banna 1983, 134). The critics of "partyism" worried that such a fractured political system would make them easy prey for the imperialist predators.

However, having cited al-Banna, al-Qaradawi puts forth his own opinion, which contradicts that of the founder of the Muslim Brothers:

> Answer: my opinion … there is no legitimate prohibition to the existence of more than one political party in an Islamic state. Such a prohibition needs a Divine text, of which there is none.

> On the contrary, this multiplicity may be a necessity in the present; as it can protect the state against the despotism of certain individuals or classes to exploit the peoples and their lives. (Al-Qaradawi 2004, 222)

Al-Qaradawi "overrules" al-Banna's view by arguing that his trepidation of the multi-party system was solely his personal opinion, and therefore, other believers are not compelled to follow it. Furthermore, he argues that the most urgent problem facing contemporary Muslim societies is corrupt despots, and therefore, the multi-party system, which imposes accountability on politicians, may be the preferred political framework.

Underlying the "partyism" controversy is a disagreement over the legitimacy of democracy. The Muslim Brothers do not reject wholesale the idea of democracy, in the same way that they do not reject outright other political concepts derived from the West (Mitchell [1969] 1993, 226, 261; Lia [1998] 2006, 77–78). As stated by al-Qaradawi:

> We are not against every innovation. We welcome any new beneficial matter and [at the same time] profit from all that is ancient and virtuous. We take from Western culture what is best such as administrative systems [...] and we add to it or subtract from it according to what fits us. (Al-Qaradawi 2009b)

Al-Qaradawi's discussion of democracy provides an important glimpse into how "adoption" is subject to "adaption" to ensure that the imported idea will be attuned to the fundamentals of Islam. At the same time his underling religious attitude is interesting and important: change is permitted unless clearly prohibited in a divine text (i.e. the Quran or the Prophetic tradition).

Islamist political thinkers are ambivalent regarding democracy because it allows humans sovereignty above Allah's. This issue was discussed by al-Qaradawi who asserted that although democracy does not necessarily contradict Islam, the notion of the sovereignty of the people must be qualified to avoid conflict with the sovereignty of God. Therefore, he argues, "There is no place for voting on matters which are definitive in the law, in fundamentals of religion and things which are clearly known. Voting can take place in [matters] which are based on interpretation ... " (Al-Qaradawi 2014). Al-Qaradawi adopts democracy, yet circumscribes it by arguing that whenever timeless moral and religious questions that have authoritative and consensual answers are at stake, there is no need to resort to elections. However, when ephemeral matters, such as nomination to public office, or declaring war and signing peace treaties, are in question, it is justified to rely on the democratic party-system. Thus, al-Qaradawi counsels selective adoption of democratic mechanisms.

In contrast to al-Qaradawi and other moderate thinkers, the militants disavow the notion of democracy. Salafi-Jihadis, for example, reject democracy outright because they view the idea of "the rule of the people" as undermining the essence of Islam. Sheikh Abu Muhammad al-Maqdisi, a leading Salafi-Jihadi thinker, explains the incompatibility of Islam and democracy:

> You should know that the root of the evil notion of democracy is Greek and not Arab ... O brothers who adhere to *tawhid* (the unity of God), [democracy] is from among the most prominent features of *kufr* (infidelity) and *shirk* (polytheism) which contradict severely and completely Islam and the religion of *tawhid*. (Al-Maqdisi, n.d.)

In the ensuing discussion al-Maqdisi spells out those features of democracy which, in his mind refute basic premises of Muslim theology. At the core of his criticism stands the notion of "legislation". When people legislate they place human will above Divine law. This tendency is aggravated with regard to man-made constitutions, which, according to al-Maqdisi, are the holiest texts of any democracy, and therefore "it is impossible to legislate a law or to promulgate a regulation unless it is in harmony with the constitution" (Al-Maqdisi, n.d.). In such a system there is no place for verses from the Quran or passages from the Prophetic tradition and thus it is at odds with Allah's instructions.

Hence, whereas al-Qaradawi understands democracy as a political mechanism that ought to be utilized after making adjustments to Islam, al-Maqdisi views democracy as a religion which inherently contradicts the principles of Islam, and must therefore be rejected.

Between theory and reality

In the ideological debates about democracy, "partyism" always had a practical side, since moderate political Islamists constantly asked themselves whether to participate in elections. Over a decade before al-Qaradawi wrote his tract about the nature of the Islamic state, the Muslim Brothers, under the leadership of `Umar Tilmisani, entered a variety of political arenas. In 1984 they participated in the parliamentary elections. In the course of the 1980s and 1990s they also ran candidates in the doctors', engineers', pharmacists' and lawyers' professional syndicates (Wickham 2013, 58–75). Approximately twenty years after they first entered the elections, in 2005, they attained nearly 20 per cent of the seats in the Egyptian parliament. This achievement seems to have unnerved the Egyptian regime, and moved them to clamp down on the Muslim Brothers. As a result, in the elections of 2010, only one of their candidates succeeded in entering the parliament. Frustrated with this political manipulation, the debate about participating in party-politics was renewed with fervour.

The "game-changer" that opened the doors of politics to the Islamist movements but eventually led to more barbarism than democracy was the Arab Upheaval. Between 2011 and 2013 the Muslim Brothers and other Islamist movements participated in Egypt's elections and won a resounding victory. However, in the summer of 2013, Egypt's military, with the help of the judiciary, unravelled the results of the elections, incarcerated Morsi – Egypt's elected president from the ranks of the Muslim Brothers, outlawed the movement and shut down many of its charitable foundations. Once again, the sphere of party-politics was closed to the Muslim Brothers. At present, it seems that most of the members oppose the use of violence, though others insist they must react with force. As a result, there are sources that claim that some of the movement's members have been resorting to limited, "smart violence", that targets the government's ability to rule, but does not target innocent bystanders (Ayyash 2015; Fahmi 2015).

The only state that successfully replaced a dictatorship with a functioning democracy during the Arab Upheaval is Tunisia. In this eleven million strong, North African state, the moderate Islamist and non-Islamist parties proved that it was possible to cooperate, and that an Islamist political party can participate in a democratic political system. After the first elections, held October,

2011, al-Nahda (Renaissance), an Islamist party which resembles the Muslim Brothers ideologically, won a plurality of the votes and shared power with non-Islamist parties (*Final Tunisian Election* 2011). Despite their victory in the elections, they agreed that Tunisia's president would be the human rights activist Moncef Marzouki. Another instance in which they demonstrated flexibility was during the debate over the place of Sharìa in Tunisia's legal system, when al-Nahda agreed that the Sharìa will not be the main source of legislation (Mersch 2014). Al-Nahda's political flexibility places it alongside other Islamist political parties, such as the Justice and Development Party in Turkey and a handful of political parties in Indonesia, all of which demonstrate that moderate Islamic parties can operate within a democratic party-system.

Although moderate Islamist movements reject the path of political violence and aspire to establish political parties that will change society through legitimate political means, they suffer at the hands of governments that tamper with the law so as to prevent the Islamists' success (Wickham 2013, 204–206, 233–234). Recently, the democratization process of Arab countries was dealt another blow in the course of the Arab Upheaval, when the break-down of most of the states that participated in it weakened moderate Islamist movements that lean towards democratic politics, and strengthened the militants that oppose democracy in principle.

Tyrannicide

The militants' espousal of violence is based on their unique perception of the essence of "Belief". They assert that in certain situations, sins remove a self-styled believer from the Muslim community. Thus, they are of the opinion that although the verbal acknowledgement of Allah and his Prophet are crucial elements of the faith, they are not enough. Actions speak as loud as words, and a person's belief is incomplete unless he is fully and persistently committed to Islamic practice (Abd al-Hadi al-Misri, n.d.).

This view is stated clearly by Shukri Mustafa, a follower of Sayyid Qutb and the founder of the violent group *al-Takfir wal-Hijra* (Accusers of apostasy and adherents of isolation), who explained to his interrogators in jail: "It is a self-evident truth that God's wish of the created [person] is that he will actually obey him and not that he will acknowledge [in theory] that He must be obeyed" (Ahmad 1991, 83). Acts weigh as much as declarations and therefore, Mustafa places a believers' deeds alongside his or her statement of faith. Mustafa's definition of belief contradicts the views of mainstream, Sunni Muslims, whom he openly criticizes: "With this self-evident truth we dismissed the position of Ahl al-Sunna [i.e. the rest of the Sunnis] which is grounded in the perception that Islam means recognition [i.e. of Allah and His religion] ... " (Ahmad 1991, 75). Once the argument that sinful acts remove a believer from the fold of the Muslim community and transform him into an apostate is put forth, it is clear why Mustafa and like-minded followers of Qutb assert that a devout Muslim is compelled to kill other Muslims whose conduct he deems impious.

The most significant act of political violence is the assassination of a ruler. Whereas the moderates, in line with traditional Sunni political thought, prohibit the killing of political leaders as well as ordinary Muslim sinners, the militants assert that when a Muslim ruler does not apply Sharìa law, fully and exclusively, he should be declared an apostate and resisted by force. As Sheikh al-Tartusi explains: "If it is clear [that the ruler committed] an act of apostasy ... and he persists in it, he must not be obeyed ... and the Islamic nation must go against him with the sword until he is deposed ... " (Al-Tartusi, n.d.). For the militant Salafis, the proclamation of apostasy (*takfir*) in this case is mandatory. What is more, eschewing it is comparable to neglecting any other religious duty, and a person who fails to proclaim apostasy against a person who clearly merits that status, such as religiously disobedient rulers, becomes an apostate himself (Al-Tartusi 2014).

The claim that it is legitimate to kill a political leader is far-reaching because it sanctions revolutions. Traditional Sunni thinkers, such as al-Qaradawi, view a ruler who implements Sharìa selectively as a sinner who does not merit excommunication as long as he does not assert that his behaviour is permitted according to Sharìa, a statement that would clearly display his rejection of the Divine law (Al-Qaradawi 2009a, 1067). In a 2004 interview "Abd al-Mun`im Abu al-Futuh, a member of the Muslim Brothers" Guidance Bureau from 1987 until 2009, presented a quietist view regarding any confrontation with Islamic regimes: " ... when there is [religious] disagreement, clash or oppression on the side of the national government [in Egypt] ... our principle is that we never raise our weapon against it" (Abu al-Futuh 2004). Hence, according to moderate Islamist thinkers killing a straying believer or sinning ruler is illegal.

When charting the attitudes of Islamist movements towards political change, two positions come into relief. On one side are the moderates who disapprove of violence and espouse party-politics that enable gradual political change, and on the other side are the militants who insist upon violent resistance and disapprove of party-politics. The moderate camp continues a long-standing tradition of political thought that goes back to the Middle Ages, rejects political violence and is willing to consider Western ideas such as the party system. By contrast, the militant camp adopts a rejectionist approach which forbids "borrowing" from other civilizations and espouses violence as a necessary means to reform society. These underlying attitudes will also determine their respective approaches to another Western creation – the nation-state and the international political order that stems from it.

States and global order

Whereas the contrasting views regarding violence against individual believers drew upon a centuries-long intra-Islamic controversy, the disagreement over the legitimacy of states and global order evolved in the post-First World War era and intensified in the 1950s and 1960s. Up until the 1950s most Islamists opposed European imperialism and supported the independence of Muslim-majority regions. Due to these concerns, questions regarding the nature of the states and global order were of secondary importance. However, after the European powers were forced out of the Middle East in the 1950s–60s, contrasting worldviews on nationalism began to surface, and the disagreements over the authority of the state and global order became much more acute.

Between the two world wars, many moderate Islamist thinkers were ambivalent about notions of nationalism and states. They placed a high premium on the Muslims' past unity and were therefore critical of the fact that nationalism parcels out the Muslim world politically (Al-Banna 1978, 22–25). At the same time, however, they recognized that nationalism is a powerful force that generates resistance to Western imperialism and is capable of expelling it from Muslim-majority lands. In the words of Hasan al-Banna:

> Although these steps [revolts against Western control] led to the concept of local nationalism, with each nation demanding its right to freedom as an independent entity, and while many of those who worked for this revival purposely ignored the idea of unity, nevertheless the outcome of these steps will be, without doubt, consolidation and a resurrection of the Islamic empire as a unified state embracing the scattered peoples of the Islamic world, ... (Al-Banna 1978, 24)

This comment illustrates the complexity of al-Banna's attitude towards nationalism. On the one hand, he is uncomfortable with the advocates of "local nationalism" who ignored the "idea of unity". On the other hand, he was convinced that in the long run they would serve the cause of unifying "the scattered peoples of the Islamic world". In order to resolve his ambivalence, al-Banna and other thinkers adopted an approach that can be labelled "critical reception", according to which Muslims can adopt Western nationalist ideas, but the latter must not clash with Muslim ideals and religious injunctions (Mitchell [1969] 1993, 264–267; Lia [1998] 2006, 79).

By the twenty-first century, notions of nationalism and state were naturalized in the Muslim Brothers' discourse and were woven seamlessly into their political statements. In a well-known document, *The Program of the Muslim Brother's Party* that was circulated in the summer of 2007, the leadership of the Muslim Brothers discuss the centrality of the Egyptian people and state in their political vision. In the introduction they write about the topics that will be addressed in the document, such as their "view about the state and its unique characteristics ... we will present the political system that we will attempt to implement on the basis of joining together the people's and government's efforts ... " (*The Program* 2007). The rest of the document is peppered with expressions such as "strengthen the Egyptian national security", "hopes of our beloved Egyptian people" and "interest of our beloved Egypt" (2007). By 2007, the notions of an Egyptian state and nation were fully integrated into their political outlook.

It is important to note that the Muslim Brothers considered all nation-states, not just Muslim-majority states, as legitimate political organizations. They viewed states in which Muslims were a minority as legitimate foci of loyalty, and therefore, when a Muslim resides in such a country he must remain loyal to the state, obey its laws and perform all its civil obligations. Such loyalty must also include enlistment in the army, even when that army is sent out to fight other Muslims. An example of this approach came up in America's campaign against terrorism, following the 9/11 attacks, which triggered a conflict of identity among thousands of Muslims serving in the United States armed forces. As American soldiers, they were obligated to fight any foe that threatened America. As Muslims, however, they felt conflicted about fighting their co-religionists such as al-Qaeda terrorists and their Afghan accomplices.

This dilemma of dual identities was raised by Captain Muhammad Abdur-Rahman, a chaplain in the American army, soon after 9/11 (Nafi 2004). In a letter addressed to the Fiqh Council of North America (FCNA), Captain Abdur-Rahman asked whether it is permissible for Muslims to participate in military operations against other Muslims in Afghanistan or elsewhere. The FCNA forwarded the question to Sheikh Yusuf al-Qaradawi, who consulted several Muslim thinkers and together they articulated a legal opinion that asserts that he can continue to serve in the American army even when it operates against Muslims (Nafi 2004, 80–82).[1] Clearly, this position recognizes, albeit implicitly, that nation-states are legitimate political units and that the international order that is based on nation-states is a legitimate political system. Furthermore, it gives priority to international law over aspects of Muslim law. The particular importance of these statements is that they go beyond recognition of Muslim-majority states and include states that are ruled by non-Muslims and in which Muslims are a minority.

From recognizing nationalism to accepting global political order

The Muslim Brothers' recognition of the legitimacy of the Egyptian state is part of a more comprehensive political outlook that accepts the nation-state as the basic unit of the global political order. Therefore, they recognize the legality of other states, the authority of international law and its institutions and the mandatory nature of international agreements. The 2007 programme states explicitly that the Muslim Brothers' intend to cooperate with the existing international entities. The document applauds international cooperation and supports "foundations and organizations that were founded by the international community to settle conflicts between the nations, especially those that are devoted to agreements of non-aggression, ... " (*The Program* 2007). Furthermore, it expresses its support for international accords and agreements and the establishment of a legal framework that would resolve conflicts. In these, and numerous other attestations, the Muslim Brothers express their commitment that Egypt, under their stewardship, would be integrated into the contemporary international order.

Evidence of their steadfast support for the principles of international law was given when the Muslim Brothers reached positions of power in Egypt (2012–13). Although before their short spell in power they had made numerous hostile declarations against Israel, once they came to power, they put aside their aggressive statements and complied by the Egyptian-Israeli Peace Treaty. Not only did the Muslim Brothers respect the Treaty, they also served as mediators between Israel and Hamas during the October 2012 hostilities, dubbed "Operation Pillar of Defense", helping to end it in eight days. Thus, the Muslim Brothers conducted Egypt's affairs in a manner that abides by international law and acted as a responsible player in this arena.

In contrast to the Muslim Brothers who recognized the legitimacy of a world order that is made up of Muslim and non-Muslim states and is regulated by international law, the Salafis-Jihadis rejected the notion of a nation-state, arguing that it is incompatible with Islam. Their view was based on the Salafi doctrine of "Loyalty and Disassociation" that requires a Muslim to have undivided loyalty to Allah, His law, the Prophet and his Companions (i.e. pious Salaf), and disassociate themselves from anyone who disagrees with them. They assert that since the idea of nationality channels loyalty to the nation, its laws and its people, it is inevitable for conflict to arise. For example, Muslim citizens will have to submit to the state's law, even if this man-made law contradicts Divine law. Similarly, a Muslim citizen will be expected to protect his nation against other Muslims, who belong to nations that are at war with his nation. This, according to Salafi-Jihadi doctrine, would be unacceptable if in the invading army participate soldiers from Muslims states, since a Muslim's loyalty is to his co-religionist and not nations or states.

In line with this outlook, the Salafi-Jihadis reacted strongly against al-Qaradawi's opinion that Captain Abdur-Rahman, mentioned above, ought to serve in the United States army even when it fights against Muslims. Abu Basir al-Tartusi published an opinion in which he vehemently opposed al-Qaradawi's legal justifications, declaring al-Qaradawi an apostate on the grounds that:

He allowed a Muslim to serve as a soldier in an army of infidelity and polytheism … [and to fight] against Muslims. This is clear apostasy according to Allah's words: "Oh you who believe, take not Jews and Christians as associates because they are associates of each other. He amongst you who turn to them [in friendship] becomes one of them" (Quran 5:51). Many other Quranic verses [also] prohibit helping the infidels against Muslims. (Al-Tartusi 2008)

In contrast to al-Qaradawi, al-Tartusi does not recognize the legitimacy of Western nation-states and their armies. Hence, the disagreement between al-Qaradawi and al-Tartusi provides an important glimpse into a crucial intra-Islamic debate about the West. Whereas al-Qaradawi assumes that Islam requires believers to accept Western states as legitimate political entities, and thus to remain loyal to their Western homeland, al-Tartusi asserts that the Divine law dictates that Muslims' loyalty must be exclusively to their co-religionists and, moreover, that Muslims must never assist non-Muslim states against fellow believers.

As in the case of democracy and the multi-party system, moderate political Islam adopts foreign ideas and institutions such as the nation-state and the international order and finds ways to weave them into their vision of Islam. Although some moderate thinkers were apprehensive about the nation-state because it has the potential to dismember the Muslim community, most of them opted for the creation of nation-states as long as they did not threaten Muslim principles and would hopefully strengthen Muslim societies in the long run. By contrast, the militants opposed the idea of the nation-state because it channels Muslim loyalty away from the Muslim *umma* (community of believers) and creates insoluble clashes of loyalties.

Political Islam, ethnicity and tribalism

Nation-states and party-systems are modern and Western phenomena. Accordingly, the debates related to them evolved around the willingness of Muslim political thinkers to be influenced by the West. Tribes and ethnic groups, by contrast, are pre-Islamic and were thought of as inconsequential social and political entities that were made obsolete by nationalism. However, despite this impression, they have remained important social and political forces. Therefore, before presenting how they interact with political Islam, it is important to note two political features that relate to them. First, tribalism is part of the power base and legitimizing force of several Arab monarchies such as Saudi Arabia, Jordan and Morocco (Ahmed 2013, 198–210). Second, peripheral tribes and ethnic groups, such as the Sinai Bedouin, North African Tuareg and Afghan Pashtun, who have a long history of suffering from administrative negligence and oppression, also have a long history of crime and political resistance against their rulers (Ahmed 2013, 180–198). These features bring into relief the political potential of tribes and ethnic groups.

There is an innate tension between the notion of tribe and ethnic group, and the idea of an Islamic *umma*. This tension appears in the Qur'an where God instructs that Islam must supersede familial and tribal relations when they conflict: "And we enjoined on man kindness to his parents, but if they force you to join with me [in worship] anything of which you have no [Divine] knowledge obey them not ... " (Quran 29:8). Yet despite Muhammad's efforts to minimize the impact of the tribes by elevating the centrality of the *umma*, he was unable to dismantle tribal and ethnic groups.

Moreover, despite the efforts made by Muslim religious leaders throughout history, they have not been able to overcome pre-Islamic ethnic and tribal worldviews and loyalties. In the words of Michael Cook: " ... our findings with regard to the interaction between religious and ethnic identity suggest that Muslim solidarity cannot override ethnic division, ... " (Cook 2014, 40). Ethnicity and tribalism have remained important political forces, and it remains to be seen how they played their hands in different political arenas. Cook observes that religious identity tended to enter ethnically divided societies and accentuate their internal tensions and conflicts (Cook 2014).

There are several case studies that confirm Cook's observation. In recent decades some members of tribes and ethnic groups that inhabit North Africa, the Middle East and Asia, have teamed up with militant political Islamists. The cooperation between militant Islamists and tribe members may come as a surprise to some observers, since their worldviews are significantly different, and some would even say opposed (Ahmed 2013, 30). In terms of religious practice many tribe members are lax practitioners of Muslim law, while the militants pride themselves on being devout practitioners. Furthermore, many tribes ascribe to mystical (Sufi) acts of devotion, while the militants abhor mystics. Lastly, most members of tribes consider their tribes the supreme foci of loyalty, while the Muslim *umma* would rank second. Such a religio-political hierarchy is unacceptable to the militant Islamists.

Nevertheless, despite this ideological gap, the militants have been able to win over small numbers of tribe members. Their success, albeit limited, is most likely an outcome of two factors. The first is that there are probably a number of militantly inclined individuals in every tribe, and the militant Islamists are able to connect with them and win them over to their cause. The second is their common enemy – the modern state. The tribes have a long list of grievances against the regimes that run many Middle Eastern, African and Asian states, due to decades of deprivation, humiliation and oppression. Therefore, they are inclined to join forces with elements that oppose their oppressors such as the militant Islamists.

The militants enter this pact in order to win over members of the tribes, enlarge their fighting force, establish enclaves of militant Islamists and further spread their religious vision in areas where established regimes have a bare nominal presence. Hence, when we examine the geographic distribution of the militant Islamists throughout the Muslim world, we find that they often chose to infiltrate tribal areas, whose inhabitants are happy to cooperate with the enemies of the state. Furthermore, usually these areas are barely policed and it is relatively easy to hide in them, train a cadre of fighters and send them out to attack targets within the country or even in other regions. They are, therefore, dysfunctional regions whose inhabitants are easily manipulated by any opponent of the state.

A close study of the militants' mode of operation in tribal regions illustrates how they infiltrate the tribes, clash with their members and bring about internal crises. The Bedouin in the Sinai Desert have been neglected by Egypt's regimes for decades. Starting in the 1980s Salafi ideas began to circulate among the inhabitants there. According to Egyptian authorities, in the year 2000, activists established the underground movement called *al-Tawhid wa-al-Jihad* (Monothesim and Jihad), whose members performed a series of attacks between the years 2004 and 2006 (Yaari 2012, 5). During the two decades that passed since the Salafi creed was introduced into Sinai, a number of developments occurred. In the course of those years a small group of young men in each tribe embraced Salafi and joined the Salafi-Jihadi groups. They altered their appearance by growing beards, and their women ascribed to stricter dress codes. They also attempted to educate their children differently and challenged the authority of their tribal elders. Most importantly, in contrast to Bedouin custom, they married across tribes. The outcome of the militants' infiltration into the tribes was detrimental to the tribes' social fabric. In the words of Ehud Yaari: "This confrontation led to splits within tribal and family units, undermining the social structure of many Bedouin communities" (Yaari 2012, 5–6).

Recently the fragmented tribes have been involved in clashes. A wave of violence initiated by militants against the Tarabin tribe prompted tribal leaders to counter with belligerent statements. Alongside these statements they brought together representatives of thirty tribes in order to establish the Sinai Tribal Federation (Awad and Abdou 2015). Whatever the results of this initiative, the Sinai Bedouin are undergoing what several other tribes have undergone at the hands of the militant Islamists: Ideological penetration; radicalization to the point of violence; terror attacks; imposition of highly conservative norms of conduct; fragmentation of the community and inter-tribal conflict. Similar dynamics that led to inter-tribal conflict occurred in several other groups such as the Tuareg of the Sahara and the Pashtun of Afghanistan.

In contrast to the militants' violent imposition of their values on tribes and ethnic groups, the moderate political Islamists were much more tolerant towards the tribes. In Yemen, for example, the Islah party, which was founded in 1990, brought together the Hashid Tribal Confederation, a Salafi network and the Muslim Brotherhood. Although they differ in their outlooks, they are able to collaborate. In essence, many moderate Islamic movements recognize the power that tribes exert over their societies and tend to keep good relations with them. In some instances, such as Yemen, the outcome is a joint political party. In others, as in Jordan, powerful tribal leaders, such as Abd al-Majid Thnaibat, are members of the local Muslim Brothers branch (*Jordan's Muslim Brotherhood* 16 March 2015).

Ordinarily, tribes and states would be considered very different social organizations. However, from the political Islamists' point of view they share an important characteristic: both constitute a focus of loyalty that competes with the Islamic *umma*. As with other non-Islamic social entities, the moderates and militants are divided. Whereas the moderates are flexible and seek ways to co-exist with the tribes, the militants' rigid intolerance moves them to wage war on any tribe member that disagrees with their religious vision.

Conclusion

The moderates' and militants' contrasting visions of change – what ought to be changed and how to bring it about – stem from their divergent, yet interrelated, views of the past and the society they strive to forge in the future.

From the moderates' point of view, the Islamic past, primarily the age of the Prophet and his companions, is a source of inspiration. As such, it guides Muslim societies as they encounter changing realities, but it does not offer specific instructions regarding governance of Muslim polities, and it certainly does not prevent them from adapting to change. By contrast, the militants view the age of the Prophet as a model that must be imitated and its institutions restored meticulously. This age is not merely a source of inspiration, but rather a blueprint for all Muslim governments. This petrified view of Islam's past causes them to resist any form of change in historical institutions, and moves them to re-establish traditional institutions such as religious police (*hisba*), courts of sharìa law and the Caliphate.

The second crucial issue that sets these orientations apart is their respective positions on the future of Muslim societies, and how they ought to be attained. The moderates view the well-being of the Muslim community (*maslaha*) as a supreme value. Such an approach places contemporary public interest above rigid ideals of history, and allows for the replacement of traditional institutions with modern, non-Muslim ones. Since the community's well-being is of critical importance, they also prohibit the use of force, be it against the ruler or in order to change its political system. By contrast, the militants place traditional values, articulated during the age of the Prophet, above contemporary interests. What is more, new political principles that require adaptation of the traditional political system are anathema to them. Therefore, they opt to preserve historical Islamic institutions, and resort to violence in order to defend them.

Note

1. Qaradawi later retracted specific elements of that legal decision, claiming he did not understand the distinctive circumstances of America. However, he did not reject the principle that a Muslim should serve in his national army even when it goes to battle with his co-religionists. Qaradawi's permission to serve in non-Muslim armies goes hand in hand with the actual conduct of Muslims in the United States, Soviet Red Army and India, that have been studied by Bleuer (2012, 1) who observes: "While these three cases are very different in numerous aspects, they do illustrate a similar phenomenon – Muslim soldiers overwhelmingly choosing to fight for the country of their citizenship over and above any potential complicating ties of Muslim solidarity".

Disclosure statement

No potential conflict of interest was reported by the authors.

References

Abu al-Futuh, 'Abd al-Mun'im. 2004. Waqi al-Qiyadat al-Hizbiyya al-'Arabiyya." [The Reality of Arabic Political Party Leaders]. *Al-Jazeera*, April 20, 2004. http://www.aljazeera.net/programs/opendialogue/2004/10/3/%D9%88%D8%A7%D9%82%D8%B9-%D8%A7%D9%84%D9%82%D9%8A%D8%A7%D8%AF%D8%A7%D8%AA-%D8%A7%D9%84%D8%AD%D8%B2%D8%A8%D9%8A%D8%A9-%D8%A7%D9%84%D8%B9%D8%B1%D8%A8%D9%8A%D8%A9.
Abd al-Hadi al-Misri, Muhammad. n.d. *Haqiqat al-Iman 'Ind Ahl al-Sunna wal-Jamàa*. [The Essence of Belief for Ahl al-Sunna wal-Jama'a]. http://www.dorar.net/enc/aqadia/3214.
Ahmad, Rif'at Sayyid. 1991. *Al-Nabi al-Musalah: al-Rafidun* [The Militant Prophet: The Rejectionist]. London: Riyad al-Rayyis lil-Kutub wa-al-Nashr.
Ahmed, Akbar. 2013. *The Thistle and the Drone: How America's War on Terror Became a Global War on Tribal Islam*. Washington, D.C.: Brookings Institute Press.
Al-Banna, Hasan. 1978. *Five Tracts of Hasan al-Banna' (1906–1949)*. Berkeley: University of California Press.
Al-Banna, Hasan. 1983. *Selected Writings of Hasan al-Banna Shaheed*. Translated by S.A. Qureshi. Karachi: International Islamic Publishers.
Al-Hudaybi, Hasan. 1977. *Dùat … La Qudat* [Preachers … Not Judges]. Cairo: Dar al-Tabàa wa al-Nashr al-Islamiyya.
Al-Maqdisi, Abu Muhammad. n.d. *al-Dimuqratiyya Din* [Democracy is a Religion]. https://archive.org/details/Democracy_201307.
Al-Qaradawi, Yusuf. 2004 (1996). *State in Islam [Min fiqh al-dawla fi al-Islam]*. Cairo: Al-Falah Foundation.
Al-Qaradawi, Yusuf. 2007. "Usul al-Iman wal-Kufr." [The Foundations of Belief and Apostasy]. *Al-Jazeera*, October 24. http://www.aljazeera.net/home/print/0353e88a-286d-4266-82c6-6094179ea26d/9ba96a17-0909-4a5b-a53b-0b6c863cf186.

Al-Qaradawi, Yusuf. 2009a. *Fiqh al-Jihad* [The Jurisprudence of Jihad]. Cairo: Maqtabat Wahba.

Al-Qaradawi, Yusuf. 2009b. "Min al-Wasatiyya Itikhadh al-Shida wal-Quwa min al-A'daa." [From the Midmay: Taking the Force and Power Away from the Enemies]. *Al-Nilin Website*, September 23. http://www.alnilin.com/157331.htm.

Al-Qaradawi, Yusuf. 2014. "Mawqaf al-Islam min al-Dimuqratiyya." [Islam's Position on Democracy]. *Al-Mawqi' al-Rasmi Yusuf al-Qaradawi*, December 16. http://qaradawi.net/new/all-fatawa/7234-2014-04-20-10-43-27.

Al-Tartusi, Abu Basir. 2008. "Limadha Kafartu Yusuf al-Qaradawi." [Why Did I Proclaimed Takfir Against Yusuf al-Qaradawi]. *Mawqi' al-Sheikh Abd al-Mun'im Mustafa Halima*, November 1. www.abubaseer.bizland.com/articles/read/a%20118.doc.

Al-Tartusi, Abu Basir. 2014. "Qa'dat Man la Yukafiru al-Kafir." [The Ruling of He Who Does Not Proclaim Takfir Against an Apostate]. *Mawiq' al-Sheikh Abu Basir al-Tartusi*, September 20. http://altartosi.net/ar/?p=4701.

Al-Tartusi, Abu Basir. n.d. "Fasl al-Kalam fi Mas'ala al-Khuruj ala al-Hakim." [Concluding Remark about the Question of Going against the Rule]. *Mawiq' al-Sheikh Abu Basir al-Tartusi*. http://tartosi.blogspot.co.il/2001/04/blog-post_11.html.

Awad, Mokhtar, and Mostafa Abdou. 2015. "A new Sinai Battle? Bedouin Tribes and Egypt's ISIS Affiliate." *Atlantic Council*, May 14. http://www.atlanticcouncil.org/blogs/egyptsource/a-new-sinai-battle-bedouin-tribes-and-egypt-s-isis-affiliate.

Ayyash, Abdelrahman. 2015. "The Brotherhood's Post-Pacifist Approach." *Sada, Carnegie Endowment for International Peace*, July 9. http://carnegieendowment.org/sada/?fa=60665.

Bleuer, Christian. 2012. "Muslim Soldiers in Non-Muslim Militaries at War in Muslim Lands: The Soviet, American and Indian Experience." *Journal of Muslim Minority Affairs* 2012: 1–15. iFirst article.

Calvert, John. 2010. *Sayyid Qutb and the Origins of Radical Islamism*. New York: Columbia University Press.

Cook, Michael. 2014. *Ancient Religions, Modern Politics: The Islamic Case in Comparative Perspective*. Princeton, NJ: Princeton University Press.

Fahmi, Georges. 2015. "The Struggle for the Leadership of Egypt's Muslim Brotherhood." *Carnegie Endowment for International Peace*, July 14. http://carnegie-mec.org/2015/07/14/struggle-for-leadership-of-egypt-s-muslim-brotherhood/idld.

"Final Tunisian Election Results Announced". 2011. *Al-Jazeera*, November, 14. http://www.aljazeera.com/news/africa/2011/11/20111114171420907168.html.

"Jordan's Muslim Brotherhood Formally Divided". 2015. *The National*, March 16. http://www.thenational.ae/world/middle-east/jordans-muslim-brotherhood-formally-divided.

Kenney, Jeffrey T. 2006. *Muslim Rebels, Kharijites and the Politics of Extremism in Egypt*. Oxford: Oxford University Press.

Lia, Brynjar. (1998) 2006. *The Society of the Muslim Brothers in Egypt: The Rise of an Islamic Mass Movement, 1928–1942*. Reading: Ithaca Press.

Mandaville, Peter. 2007. *Global Political Islam*. London: Routledge.

Mersch, Sarah. 2014. "Tunisia's Compromise Constitution." *Sada, Carnegie Endowment for International Peace*, January 21. http://carnegieendowment.org/sada/?fa=54260.

Mitchell, Richard. (1969) 1993. *The Society of the Muslim Brothers*. New York: Oxford University Press.

Nafi, Basheer M. 2004. "Fatwa and War: On the Allegiance of the American Muslim Soldiers in the Aftermath of September 11." *Islamic Law and Society* 11 (1): 78–116.

The Program of the Muslim Brother's Party (Barnamaj Hizb al-Ikhwan al-Muslimin). 2007. *Islamonline*. Accessed September 25, 2015. https://ar.wikisource.org/wiki/%D8% A8%D8%B1%D9%86%D8%A7%D9%85%D8%AC_%D8%AD%D8%B2%D8%A8_% D8%A7%D9%84%D8%A7%D8%AE%D9%88%D8%A7%D9%86_%D8%A7%D9% 84%D9%85%D8%B3%D9%84%D9%85%D9%8A%D9%86.

Qutb, Sayyid. 2005. *Fi Zilal al-Quran* [In the Shade of the Quran]. Cairo: Dar al-Shuruq.

Qutb, Sayyid. n.d. *Milestones*. http://holybooks.lichtenbergpress.netdna-cdn.com/wp-content/uploads/Milestones.pdf?b5c044.

Watt, Montgomery W. 2002. *The Formative Period of Islamic Thought*. Oxford: Oneworld.

Wickham, Carrie Rosefsky. 2013. *The Muslim Brotherhood: Evolution of an Islamist Movement*. Princeton, NJ: Princeton University Press.

Yaari, Ehud. 2012. *Sinai: A New Front*. The Washington Institute for Near East Policy 9. http://www.washingtoninstitute.org/uploads/Documents/pubs/PoilicyNote09.pdf.

Zollner, Barbara H. E. 2009. *The Muslim Brotherhood: Hasan al-Hudaybi and Ideology*. London: Routledge.

The "ethnic" in Indonesia's communal conflicts: violence in Ambon, Poso, and Sambas

Kirsten E. Schulze

ABSTRACT
This article looks at the communal violence in Ambon, Poso, and Sambas in post-Suharto Indonesia from a comparative perspective. It explores why Ambon and Poso were seen as religious while Sambas was seen as ethnic despite the fact that in all three conflicts different religions and ethnicities fought each other. Examining the "ethnic" elements, this article advances three arguments: First, that the Poso and Ambon conflicts were no less ethnic than the Sambas conflict as they had similar "ethnic causes". Second, that the religious narrative dominated in Ambon and Poso because it reflected the Islamic resurgence in Indonesia since the 1990s while the narrative in Sambas reflected that it was the latest round of a pre-existing anti-Madurese conflict which had already been "defined" as "ethnic". Third, that the narratives were framed strategically, thus influencing the trajectory of the conflict but also responding to it.

After the fall of Suharto in May 1998, Indonesia experienced an upsurge in Islamist, separatist, and communal violence. This violence erupted in the context of the transition from authoritarianism to democracy which saw a drawn-out struggle in Jakarta between the "old" elites associated with the New Order regime and the reformist challengers (Crouch 2010). This political transition provided an opportunity for separatists to push for independence as seen in East Timor (Kingsbury 2000; Martinkus 2001; Greenlees and Garran 2002) and Aceh (Schulze 2004; Davies 2006; Aspinall 2009), for radical Islamists to challenge the nature of the state (Conboy 2005; Sidel 2006; Solahudin 2013), for communities to reshape local socio-political and economic constellations (Van Klinken 2007; Davidson 2008; McRae 2013), and for politicians, military officers, and businessmen to stir up and manipulate these conflicts for their own ends (Tomagola 2001; Aditjondro 2004). While the fall of Suharto set the ball rolling, the roots of violence in Indonesia lay far deeper, in the narrow conception of the Indonesian nation and the way in which this was institutionalized (Bertrand 2004; Tajima 2014). New Order policies of development, transmigration, and "uniformization" resulted in resource exploitation and cultural marginalization outside Java and were perceived as "Javanese colonialism".

This article is a comparative study of three of Indonesia's communal conflicts – Ambon (in Maluku province), Poso (in Central Sulawesi province), and Sambas (in West Kalimantan province) – which the literature on post-Suharto violence has either looked at separately or referred to only in passing in the analysis of the broader transition dynamics. These three conflicts erupted within weeks of each other late 1998/early 1999. They erupted in the urban centres and spread from there to neighbouring villages, and in the case of the Ambon conflict to neighbouring islands. All three conflicts had multiple causes – ethnic, religious, political, social, and economic. In all three conflicts, there were clear links between the violence and local politics both in terms of timing and mobilization (Aragon 2001; Van Klinken 2007; Davidson 2008; McRae 2013). All three saw clashes between locals and migrants as well as between Muslims and non-Muslims. Yet the Indonesian newspapers such as *Kompas*, *Merdeka*, *Media Indonesia*, *Republika*, or *Suara Pembaruan* described the violence in Ambon and Poso as "*konflik antaragama*" (religious conflict), identifying the actors as Muslims and Christians, while the Sambas conflict was described as "*perang antaretnis*" (ethnic warfare) and the actors were identified as Dayak, Malays, and Madurese. This categorization is also present in other observer narratives such as reports by human rights organizations as well as in the academic literature. The Sambas conflict, which lasted from 19 February until May 1999, is seen as having started with a Malay offensive followed by a joint Malay–Dayak offensive. The Poso conflict, which lasted from 24 December 1998 until 2007, is described as having had two phases of urban Christian–Muslim clashes, followed by a short Christian offensive, a lengthy Muslim offensive, and post-agreement terrorism. The Ambon conflict, which lasted from 19 February 1999 until 2003, is depicted as comprising three phases of Christian–Muslim violence in 1999, followed by a Muslim offensive in 2000, and post-agreement terrorism. Moreover, analyses of the Ambon conflict have often focused on the role of religion (Bartels 2003; Gaspersz 2005; Al-Qurtuby 2015), the role of the Protestant church (Hehanussa 2013), and the role of Laskar Jihad (Schulze 2002; Bräuchler 2005; Hasan 2006). Jihadist violence has also been the focus of analyses of the Poso conflict (Karnavian 2008; McRae 2013).

This article does not discuss the general causes of these conflicts, their timing, or the role of religion as these have already been addressed in the existing literature. Instead it examines the "ethnic" dimension from a comparative perspective, starting with the question of whether the Ambon and

Poso conflicts were indeed less ethnic than Sambas. "Ethnic" refers to the identity markers of a particular *suku* (ethnic group) such as *adat* (customs) as well as common ancestry, culture, history, and beliefs. The analysis of the ethnic dimension focuses on "ethnic" causes, "ethnic" narratives, and "ethnic" violence. Here it is argued that the Ambon and Poso conflicts were no less ethnic than the Sambas conflict as they shared many of the same ethnic causes and, the ethnic narratives that were advanced, were similar. This article then looks at the conflict narratives, exploring why the religious narrative dominated in Ambon and Poso despite the involvement of different ethnic groups and why the ethnic narrative dominated in Sambas despite the involvement of different religions. It also reflects on why the ethnic conflict narrative was advanced mainly by non-Muslims, and whether the narrative framing had direct implications for the trajectory of the conflicts. Here two arguments are advanced: First, that the conflict narrative in Ambon and Poso was religious because it reflected the broader national religious tensions resulting from the resurgence of Islam in Indonesia since the 1990s while the ethnic narrative dominated in Sambas because it was the latest round of periodic anti-Madurese violence since the 1960s. The latter was "defined" as "ethnic" at a time when Islam was in a weakened position in Indonesia with the defeat of the Darul Islam (DI) rebellions in 1962. Second, that the narratives were also framed and re-framed strategically, the latter accounting for the shift from an ethnic narrative to a religious one among Christians in Ambon and Poso. They thus influenced the trajectory of the conflict and were influenced by it.

Ethnic causes

When looking at the causes of the Ambon, Poso, and Sambas conflicts, it is impossible to overlook the changes in the ethnic composition of these three areas in the decades preceding the eruption of the violence. The in-migration of other ethnic groups changed the demographic balance leading to the marginalization of the indigenous, resulted in the loss of ancestral land, and eroded local customary *adat* structures. All of these thus became "ethnic" causes of conflict.

In-migration and the marginalization of the indigenous

Driven by the need to address overpopulation on Java, Bali, and Lombok, the central government pursued a transmigration policy to redistribute people from high population density areas to those with smaller populations (Hardjono 1977; Fasbender and Erbe 1990). The resettlement of transmigrants on the outer islands, however, was problematic as both the colonial and post-colonial government had fostered the sense that people of different regions were of different ethnicity. Indeed, ethnicity and locality overlapped to such an extent that they were assumed to be a single concept, what Tom Boellstorff refers to as ethnolocality (Boellstorff 2002, 25). Transmigrants were thus not seen by locals as fellow Indonesians, but as "others" and as their numbers grew, so did the competition and fears that locals were losing out.

Between 1975 and 1990 Central Sulawesi saw the influx of 181,696 transmigrants, Maluku the influx of 139,465 transmigrants, and West Kalimantan the influx of 102,520 transmigrants (Bertrand 2004, 93). This transmigration was perceived by locals as a fundamentally unequal process in which local land was appropriated by the state and given to migrants along with government assistance in the form of tools and seed. In Maluku, this resulted in the transmigrant farmers being seen as more competitive than locals who were not familiar with "modern" agriculture.[1] In West Kalimantan, it was believed to have led to the loss of land as well as jobs and when the local Dayak complained, they were ignored or simply labelled as "lazy".[2]

The transmigrants, who were mainly Javanese farmers, were followed by significant numbers of "spontaneous" migrants of other ethnicities. The latter were not organized by the state but went on their own buoyed by the general pro-migration mood as well as the increased access to remote areas as new roads were constructed in accordance with the New Order's developmentalist policies. The construction projects themselves attracted large numbers of spontaneous migrants who worked on the sites. The completed roads brought further migrants, small traders lured by the possibility of new markets.

In Central Sulawesi the migrants flocked to the extractive industries such as ebony as well as cash crops soon dominating the clove, cacao, coffee, and copra trade. They also owned the majority of small shops (HRW 2002, 6). Even the market in the Protestant highland stronghold of Tentena became dominated by Bugis, Gorontalo, and Arab descent migrants with the effect that pork could no longer be purchased as the traders were Muslim (Damanik 2003, 44). By the 1990s the key sectors of the economy were dominated by migrants because local Christians were more interested in civil service positions while the migrants were able to tap into existing ethnic trade networks.

In West Kalimantan the spontaneous migrants were Bugis and Madurese. The latter became a particular thorn in the eyes of local Dayaks and Malays as they had followed Madurese transmigrants (*DR*, 29 March–3 April 1999). This made them the largest migrant community. Moreover, according to locals, the Madurese, unlike the Bugis, did not integrate with society.[3] And in terms of employment they seemed to be everywhere. They worked as port labourers, on construction sites, on plantations, in coffee shops, and commerce. Their employment by logging companies and illegal loggers as well as construction companies that "opened the jungle" by building roads put them on a collision course with the rural Dayaks who sought to protect their resources. In the cities the Madurese were particularly numerous in the transport sector. In Pontianak they took over the *becaks* (pedicabs) from the Chinese[4] while in Sambas they pushed out the Malays. They also competed with Malay small traders and peddlers.

In Maluku the majority of spontaneous migrants were Bugis, Butonese, and Makassar – referred to as BBM. The BBM initially filled the emerging gaps in the economy as Ambonese Muslims climbed up the educational ladder. Butonese migrants in the 1960s worked as labourers in the harbour.[5] By the 1980s, they had also moved into fishing. Bugis migrants worked as *becak* drivers and soon dominated local transport. By 1996, locals found that they were losing in the competition with the outsiders and started blaming the migrants for problems ranging from the pollution of Ambon's harbour,[6] to rising Muslim Ambonese unemployment, and declining economic opportunities for Christian Ambonese (Bertand 2002, 73).

The loss of ancestral lands

In-migration also resulted in the loss of *tanah adat* (customary/ancestral lands) in West Kalimantan and Central Sulawesi. The encroachment by the state on ancestral lands began with the Basic Agrarian Law 5/1960 which stated that customary land tenure only applied to the extent that it did not conflict with "national interests" (ICG 2001, 15). Under Suharto further legislation was introduced with the specific purpose of appropriating the land for development. Basic Forestry Law 5/1967 claimed the country's forests as state property. Basic Mining Law 11/1967 enabled the state to become the ultimate judge on land use. And in 1973 presidential instruction number 2 designated ten outer island provinces as new transmigration sites. For this, too, land was set aside. Thus, the New Order systematically appropriated *adat* land.

In Central Sulawesi it was primarily Pamona *adat* land that was used for transmigration sites while hundreds of hectares of Mori *adat* land were taken for palm oil plantations (Damanik 2003, 44). Government officials sold land and exploited the resources, including areas of *hutan lindung* (protected forest) resulting in repeated protests by the indigenous populations (Forum Cheq and Recheq n.d., 2). Not surprisingly, during the last decade of the New Order there were intermittent outbreaks of violence between the indigenous population and transmigrants which were put down by the military.

From the 1990s onwards, spontaneous migrants also started to push into the interior of Poso district searching for land especially for cacao plantations (Damanik 2003, 44). This rose dramatically after the 1997 Asian financial crisis when cacao became the "'hot' export crop because it was pegged to the US dollar" (Aragon 2001, 56). Some migrants did not even bother to purchase land but simply entered Pamona ancestral forests with chainsaws and cut down the trees to clear fields for cacao and other cash crops (HRW 2002, 6).

In West Kalimantan it was Dayak *adat* land that was appropriated by Jakarta for transmigration, the logging industry, and plantations. Most Dayak land was communally owned but this was not recognized by the central government as "there are no formal land titles".[7] In many cases, this meant the eviction and destruction of whole villages without compensation by the state (Dove 1997, 1). They were then relocated to new "modern" villages with "modern" houses, often forcibly by the army and police.[8] It is estimated that as many as 2.5 million Dayaks were displaced throughout Kalimantan.

The land taken by the state was then given as concessions to logging and plantation companies. Between 1968 and 1973 timber production in West Kalimantan increased 25-fold from 127,894 to 3.3 million cubic metres (Davidson n.d., 4). In the 1980s around three million hectares were given for large-scale, mainly palm oil plantations (Bappeda 1993, 11, table 1.5). This land, too, was taken with little or no compensation or consultation.[9] The destruction of the forest by logging and plantation companies was further compounded by illegal logging, usually facilitated by corrupt local officials and protected by elements in the security forces.

Like the Pamona, Mori, and Lore in Central Sulawesi, the Dayak protested their dispossession only to be accused of "obstructing national development" (ICG 2001, 20) and to be labelled as "primitives" (Djuweng 1997, 25–26). At the same time, whenever a Dayak felled a tree to meet household needs, he was treated like a criminal (*The Jakarta Post*, April 20, 1999). Not surprisingly "the frustration of the Dayaks seeing the greedy exploitation of Kalimantan, the felling of trees and damage to the environment and all the wealth that was enjoyed in Jakarta"[10] became one of the key reasons for the periodic Dayak violence.

Conflict erupted with those migrants who were seen as collaborators in this process of dispossession: the Madurese. They were seen as being at "the forefront of the land grab" from 1967 onwards.[11] They were also working for the construction companies that were clearing the land and building roads into West Kalimantan's interior. And when the logging companies arrived, it was the Madurese who cut down the trees the Dayaks saw as theirs.

The loss of *adat* land had a traumatic impact on the indigenous communities in both Central Sulawesi and West Kalimantan as land was intrinsically connected to the ancestral religions. In these animistic belief systems soil, trees, plants, stones, and rivers were imbued with spirits living in harmony with man, constituting a "greater whole". Nature and resources were not economic assets and not subordinate to man but existed in harmony with him (Djuweng 1997, 12–14). This interconnectedness with the land had not changed when the Pamona, Lore, and Mori had become Protestants or when the Dayak had become Catholics. The land was still considered sacral. It was the "proof of the existence of their ancestors before them, a base on which to continue life at present, a future heirloom to be handed down to the next generation" (Djuweng 1998, 6).

Undermining and violating local adat

While the loss of ancestral lands was central only to the growing ethnic tensions in West Kalimantan and Central Sulawesi, the "loss" of *adat or* violation of *adat* played a key role in the eruption of violence in all three conflicts. During the New Order local *adat* was systematically undermined by the state's nation-building efforts through centralization, "uniformization", and bringing all constituent elements of the Indonesian nation in line with the New Order's national imaginary, which had a Javanese and "modern" face. The policy which had the greatest impact on local *adat* was Law 5/1979 on Village Governance. Its purpose was to standardize village government across the archipelago as well as to replace "outdated" traditional village systems with a "modern" one. This was detrimental for the vast majority of communities in Indonesia as this legislation was not ethnically neutral; it imposed the Javanese system, as the chosen model, on non-Javanese areas.

The Law on Village Governance removed power from customary leaders as well as customary councils of elders and placed it in the hands of the national civil service, increasing political control by outsiders and engineering new socio-political hierarchies. In West Kalimantan the communally elected Dayak *kepala adat* (customary leader) was replaced by a politically elected *kepala desa* (village head). The requirement of a high school degree for candidates for village head, excluded most customary leaders from running (ICG 2001, 18–19). However, it was not just village governance that was standardized but also village size. This led to the merger of distinct communities with "the component parts of the new villages ... sometimes as much as eight or ten kilometres apart with the result that some villagers did not even know the village head" (ICG 2001, 18–19).

In Ambon, the impact of these administrative reforms was fourfold: first, the traditional *raja negeri* (village head) had to change his title to *kepala desa*, trading a title legitimated by *adat* for a purely administrative one. Second, under the new system, all adults living in a village had the same right to become *kepala desa* unlike the *raja* which had been an "ascribed status" (Pariela 1996, 116). Third, the assault on *adat* weakened Ambon's *pela* alliance system which tied together two or three different villages, irrespective of religion, into a brotherhood (Bartels 2010, 219). *Pela* relations created "cultural harmony" which counter-balanced what one Ambonese referred to as "the silent religious conflict since the arrival of Christianity during the colonial era".[12] And fourth, the introduction of the elected *kepala desa* resulted in the loss of moral authority as most *kepala desa* were associated with the increasingly corrupt governing Golkar party. This, in turn, meant that when the conflict erupted in January 1999, local leaders had no capacity to calm the situation.

The systematic erosion of local *adat* by the New Order regime was exacerbated by the in-migration into Ambon, Poso, and West Kalimantan of other ethnic groups with their own, different customs. This caused tensions when local *adat* was disrespected. As Albert Tumimor, the grandson of the *raja* of Poso, recalled his grandfather saying: "I did not invite you [the migrants]. But if you want to stay here, respect our traditions." Tumimor then remarked that the migrants "did not behave like guests or what you would expect from newcomers. When they were here for a while and had become rich, they started to suppress the indigenous".[13] Many locals also felt that there was a tendency for migrants to feel more cultured than the locals and to behave arrogantly (Damanik 2003, 43).

While disputes over land in the rural areas gave rise to "chronic" conflict dynamics between locals and both transmigrants and spontaneous migrants, it was in the urban areas like Ambon city, Poso city, and Sambas town where the incendiary mix of a high concentration of spontaneous migrants, high population density, high unemployment, and a high proportion of male youths created the "acute" conflict that erupted in December 1998 and January 1999. Here customs from the various migrant communities collided with local *adat* structures and the close proximity of indigenous and migrants combined with the political, economic, and social competition heightened ethnic identity and "sharpened" indigenous responses to transgressions of local *adat* by outsiders. At the same time, traditional structures as a whole, both migrant and indigenous, were challenged by modernity and youthful rebellion which resulted in the disrespect of any *adat* or indeed authority.

As can be seen from this discussion, the Ambon, Poso, and Sambas conflicts clearly drew upon "ethnic" grievances resulting from in-migration, the loss of ancestral land, and the erosion or violation of local *adat* in the years preceding the violence. The cumulative effect was a direct cultural or "ethnic" threat which was a key cause of all three conflicts.

Ethnic violence

To assess the extent to which the violence in Ambon, Poso, and Sambas was "ethnic" it is useful to look at the targets, the motivation, and the *modus oper-andi*. In all three conflicts, there was ethnic targeting. In the Ambon conflict, this was most visible during the first few days when, in the context of the broader conflict in which violence was perpetrated against both Christians and Muslims, Christian Ambonese systematically attacked the BBM. On 19 January 1999, they burnt the kiosks and then the *becak* owned by the Bugis and Butonese. On 20 January, Ambonese Christians burnt the overwhelmingly Bugis owned stalls in Ambon city's markets while taking care not to attack the shops of the Chinese (Rahawarin 2000, 3–4). They also burned a Butonese settlement and stopped public buses and *becak* as symbols of the BBM. There were calls for the BBM to leave Maluku[14] as well as anti-BBM banners and slogans. Former Ambon mayor Dicky Wattimena, who was known for his anti-BBM politics, was seen giving orders during the violence and telling the BBM to go home (*Ummat*, February 15, 1999). By the end of the first phase of the conflict in May 1999, the overwhelming majority of BBM had fled to Sulawesi.

The BBM were targeted because they had demographically increased the Muslim share of the population in a precariously balanced Muslim–Christian society. They were blamed for the consequent decrease in the Christian share of the local resources in the decade preceding the conflict and, with the impending June 1999 elections, it was feared that the BBM would increase the vote for the Muslim parties (Van Klinken 2001, 22). They were also seen as a cultural threat,[15] diluting and undermining Ambonese *adat*. Ambonese Christians further believed that Ambon's Muslims would like to see them leave to reduce the economic competition, but were too polite to say so.

Ethnic targeting also occurred in the Poso conflict, in this case by both indigenous and migrants. In the first two phases – 24–29 December 1998 and 15–20 April 2000 – street battles were fought between the migrant Bugis residents of Kayamanya and the Pamona and Mori residents of the Sayo and Lombogia neighbourhoods of Poso city (Aragon 2001, 60). In both phases most of those injured, most of the houses destroyed, and most of the displaced were Pamona and Mori. The third phase in May–June 2000, was an organized and planned attack by the Pamona. One of the areas targeted was the village of Sintuwulemba where prospering migrant cacao farmers were "the focus of jealousy" by their indigenous Pamona neighbours "who had watched their ancestral holdings shrink as the migrants continued to purchase more land" (Aragon 2001, 68). On 28 May, Sintuwulemba was attacked, 200 houses burnt down, and those migrants who did not manage to flee were hacked to death.[16] Over the next couple of days the Pamona fighters proceeded to round up those who had fled into the nearby forest. One Pamona youth, who had participated in the attack "returned to Tentena with 50 identity cards which he had taken off the people he had killed"[17] – they were all migrants.

The motivations for targeting the migrants in the Poso conflict were similar to those in the Ambon conflict. "They targeted the Bugis, Gorontalo and Javanese because they were an economic threat … and because they were aggressive."[18] The Pamona retribution in the third phase of the conflict, moreover, was explained as a response to the fact that virtually all of the destruction in the first and second phases was of Pamona property. It was also a response to the role played by the migrants in that violence, the cultural marginalization and dislocation of locals (Aditjondro 2004).

The Sambas conflict, too, saw ethnic targeting. The conflict erupted when some 200 Madurese attacked the Malay village of Paretsetia over the detention of a Madurese who had been caught burgling a house the previous day. The lack of capacity of the police to deal with the Madurese attackers (*Kompas*, January 22, 1999) gave rise to the mobilization of Malays throughout Sambas district. On 21 February 1999, armed with traditional weapons such as spears and swords they went in search of Madurese. They burnt down 20 houses in the villages of Sebangkau Semparuk and Tebas Sungai (*Suara Karya*, February 24, 1999). Later they killed two Madurese in Sungai Kelambu. On the night of 23 February, a crowd of Malays attacked the local police station (*Merdeka*, February 25, 1999) where Madurese had taken shelter. When this round of violence subsided sixteen people had been killed and eighty-one houses and two trucks burnt (*Kompas*, February 23, 1999). It had also triggered a Madurese exodus from Sambas district.

The second phase of the Sambas conflict started on 15 March and the Malays were now joined by the Dayaks in targeting the Madurese. The Dayaks attacked the Madurese who lived in the villages of Pantai, Semparuk, Harapan, Lonam, and Serapan. They then joined the Malays and headed for Madurese settlements with jerry cans filled with petrol (*GAMMA*, March 28, 1999). Throughout Sambas roadblocks were set up and every car was stopped and searched for Madurese (*Tempo*, March 28, 1999), who were then beheaded. Open trucks carried triumphant men holding up heads as crowds cheered and shouted "Long live the Malays" while brandishing spears and long knives (*The Sunday Times*, March 21, 1999). By early May, with the Madurese expelled from Sambas district, Dayak and Malay combatants ran out of targets and the mobilizations ceased (Davidson 2008, 134). According to official statistics at the end of the conflict 35,000 Madurese had been displaced and more than 2,500 houses burnt (*The Jakarta Post*, July 20, 1999).

The reasons for targeting the Madurese in Sambas shared many similarities with reasons for targeting migrants in Poso and Ambon: economic competition, disrespect of local *adat*, usurpation of indigenous land. The *modus operandi* of Malays and Dayaks, however, appeared to be more distinctly ethnic, and, interestingly, tied only to Dayak customs. Indeed Dayaks held *adat*-based war ceremonies before they attacked. They also explained the beheadings and triumphant display of heads by pointing to their "headhunting" heritage. This was echoed by much of the contemporaneous media. Academic analyses in comparison see the Dayak violence as drawing upon a "reimagined" headhunting past.

The divergence between the participant narratives and observer narratives on the Malays is even greater. Malay explanations for adopting "headhunting" practices revolved around the Madurese being aggressive, rude, dishonest, hot tempered, individualistic, and lacking respect for other people's traditions and property.[19] The "brutality" of the violence was thus the result of extreme anger. Dayaks explained the Malay behaviour as the result of Dayak traditions having been introduced into the Malay community by the "large number of Dayaks who converted to Islam and thus became Malay".[20] These Malays were of Dayak origin, shared the Dayak ancestors and were tied to Dayak *adat* which "explains why the Malay–Madurese conflict followed a similar pattern including the eating of human flesh and the drinking of blood".[21] Scholars such as Davidson and Van Klinken argue that the appropriation of Dayak war practices was a reaction to earlier Dayak ethnic mobilization in 1997, with the aim of asserting equality in indigeneity (Davidson 2008) and reclaiming lost positions in local government (Van Klinken 2008, 1). What ties participant and observer narratives together is indeed indigeneity. This is conferred either through genealogy or through emulation and, arguably, the Dayak narrative portraying the Malays as being of Dayak origin is recognition of the indigenous status of the Malays.

Conflict narratives: ethnic vs. religious

The violence which erupted in Poso, Ambon, and Sambas in 1998/1999 clearly had an ethnic dimension as the above discussion demonstrates. It also, however, had a religious dimension which was not about religion *per se* but about what Lorraine Aragon in her analysis of the Poso conflict termed "the political economy of being Protestant or Muslim" (Aragon 2001, 47). The in-migration into all three areas was overwhelmingly Muslim which changed the local religious balance and led non-Muslims in Maluku, Central Sulawesi, and West Kalimantan to speculate about the "real" agenda of Jakarta. Many Dayaks believed that the government wanted "to reduce the indigenous people"[22] and to keep "the Christian population small".[23] The belief that transmigration aimed at the Islamization of areas with historically large Christian populations was also widespread.[24] This speculation was grounded in the changes in Indonesia in the 1980s and 1990s which saw a resurgence of Islam at a popular level followed by a shift in attitude of the central government which led to the establishment of the Indonesian Muslim Intellectuals Association or *Ikatan Cendikiawan Muslim Indonesia* (ICMI) headed by Vice-President BJ Habibie. ICMI actively sought to increase the number of Muslims in leading positions in government and society in the eastern provinces.

Against these developments at national level the increasing number of Muslim migrants placed considerable strain on the informal Christian–Muslim power-sharing arrangements in Central Sulawesi and Maluku. Poso district saw a shift from a fairly evenly balanced population[25] to a 57.2 per cent Muslim majority by the end of the New Order. Moreover, between 1989 and 1999 the top fifty positions in the office of the *bupati* (regent), the heads of offices, agencies, divisions, and sub-districts saw the percentage of Christian office holders drop from 54 per cent to 39 per cent (Mappangara 2001, appendix 2). Dating from the appointment of Arief Patanga as *bupati*, it was not only the number of Muslim bureaucrats which increased but practically all leaders of the executive and legislative were members of ICMI (Damanik 2003, xxxvii), including many migrants.

Similarly, between 1971 and 1990 the percentage of Muslims in Maluku province grew from 49.9 to 56.8 (Van Klinken 2001, 12). By 1997, it had reached 59.02 per cent (ICG 2002, 1). While at provincial level the balance shifted from 50/50 to 40/60 in favour of the Muslims, in Ambon city the religious balance shifted from a Christian majority of 57.5 per cent to just under 50 per cent which included at least 50,000 Muslim migrants from South Sulawesi (Jubilee Campaign UK 1999, 4). These changes dated back to the first Muslim governor Akip Latuconsina in 1992 who was also the provincial head of ICMI. His appointment was seen as the start of the political marginalization of Ambon's Christians as Latuconsina "reformed" Maluku's civil service by removing "top bureaucrats with Christian names", replacing them with Muslims (Van Klinken 2001, 19).[26] By 1996, all the *bupatis* in Maluku province were Muslim (Bertrand 2004, 118). Most new teachers hired by the government were Muslims. Moreover many originated from outside Maluku.

In light of this religious dimension, the question arises why non-Muslims in Ambon and Poso advanced an ethnic narrative when the conflicts erupted as exemplified by Ambonese Christian "commander" Emang Nikijuluw's explanation that the Ambon conflict "was not a clash between Ambonese Muslims and Christians but between Ambonese Christians and the BBM".[27]

The ethnic narrative appealed for three key reasons: First, it more accurately reflected the multiple grievances and complex causes of the conflicts rather than reducing them to religion as the sole factor. Second, it allowed the Christians to frame their fears with respect to the Islamic resurgence in a way they believed would not upset indigenous Muslims with whom relations were largely harmonious, aided by the fact that they had a shared local history, culture, and even ancestors. Third, it allowed them to put forward their grievances in a "neutral" way in country in which the Islamization had considerably narrowed the space for Christians to advance a "religious narrative" as many Muslims associated Christians not just with colonial history but the more recent appearance of aggressive evangelical missionaries and the policies of "western imperialists".

Muslims in Ambon and Poso from the beginning of the two conflicts advanced a religious narrative. This narrative in Ambon emphasized that the attack against Muslims, who were celebrating Idul Fitri, had been planned by Christians in the Protestant Maranatha church.[28] The violence was referred to as "Idul Fitri *berdarah*" (bloody Idul Fitri). In Poso Muslims emphasized that a Muslim youth had been stabbed in a mosque by a Christian on Christmas Eve.[29]

Why did Muslims in Ambon and Poso advance a religious narrative? First, for most local Muslims this was simply a reflection of reality as they saw it, evidenced by the violence erupting on religious holidays and the targeting of religious buildings. Second, the shift away from distinctly local Muslim practices towards a more universal Islam over the previous two decades, had created a religious solidarity between local Muslims and Muslim migrants, although their relationship remained complicated on an ethnic, social, economic, and political level. Third, the Islamic resurgence in Indonesia in the years immediately preceding the conflict had strengthened Muslim identity to such an extent that it had become the core identity for many Muslims in Ambon and Poso. And fourth, the religious narrative provided local Muslims with a vehicle for appealing to Muslims in other parts of Indonesia for humanitarian assistance after the conflict erupted. For Ambonese Muslims there was an additional, fifth, reason: they were not convinced that the BBM were targeted for ethnic reasons and feared that they would be next.[30]

In 1999 the first volunteers from Jemaah Islamiyya (JI) and Kompak arrived in Ambon followed by Laskar Jihad in 2000; JI and Kompak arrived in Poso in 2000; and Laskar Jihad in 2001. They came to provide humanitarian aid, to defend their fellow Muslims and for *dakwa* (proselytization). The arrival of these *mujahedin* reinforced the religious narrative by recasting the conflict as a *jihad*. Their participant narrative diverged somewhat from that of most local Muslims in that it added *salafi* notions of puritanism as well as international *jihadi* notions of conflict between Islam and the Zionist–Crusader alliance. Laskar Jihad's extreme anti-Christian rhetoric, moreover, played a key role in shifting the narrative advanced by Christians in Ambon and Poso from an ethnic one to a religious one. It also resulted in a shift from trying to appeal to the Indonesian government for help to appealing to the Christian World as well as the United Nations (Damanik 2003, 78). Here the key role was played by the churches (Hehanussa 2013, 226), further reinforcing the reframing of the narrative along religious lines.

This shift is interesting as it shows that narratives can influence the trajectory of the conflict – as the arrival of the *mujahedin* proves – and that changes in the trajectory of the conflict can, conversely, reframe existing narratives. It also reveals that narratives can be a strategic choice. The shift in the Christian narrative was not just a response to the attacks on their religion but it was also a strategic reframing of the narrative signalling "giving up" on waiting for help from the Indonesian government in favour of trying to get help from the international community. It reflected the recognition that while Christians had little to gain from a religious (Christian) narrative in an Indonesian national context, a religious narrative served them better than an ethnic one in an international context as it tapped into increasing, mainly western, concerns about militant Islam and the persecution of Christian minorities.

This leaves the participant narratives in the Sambas conflict which were and remained ethnic, partially because this was a much shorter conflict with fewer opportunities for a narrative shift but also because there was a clear victor from the outset. The Dayak narrative emphasized the Madurese violation of *adat*, their cultural incompatibility, and their lack of indigeneity. The Malay narrative similarly pointed to the "Madurese character" as aggressive and disrespectful, stereotyping them as thieves, and stressing their migrant origins. The Madurese narrative portrayed the Madurese as helpless victims of "primitive barbarity" who had been forsaken by the Indonesian government and security forces.

Why was the Sambas conflict seen as ethnic despite the fact that the actors were Catholic and animist Dayaks, Muslim Malays, and Muslim Madurese? Moreover, why did the Malays as Muslims fight alongside the non-Muslim Dayaks against their fellow Muslim Madurese?

There are five interconnected explanations: First, the Sambas conflict must be viewed not as a stand-alone conflict but as an episode of the broader anti-Madurese violence in West Kalimantan since the beginning of the New Order. This conflict had started as one over land and land was at the heart of at least 11 outbreaks of anti-Madurese violence between 1967 and 1997 (*DR*, 29 March–3 April 1999). However, it was also seen as a Madurese assault on the rural Dayak way of life and everything that defined "being Dayak". It thus was cast not simply as an indigenous-migrant or a land conflict but as an ethnic struggle. Second, the broader Madurese-Dayak conflict erupted at a time when the Indonesian national mood had swung against Islamism. The defeat of theDI rebellions, which had challenged the Indonesian state from 1948 to 1962, as well as the relegation to the political periphery of Muslim groups involved in the violence of 1965–66, effectively closed the door to a narrative of "religious violence". Religion, in general, and Islam, in particular, were portrayed as a force in retreat by Jakarta while "secular" nationalism and developmentalism were hailed. This made it "un-strategic" for the Madurese to cast the conflict in Muslim–Christian terms and allowed the Dayak to shape the conflict narrative as an ethnic one. Third, moving on specifically to Sambas, the initial violence was between two Muslim groups. Constructing a narrative around "Idul Fitri *berdarah*" was thus difficult despite the fact that the violence, like that in Ambon, erupted on Idul Fitri. What set the Malays and Madurese apart was ethnicity as well as the latter's clear status as migrants – not religion. Fourth, the Malays felt closer to the Dayak than the Madurese as they had a shared, albeit separate, history in West Kalimantan but also cultural and family links through Dayak conversions to Islam and inter-marriage. And finally, fifth, Muslim Malays sided with non-Muslim Dayaks against Muslim Madurese because they not only felt economically threatened in the cities with the Madurese moving into urban areas in large numbers, but they also wanted to strengthen their position in local politics vis-à-vis the Dayaks and the only way to do this was through asserting indigeneity as Davidson has argued (Davidson 2008). That then explains the "Dayak-like" headhunting and the thoroughly un-Islamic drinking of blood and consumption of human flesh despite the admonishment by the *ulama*.[31]

Conclusion

The Ambon, Poso, and Sambas conflicts erupted during Indonesia's transition from authoritarianism to democracy. They were linked to the struggle for political power and control over resources in the context of decentralization. All three conflicts shared similar causes resulting from the in-migration of other ethnic groups and the disrespect of local *adat* by migrants coupled with social, economic, and political competition between locals and migrants. In all three cases violence by indigenous actors specifically targeted migrants in order to defend their local resources, particularly land, from encroachment by migrants and the Indonesian state. Thus, there is little to suggest that the Sambas conflict was somehow inherently more ethnic than the other two. Indeed, the ethnic narratives advanced by the non-Muslims in all three conflicts were broadly similar in their emphasis on the indigenous experience of physical, social, cultural, and political displacement by migrants from other ethnic backgrounds. Yet, participant and observer narratives on the Ambon and Poso conflicts were largely framed in religious terms while those on the Sambas conflict cast the violence as ethnic.

It has been argued here that at a broader level, the religious narrative dominated in the Ambon and Poso conflicts because it reflected the religious tensions nationally resulting from the resurgence of Islam in Indonesia since the 1990s while the ethnic narrative dominated in the Sambas conflict because there was an extant historical narrative, which was ethnic as it predated this resurgence.

The ethnic narrative was retained in Sambas because the first phase of the violence pitted Muslims of different ethnicity against each other which precluded a religious narrative. The entry of the non-Muslim Dayaks into the conflict in the second phase did not result in a narrative shift because the political, economic, and social interests of the Malays lay in emphasizing shared indigeneity with the Dayaks rather than shared religion with the Madurese. Moreover, the fact that the conflict overall was quite brief, when compared with the Ambon and Poso conflicts, limited the scope for an "evolving" narrative. And finally, the episodic nature of the broader anti-Madurese violence in West Kalimantan not only reinforced the existing narrative but self-validated it.

In comparison, the Ambon and Poso conflicts were of recent nature, following several decades of peaceful co-existence between local Christians and Muslims. They erupted at a time of Islamic resurgence leading local Muslims to almost automatically adopt a religious narrative as it reflected their core identity at the time and resonated with broader Muslim grievances resulting from the first two decades of the New Order. Local Christians advanced an ethnic or mixed narrative which then shifted to a religious narrative as the conflicts progressed over years. This shift reflected a change in the conflict trajectory with the arrival of the *mujahedin* and particularly the arrival of Laskar Jihad, which resulted in the Christians seeing themselves as victims of religious aggression but also in a strategic reframing of the narrative in order to appeal to the international community.

More generally, the comparison of these three conflicts has shown the impact and importance of national and even global dynamics on the shaping of local conflict narratives as well as why some narratives have historical durability. It has also illustrated that narratives, particularly in protracted, on-going conflicts, are often reframed to reflect developments on the ground or strategic needs, resulting in the emergence of a particular narrative even when a different one was equally valid. And finally, it has been demonstrated that the competing interests of the actors result in a contest of narrative framing. It is this area which has considerable scope for further research by delving more deeply into the question of which actors get to frame or reframe the narrative, which ones are excluded from the process, and why.

Notes

1. Interview with Jacky Manuputty, Ambon, April 1, 2005.
2. Interview with Mgr A. Agus, Apostolic Administrator (Sintang), Pontianak, West Kalimantan, September 3, 1999.
3. Interview with Father Jeremias, Menyalin, West Kalimantan, September 5, 1999.
4. Interview with Father Petrus, Pontianak, West Kalimantan, September 4, 1999.
5. Interview with Jusuf Kalla, Coordinating Minister for People's Welfare, Jakarta, April 11, 2003.
6. Interview with Des Alwi, Jakarta, June 18, 2001.
7. Interview with Father Petrus, Pontianak, West Kalimantan, September 4, 1999.
8. Interview with Father Sekundus, Pontianak, West Kalimantan, September 3, 1999.
9. Interview with Stepanus Djuweng, Institute of Dayakology, West Pontianak, Kalimantan, September 6, 1999.
10. Interview with Lt. Gen (ret.) Z. A. Maulani, former head of BAKIN, Tangerang, April 24, 2001.
11. Interview with Prof. Dr Y. C. Thambun Anyang, SH, Pontianak, West Kalimantan, September 4, 1999.
12. Interview with Jacky Manuputty, Ambon, April 1, 2005.
13. Interview with Albert Tumimor, district attorney, Tentena, January 13, 2003.
14. Interview with Jacky Manuputty, Ambon, April 1, 2005.
15. Interview with Jacky Manuputty, Ambon, July 31, 2012.
16. Interview with Reverend Nelly, Silancar village, January 11, 2003.
17. Interview with Reverend Tobundo, Synod Head, Tentena, January 12, 2003.

18. Interview with Reverend Irianto Konkoli, Palu, January 8, 2003.
19. Interview with Sanussi M. Asri, SH, Pontianak, West Kalimantan, September 6, 1999.
20. Interview with Father Jeremias, Menyalin, West Kalimantan, September 5, 1999.
21. Interview with John Bamba, Institute of Dayakology, Pontianak, West Kalimantan, September 6, 1999.
22. Interview with Prof. Dr Y. C. Thambun Anyang, SH, Pontianak, West Kalimantan, September 4, 1999.
23. Interview with Father Sekundus, Pontianak, West Kalimantan, September 3, 1999.
24. Interview with Albert Bisalemba, Lucas und Rasip Ley, Kelompok Merah (Red Forces Christian vigilante group), Tentena, January 13, 2003.
25. Interview with Reverend Tarau, Partai Kristen, DPRD, Palu, January 8, 2003.
26. Interview with Jacky Manuputty, Ambon, April 1, 2005.
27. Interview with Emang Nikijuluw, Christian grassroots (vigilante) leader, Ambon, February 22, 2011.
28. Interview with Ali Fauzi, Ambon, December 20, 2001.
29. Interview with Hj Adnan Arsal, Poso, January 11, 2003.
30. Interview with Ali Fauzi, Ambon, December 20, 2001.
31. Interview with Sanussi M. Asri, SH, Pontianak, West Kalimantan, September 6, 1999.

Acknowledgements

I would like to thank the four anonymous reviewers and the two special issue editors Ayelet Harel-Shalev and Arthur Stein for their extremely useful comments.

Disclosure statement

No potential conflict of interest was reported by the author.

References

Aditjondro, George Junus. 2004. "Kerusuhan Poso dan Morowali, Akar Permasalahan dan Jalan Keluarnya." Paper presented at the Discussion on 'The State of Emergency in Aceh, Papua, and Poso', Propatria, Jakarta, Januari 7.
Al-Qurtuby, Sumanto. 2015. *Religious Violence and Conciliation in Indonesia: Christians and Muslims in the Moluccas*. London: Routledge.
Aragon, Loraine. 2001. "Communal Violence in Poso, Central Sulawesi: Were People Eat Fish and Fish Eat People." *Indonesia* 72: 45–79.
Aspinall, Edward. 2009. *Islam and Nation: Separatist Rebellion in Aceh, Indonesia*. Stanford, CA: Stanford University Press.
Bappeda. 1993. *Pendapatan Regional Propinsi Kalimantan Barat, 1985-1992*. Pontianak: Bappeda Propinsi Daerah Tk I Kalbar dan Biro Pusat Statistik Kalimantan Barat.
Bartels, Dieter. 2003. "Your God Is No Longer Mine: Moslem-Christian Fratricide in the Central Moluccas (Indonesia) After a Half-Millennium of Tolerant Co-existence and Ethnic Unity." In *A State of Emergency: Violence, Society and the State in Eastern Indonesia*, edited by Sandra Pannell, 128–153. Darwin: Northern Territory University Press.

Bartels, Dieter. 2010. "The Evolution of God in the Spice Islands: The Converging and Diverging of Protestant Christianity and Islam in the Colonial and Post-colonial Periods." In *Christianity in Indonesia*, edited by Susanne Schröter, 225–258. Berlin: Dr. W. Hopf.

Bertand, Jacques. 2002. "Legacies of the Authoritarian Past: Religious Violence in Indonesia's Moluccan Islands." *Pacific Affairs* 75 (1): 57–85.

Bertrand, Jacques. 2004. *Nationalism and Ethnic Conflict in Indonesia*. Cambridge: Cambridge University Press.

Boellstorff, Tom. 2002. "Ethnolocality." *The Asia Pacific Journal of Anthropology* 3 (1): 24–48.

Bräuchler, Birgit. 2005. *Cyberidentities at War: Der Molukkenkonflikt im Internet*. Bielefeld: Transcript.

Conboy, Ken. 2005. *Second Front: Inside Asia's Most Dangerous Terrorist Network*. Jakarta: Equinox.

Crouch, Harold. 2010. *Political Reform in Indonesia after Soeharto*. Singapore: ISEAS.

Damanik, Rinaldy. 2003. *Tragedi Kemanusiaan Poso: Menggapai surya pagi melalui kegelapan malam*. Palu: PBHI & LPS-HAM.

Davidson, Jamie. 2008. *From Rebellion to Riots: Collective Violence on Indonesian Borneo*. Madison: University of Wisconsin Press.

Davidson, Jamie. n.d. "The Dukun, Kraton and Barongsai: Ethnic Violence and Its Politics in West Kalimantan." Unpublished paper.

Davies, Matthew. 2006. *Indonesia's War over Aceh: Last Stand on Mecca's Porch*. London: Routledge.

Djuweng, Stepanus. 1997. *Indigenous Peoples and Land Use Policy in Indonesia: A Dayak Showcase*. Pontianak: Institute of Dayakology.

Djuweng, Stepanus. 1998. "The Dayak: Children of the Soil." *Kalimantan Review* 1: 6–8.

Dove, Michael. 1997. "Dayak Anger Ignored." *Inside Indonesia* 51 (July–September). www.insideindonesia.org/dayak-anger-ignored.

Fasbender, Karl, and Susanne Erbe. 1990. *Indonesia's Managed Mass Migration: Transmigration Between Poverty, Economy and Ecology*. Hamburg: Verlag Weltarchiv.

Forum Cheq and Recheq. n.d. "Report Tragedi Kemanusiaan di Poso: Kerusuhan Bernuansa SARA di Kota 'Citra' Poso dan Sekitarnya."

Gaspersz, Steve G. C. 2005. "Church and Religious Conflict: Some Experiences of Theological Reflection During Years of Riots in Maluku." In *Christian Faith and Violence*, Volume 1, edited by Dirk van Keulen and Martien E. Brinkman, 282–292. Zoetermeer: Meinema.

Greenlees, Don, and Robert Garran. 2002. *Deliverance: The Inside Story of East Timor's Fight for Freedom*. Crows Nest, NSW: Allan & Unwin.

Hardjono, Joan M. 1977. *Transmigration in Indonesia*. Kuala Lumpur: Oxford University Press.

Hasan, Noorhaidi. 2006. *Laskar Jihad: Islam, Militancy and the Quest for Identity in Post-New Order Indonesia*. Ithaca, NY: Cornell Southeast Asia Program.

Hehanussa, Jozef M. N. 2013. *Der Molukkenkonflikt von 1999: Zur Rolle der Protestantischen Kirche (GPM) in der Gesellschaft*. Műnster: LIT.

HRW (Human Rights Watch). 2002. *Breakdown: Four Years of Communal Violence in Central Sulawesi*. New York, NY: Human Rights Watch.

ICG (International Crisis Group). 2001. *Communal Violence in Indonesia: Lessons from Kalimantan*. ICG Asia Report 19.

ICG (International Crisis Group). 2002. *The Search for Peace in Maluku*. ICG Asia Report 31.

Jubilee Campaign UK. 1999. *Analysis of the Sectarian Conflict in Maluku and Its Role in the Islamisation of Indonesia*. Report.

Karnavian, Tito. 2008. *Indonesian Top Secret: Membongkar Konflik Poso*. Jakarta: PT Gramedia Pustaka Utama.

Kingsbury, Damien, ed. 2000. *Guns and Ballot Boxes: East Timor's Vote for Independence*. Clayton: Monash Asia Institute, Monash University.

Mappangara, Suriadi, ed. 2001. *Respon Militer Terhadap Konflik Sosial di Poso*. Palu: Yayasan Bina Warga.

Martinkus, John. 2001. *A Dirty Little War*. Sydney: Random House.

McRae, Dave. 2013. *A Few Poorly Organised Men: Inter-religious Violence in Poso, Indonesia*. Leiden: Brill Academic.

Pariela, Tony. 1996. "Social Tansformation in Soya Atas Village." In *Remaking Maluku: Social Transformation in Eastern Indonesia*, Special Monograph 1, Centre for Southeast Asian Studies, edited by David Mearns and Chris Healy. 106–120, Darwin: Northern Territory University.

Rahawarin, M. Nasir. 2000. *Konflik Maluku Dan Solusinya*. Muslim position paper. Ambon.

Schulze, Kirsten E. 2002. "Laskar Jihad and the Conflict in Ambon." *The Brown Journal of World Affairs* IX (1): 57–69.

Schulze, Kirsten E. 2004. *The Free Aceh Movement: Anatomy of a Separatist Organization*. Washington, DC: East West Centre.

Sidel, John. 2006. *Riots, Pogroms, Jihad: Religious Violence in Indonesia*. Ithaca: Cornell University Press.

Solahudin. 2013. *The Roots of Terrorism in Indonesia: From Darul Islam to Jema'h Islamiyah*. Ithaca: Cornell University Press.

Tajima, Yukhi. 2014. *The Institutional Origins of Communal Violence: Indonesia's Transition from Authoritarian Rule*. Cambridge: Cambridge University Press.

Tomagola, Thamrin Amal. 2001. "Ambon Terbakar." In *Ketika Semerbak Cengkih Tergusur Asap Mesiu: Tragedi Kemanusiaan Maluku di Balik Konspirasi Militer, Kapitalis Birokrat, dan Kepentingan Elit Politik*, edited by Zairin Salambessy and Thamrin Hussain, 18–23. Jakarta: Tapak Ambon.

Van Klinken, Gerry. 2001. "The Maluku Wars: Bringing Society Back In." *Indonesia* 71: 1–26.

Van Klinken, Gerry. 2007. *Communal Violence and Democratisation: Small Town Wars*. London: Routledge.

Van Klinken, Gerry. 2008. "Blood, Timber, and the State in West Kalimantan, Indonesia." *Asia Pacific Viewpoint* 49 (1): 35–47.

Gendering ethnic conflicts: minority women in divided societies – the case of Muslim women in India

Ayelet Harel-Shalev

ABSTRACT

This article explores the practical and theoretical significance and long-term consequences of the failure to incorporate women's interests in post-conflict negotiations by examining the case of Muslim women in India. Analyses of deeply divided societies must recognize that political competition and political violence do not affect all citizens equally. Also, the "larger picture" depicted by inter-community conflicts should not overshadow the effects of intra-community conflicts, which are no less important. Evident within each community conflict are the winners and the losers of the political accommodation process, in which the marginalized and weaker sections of each "side" of the conflict may be the real "losers". Gendered analysis of ethnic conflicts and ethnic conflict resolution demands a reorientation of the concepts of conflict and security – Whose conflict is being solved and who is being secured?

Introduction

A substantial number of studies have addressed the puzzle of the survivability of India's democracy in light of the high incidence of ethnic and religious conflicts in the country. Scholars debate whether or not the Indian political system includes an effective mechanism of power-sharing between the country's Hindu and Muslim citizens (see, for instance, Brass 1991; Lijphart 1996; Wilkinson 2000; Harel-Shalev 2010). Moreover, researchers have indicated that during post-conflict situations, the political space needed to change the balance of power between and within communities is available (Moran 2010). This paper will delve into these issues by focusing on the failure to incorporate women's interests in formal and informal negotiations regarding the ongoing Hindu–Muslim conflict in post-independence India and its long-term consequences.

The main argument in the current research is that a consideration of the gendered aspects of ethnic conflicts and ethnic conflict resolution is crucial to the understanding of ethnic conflicts – from their beginnings through their evolution and extending to their resolution. In deeply divided societies, the communities from the two (or more) sides of the division challenge each other, are involved in severe conflicts, and disagree on the main character-istics of the state (Harel-Shalev 2010; Guelke 2012), and the corresponding political competitiveness and violence that erupt do not affect all citizens equally. Moreover, communal competition and conflict have distributional consequences both within and between each community. Accordingly, the marginalized and weaker sections of each "side of the conflict" may be the real "losers" among the competing sides. In light of the earlier writings of scholars such as Tickner (1992), Yuval-Davis (1997), Enloe (2000), Hansen (2000b), Shachar (2001), and Sjoberg (2013), this research assumes that women and gender factors should not be invisible in conflict analysis and that, accordingly, the gendering of conflict analysis is called for.

To emphasize the significance of the "absence" of women's interests, particularly those of minority women, from conflict analysis and the post-conflict negotiations over rights and to emphasize the necessity of incorporating gendered analysis into mainstream conflict studies, I will analyse the status of Muslim women in the post-independence environ-ment of India from the perspectives of several schools of thought: (1) Studies associated with ethnic conflicts in deeply divided societies and pro-posals for ethnic conflict resolutions; (2) studies (based predominantly on law) that address multiculturalism, communities and the law; and (3) fem-inist theories in general, and feminist international relations (IR) and femin-ist security studies in particular, that aim to trace women's agency and women's voices in world politics and global conflicts. Although these aca-demic approaches have evolved as separate disciplines, they must be com-bined to reorient the discussions of ethnic conflict and conflict resolution towards a discourse that is not gender-blind.

Ethnic conflicts and their resolutions in deeply divided societies

Destructive ethnic conflicts constitute a prominent feature of the post-cold-war world (Ross 2000, 1002). In fact, most political violence in the current global political environment is internal, and governments must cope with the inter-communal conflict that threatens both their internal political stability and their interstate relations. By dealing with minority communities, govern-ments must, perforce, balance considerations of internal governance with concerns about the international ramifications of their decisions (Stein and Harel-Shalev, *Introduction to the special issue*, 2017).

Deeply divided societies typically comprise several homeland communities (or communities that perceive themselves as such), each with its own inherent ethnic, national, and/or religious identity (Esman 1985; Kymlicka 2007; Harel-Shalev 2010). Homeland communities (also known as "old communities" or indigenous communities) view themselves as possessing rights to their country and homeland from time immemorial, and as such, they are inclined to demand a wide range of rights, including collective rights, from the governing state (Connor 1987; Peleg 2007). The constant exposure of minority communities in deeply divided societies to ethno-national discourses marred by the resistance of the majority to sharing power with the minority is likely to cultivate in the latter a collective, ethno-national consciousness that may subsequently help destabilize the existing political structures as the minority communities campaign for autonomy, regionalism, or sovereignty (Hechter and Levi 1979; Connor 1992). Moreover, homeland minorities often demand a status that reflects nothing less than an equal share in the majority community's power (Harel-Shalev 2010). In the existing global socio-political reality, however, majority communities typically reject these demands, a scenario that can lead to violent conflicts.

A range of theories and practices designed to promote peaceful resolutions of internal ethno-national conflicts have been offered (Ramsbotham, Miall, and Woodhouse 2011). Power-sharing, considered one of the most viable and just solutions to internal conflict, delineates a political system in which communities formally or informally share power (Lijphart 1977, 1996). Key to power-sharing is acknowledgement that majority rule may not be the best governing solution for deeply divided societies and that minorities should have assured access to power and be able to influence public policy.

According to the theoretical literature, a conflict is considered resolved only after a ceasefire has been achieved, the incidence of direct violence declines, and an agreement (either formal or informal) has been reached. In some cases, normalization and reconciliation follow these phases (Ramsbotham, Miall, and Woodhouse 2011, 13–14). Galtung (1990) further distinguished between two categories of resolutions, negative and positive peace. The former is signified primarily by the cessation of direct violence without any substantial secondary gains, whereas the latter also entails the elimination of structural and cultural violence (Galtung 1990; Ramsbotham, Miall, and Woodhouse 2011). The current research aims to add significant nuances to the "positive peace" category and "power-sharing" by investigating conflicts through the prism of gendered analysis.

Multiculturalism, communities and the law

Historically, ethnic minority demands in post-conflict situations in deeply divided societies have involved not only the elimination of classic discrimination, to which minorities are often exposed, but also claims that their special needs be accommodated. The reasoning underlying the demands for special rights and accommodations for ethnic and religious minorities is that minority cultures are typically at a substantial disadvantage, in that all aspects of everyday life are dominated by the majority culture as reflected in, for example, the state's official language, holidays, and symbols, all of which typically suppress the culture of the minority community whose members consequently suffer grievous harm (Kymlicka 1995; Stopler 2007, 323).

Over the last twenty years, interest in what is termed group-differentiated rights has grown steadily (Kymlicka 1995, 2012; Mahajan 2005; Shachar 2010; Bhargava 2011). Political theorists disagree about what defines the most appropriate policy, in terms of what is most just and ethical, for entitling individual and group rights in deeply divided societies. Communitarian scholars claim not only that minority communities should be protected, but also that the members of these communities themselves should take action to protect their group identity practices when the state attempts to marginalize them (Selznick 1992; Etzioni 1995). Liberal theoreticians (Kukathas 1995; Barry 2000), on the other hand, argue that whereas individuals in most communities usually enjoy some level of personal autonomy and protection, it is acceptable (and even advisable) that the state compel them to relinquish their collective identities (Harel-Shalev 2009).

Despite their belief in the indispensability of group rights, however, critical communitarian scholars acknowledge the dilemma inherent in the implementation of two sets of rights, namely, individual and group rights: when a state awards a community jurisdictional powers, it creates greater group autonomy and empowerment, but at the same time, it also exposes certain individuals within the group to systematic, in-group rights violations (Kymlicka and Norman 2000; Barzilai 2003; Harel-Shalev 2010). Indeed, critical communitarianism warns that the implementation of group-differentiated rights can potentially infringe on the rights of marginalized individuals and groups within the community. The current research follows critical communitarianism in analysing internal ethnic conflicts and focuses on the status of women. The granting of group rights can further deny the rights of women, and therefore, women's voices should play a substantive part in the discourse regarding the implementation of group rights (Okin 1999; Shachar 2001; Benhabib 2002; Harel-Shalev 2013).

The contribution of gendered analyses of international and global politics

Feminist theorists such as Irigaray (1985) vigorously challenged patriarchal mythologies. MacKinnon (2006) produced gendered critique, then took it to the international plane and exposed the far-reaching consequences and significance of the systematic maltreatment of women and its systemic condonation. In Mackinnon's view, the ability to see and really understand what a subordinated group of people is deprived of, subjected to, or delegitimized by first requires that these people be seen as real and important to those holding the positions of institutional power, including scholars. From MacKinnon's perspective, the perception of gender equality could only be created if wrongs against women as women were forbidden by law and perpetrators were pursued, brought to justice, and punished accordingly in the same manner as other "human rights" are protected.

Consequently, gendered analysis forces scholars to re-evaluate traditional security politics and the framework of ethnic conflict analysis. Whereas security is traditionally understood to be at the top of the state's list of priorities, and securitization is perceived as the domain of extraordinary measures defined by perceived threats to the state (Enloe 2000; Hoogensen and Vigeland Rottem 2004, 168), gendered analysis focuses on the meaning of security and asks who is being secured. And whose conflict is being solved? The inherently unfair phenomenon of discrimination against women, that is, gender inequality, should be perceived to be as unjust, severe, and devastating as discrimination on the basis of race, caste, ethnicity, or religion (Stopler 2003). Feminist theorists have repeatedly claimed that gender should be incorporated into studies of war and peace (Confortini 2006; Naraghi Anderlini 2006) and that gender-based security and insecurity (Hansen 2000a) should be taken into account in analyses of ethnic conflicts and ethnic conflict resolution.

Accordingly, feminist theorists have emphasized the need to deconstruct the categories of gender and to discuss the varied and multi-layered constructions of women's citizenship (Yuval-Davis 1999, 120; Narayan 2013). Analyses of ethnic conflicts done without the gender lens may skew our understanding of the situation under study while neglecting critical societal elements (Yuval-Davis 1999; Naraghi Anderlini 2006). Feminist scholarship, then, looks at the world through "gender lenses" and aims to trace the ways in which gender is central to understanding international processes (Steans 1998; Sjoberg 2016) while sharing a normative and empirical interest in the gender-hierarchical nature of the international system (Sjoberg 2016).

Although post-war or post-conflict periods are perceived by many feminist scholars as times when gender, gender roles, and gendered power relations can be radically de/reconstructed (Moran 2010, 266; Speake 2013), women's involvement in formal missions and talks remains low (Diaz 2010, 1). Indeed, advocates of a transformative gendered approach to peacebuilding and con-flict resolution have voiced their concerns that despite the opportunity afforded by negotiations to incorporate gender issues, formal peacebuilding, and conflict resolution initiatives continue to ignore or marginalize them (Strickland and Duvvury 2003). Those initiatives that do consider issues of gender scarcely address the structural inequalities and power dynamics that constitute the foundation of gender discrimination (Strickland and Duvvury 2003; Speake 2013). Applying gender analysis to the evaluation of the status of Muslim women in post-Independence India will assist us in reinter-preting Hindu–Muslim relations in India.

Uniting the three theoretical perspectives based in ethnicity, law and fem-inist IR in a single analysis can help elucidate the defining aspects of ethnic conflicts and ethnic conflict resolution. Moreover, as this study suggests, not only does the gender-skewed approach to post-conflict power-sharing and resolution have the potential to be detrimental to women's status in society, its impact on the status of minority women may be even greater. As Okin claimed, "Unless women … are fully represented in negotiations about group rights, their interests may be harmed rather than promoted by the granting of such rights" (Okin 1999). The verity of this assertion will be emphasized by my analysis of the status of Muslim women in post-indepen-dence India.

Since conflict resolution affects different communities in varied ways, in fact, both the distinction by Galtung between negative and positive peace (Galtung 1990) and Lijphart's (1977) notion of power-sharing can be inter-preted differently. Although conflict resolution can solve problems of inter-community inequality, it may simultaneously promote inequality within certain communities. Ultimately, a solution perceived by the dominant parties of the communities involved in the conflict as peaceful may affect the marginalized groups within these communities, particularly minority women, in decidedly different ways.

Ethnic conflicts and Muslim women in India

The process of the partition of India and the creation of Pakistan uprooted entire communities and left unspeakable violence in its path (Talbot and Singh 2009). India was created in the midst of a violent partition characterized by acute conflict between Hindus and Muslims (Menon and Bhasin 1998). Uncompromising disagreements arose between the leaderships of the two groups in colonial India. During the 1940s, one of the main controversies that arose in the lead up to India's independence surrounded the demand of the Muslim League, the dominant Muslim party in colonial India, for separ-ate electorates and power-sharing as a form of government. Refusing to acquiesce, the Congress Party rejected the demand for separate electorates and chose instead to institute the majority-rule system, a step that led the Muslim League to call for a separate independent Muslim state – Pakistan. The creation of independent India and Pakistan in August 1947 exacted a heavy price. The communal violence between Muslims, Hindus, and Sikhs led to one of the largest and most violent exchanges of population ever (Pandey 1994). The truly immeasurable extent of the violence is reflected in wide-ranging casualty estimates by historians, who put the number at between half a million and two million (Talbot and Singh 2009). The partition and the immediate attempts at conflict resolution continue to affect Indian citizens to this day.

The partition of the sub-continent created multi-layered conflicts at the international, national, and regional levels. Chief among these were the international conflict between the newly created states of India and Pakistan and the strife between India's communities, particularly between Hindus and Muslims. The processes of negotiations and deliberations between Hindus and Muslims in India are well documented in the protocols of constituent assembly debates and of discussions between other formal committees, both before and after partition. The constitution of the newly formed Indian state was created in the midst of the severe conflict and ongoing violence associated with the partition.

Among the remaining citizens of post-colonial India, the struggle between Hindus and Muslims revolved around heated debates about rights. The most contentious discussions related to: (a) Representation of the Muslim population in politics and in the public sphere in the independent state; (b) official languages and the status of the Urdu language; and (c) cultural and religious rights of the Muslim community.

In the newly born Hindu-dominated nation-state, the leading elites of the Congress Party refused to create a political regime based on a power-sharing framework of proportional representation, preferring "one vote for one citizen" instead of a consociational regime. They also refused the demands of Muslim representatives for any kind of proportional representation mechanisms (e.g. quotas or affirmative action) for the Muslim community as a whole, although heated debates were held discussing appeals from the Muslim community to reserve seats for Muslim candidates (*Constituent Assembly Debates* (CAD) V, 294–297). Although affirmative action is extended in India to members of the lower caste Hindus, the Muslims – despite their collective status as a separate, weak, and underrepresented community – are ineligible for its benefits.[1] Indeed, since India gained its independence and until today, every call that affirmative action be implemented for the entire Muslim community has been perceived as a demand to further partition India (Bhargava 2007). However, the minority representatives, who raised the issue of Muslim representation on various occasions, did not initiate a fierce struggle at any time over the years (Wilkinson 2006).

The issue of language, another source of intense conflict, was among the other important struggles between Hindus and Muslims. In the early days of independence, debates raged over the future status of Urdu, which is spoken by half the Muslim citizens of India and considered a Muslim language (Wright 2002; Harel-Shalev 2006, 2009). Although Urdu and Hindi were supposed to be the official languages of the newly formed state, instead, Hindi received that status, and Urdu was stripped of the formal status that had initially been agreed upon. In the original plan, Hindustani (an oral tongue that combines Hindi and Urdu and is written in two different scripts, Devanagari and Arabic-Persian) was designated the national language. Following the confirmation of the partition in 1947, many Hindus felt the need to cancel the official status of Urdu. Members of the Constituent Assembly proposed deleting Urdu from the draft constitution. Although Muslim members of the assembly vigorously opposed this action (CAD; IX 34, 1339–458), an overwhelming majority of delegates voted in favour of legislation approving Hindi written in the Devanagari script as the sole official language of the union (CAD; IX 34, 1486–91; Schedule 343 (1)). Urdu was later acknowledged as one of the scheduled languages (minority languages), rather than an official national language, of the union.[2] Again, as in the sphere of representation, minority representatives unsuccessfully challenged the relegation of the Urdu language to its inferior status (Farouqui 1994; Wright 2002), but their struggle proved fruitless.

The situation surrounding religious community rights was markedly different. In the country's early days, in accordance with India's principles of secularism and equality and with its self-definition as a civic nation, the Indian Constituent Assembly pushed for the legislation of "uniform personal laws" for all Indian citizens. The ultimate outcome of the discourse on religious community rights was Article 44 of the Indian constitution, "Uniform Civil Code for Citizens": "The state shall endeavour to secure for citizens a uniform civil code throughout the territory of India." Due to fierce conservative Muslim opposition to its implementation, however, this article was formulated as a recommendation and not as actual policy or law (CAD, VII, 303-782). In parallel with Article 44, Article 372 of the Indian constitution states that existing family laws for each religious community will remain intact until Parliament revises the original laws.

In later periods, several attempts by the state and its institutions to pass legislation that would promote a uniform civil code were adamantly rebuffed by the leading conservative Muslim representatives. One case in particular, commonly known as "The Shah Bano affair", enraged the conservative Muslim leadership, which threatened that if the decision to intervene in Muslim religious autonomy and to force a husband to pay alimony to his divorcee was not reversed, Muslims would treat the Indian Republic Day as a "black day" (Baxi 1994; Mullally 2004; Harel-Shalev 2010; Agnes 2012). In the aftermath of the Shah Bano affair, debate of the Uniform Civil Code not only became entangled in the wider political controversies between Hindus and Muslims, it also pitted conservative Muslims on the one side, against advocates of liberalism, a gender-just interpretation of Islam, and women's rights, on the other.[3]

Like minority communities in other deeply divided societies, the elite of the Muslim community in India demanded numerous rights from the state, including group rights. Among these, language rights, rights to representation as a community, and religious and cultural group rights were the bases of some of the most important demands raised by the Muslim community in the newly founded state. The responses of the fledgling Indian state – which included, on the one hand, the cancellation of the national status of Urdu and a prohibition on quotas for proportional representation for Muslims, but, on the other, the granting of religious autonomy – raise several questions. Why did the Muslim community insist on these particular issues? Why was the state willing to "give up" its plan to institute a uniform civil code and at what cost? And what are the gendered implications of these decisions? A close reading of these processes indicates that the approach used to resolve the main conflicts between Hindus and Muslims has significant, lasting effects on the country's gender power relations (Ganguly 2003).

Although the Indian Constitution guaranteed the equality of individuals before the law, regardless of their gender or religion (Article 14 of the constitution), it was summarily undercut by granting power to religious authorities in certain domains. A complicated system of parallel, personal laws was thus created. Intended to provide guidance specific to each religious community in the areas of marriage, divorce, and inheritance (Basu 2003; Jones 2010), it allocated different rights to different communities.

In addition to guaranteeing religious autonomy to its minorities (until Article 44 will be realized), the Indian Constitution also grants them the freedom to manage their religious affairs. For Hindus – the majority population – the state established a form of civil law that adapted Hinduism to democratic principles and that was applied to all castes (Galanter 1989, 1997; Weiner 1997; Jacobsohn 2003; Harel-Shalev 2009), despite resistance from conservative Hindus, which was disregarded. In contrast, Muslims live under a particular interpretation of Sharia law (known as Shariat in India), and despite sporadic efforts by the state and liberal Muslims, India's legal and political institutions have thus far failed to similarly democratize Muslim marriage and religious laws (Raghubir 1986; Baxi 1994; Engineer 2009).[4] This reality has cultured a potent source of ideological conflict that also drives resource competition between Hindus and Muslims in India. While the Indian Constitution guarantees equality before the law, the Indian policy of differential religious group rights constitutes a barrier to that equality in Indian society. The debate over whether uniform vs. separate family laws[5] should be implemented evolved to become one of the most contested issues in India (Hasan and Menon 2005).

Although women's status in India has steadily improved over time (Hasan and Menon 2005), the traditional norms of Indian society continue to marginalize them, both in the private (within the family) and in the public spheres (Wolkowitz 1987). An examination of the policy decisions by the state in its early days shows that the status of Muslim women in India is even more troublesome than that of Hindu women. As will be illustrated below, Muslim women's status and position in society are intrinsically linked not only with the sensitive, often volatile and politically contentious Hindu–Muslim relations (Basu 1993; Hasan 1993; Ganguly 2003), but also with internal conflicts of interests within the Muslim community (Rajgopal 1987; Varshney 2002; Brass 2005; Wilkinson 2006).

Gendering conflict analysis – bringing Muslim women's interests back in

Lijphart (1977), a renowned political scientist, is an advocate of power-sharing in deeply divided societies. He strives to theorize a model, which is both stable and just for divided societies. He further suggested (1996) that the negotiation process between the Hindu and Muslim communities, which resulted in the granting of minority religious autonomy and the reversal of the Shah Bano verdict (which initially put state law above family religious laws), is a testimony of the successful implementation of power-sharing in India. In fact, according to Lijphart's analysis, this move is an indication of at least one instance of successful conflict resolution in India. However, it also elicits several questions in the realm of gendered conflict analysis. What was the underlying matrix within which the courts made their decisions? Whose conflict was resolved? Whose security benefited? Who was disempowered by these processes? Who was empowered?

However, what Lijphart sees as successful power-sharing has adverse consequences. A close examination of the Hindu–Muslim negotiations over rights from the perspectives of critical communitarianism thinking and feminist theories suggests that the analysis by Lijphart (1996) does not focus on the hegemony and the exclusivity enjoyed by the conservative elite of the Muslim community in India. Likewise, it disregards the greater ramifications of the state's preferential treatment of the Muslim conservative elite, which includes the marginalization of other groups within the community and the low status afforded Muslim women relative to other women in India. Whereas various Muslim groups within India were calling for a more gender-just interpretation of Muslim personal law, the informal power-sharing arrangements conferred hegemony on the conservative elite, who were unwilling to implement any change to the benefit of Muslim women. This move was detrimental to the balance of power within the minority community. Perhaps from the perspective of the conservative Muslim elite in India, the negotiation process, which led to a "positive peace" and so-called "efficient power-sharing", could be considered a success. For Muslim women, however, the outcome of these processes, far from *positive*, reflects their disempowerment (Alam 2008).

Religious and cultural norms continue to be the most prevalent and widely accepted justifications in India for discrimination based on sex/gender (Stopler 2003). An examination of family law policies should therefore not only focus on the myriad conflicts that have erupted between the state and its minority communities, but also highlight in-group rivalries and address the interests of the weaker groups among the minority denominations. India's policies towards religious minorities have affected gendered categories among Indians. The government's decision to grant religious rights to the communities at the expense of other rights and the state's preference for "non-intervention" in religious affairs have been sustained for decades to the detriment of women's rights, which have been sacrificed for so-called "inter-communal peace" (CAD VII, 550–552; Aslam 1989; Hasan 1993; Chatterjee 1995).

Indeed, current debates about legislative reform related to "personal status" in India cannot overlook the socio-political and legal dimensions of the Indian polity, which are expressed first and foremost by the fiery political conflict between Indian Hindus and Muslims. In addition, the dynamic struggle between Hindu right- and left-wing groups, which inevitably intensifies overall conflict levels in the country, must be taken into account (Asad 1999; Van Der Veer and Lehmann 1999). Likewise, the same can be said for the friction among India's Muslim groups (Alam 2008; Shani 2010). The sustained acceptance, by the state and ruling Hindu elites, of conservative Muslims as the dominant voice of the community, however, continues to beget the outright neglect of Muslim women's interests.

Many scholars (such as Moran 2010; Narayan 2013) perceive of post-conflict situations as windows of opportunity to change gender relations and gender hierarchies. In the case of India, however, this potential has not borne any fruit for Muslim women. Although India succeeded in democratizing Hindu Law in the early 1950s – a move that increased, to some extent, the rights granted to Hindu women (Newbigin 2009) – it was unable to institute a similar process within Islam. The informal compromise (i.e. preservation of the "status quo") between the Hindu and Muslim elites, initially formulated during the early days of independence, has apparently been upheld to this day.[6]

Scholars who have investigated the initial negotiations between Muslims and Hindus have claimed that at the time of independence, Muslims were in a position neither to demand representation nor to secure official status for the Urdu language. How then were they strong enough to insist on and obtain religious autonomy? And why has the conservative Muslim community been so stubborn and uncompromising in its fight to preserve Muslim religious autonomy? The staunchest opponents to a uniform civil code, Muslim conservatives (Hasan 2010), whose aims comprised the preservation of their position of power and the maintenance of limits on the rights of Muslim women, are considered by the Indian leadership to represent the voice of the Muslim community. Were the state and its judicial system willing to listen to the voices of Indian women, particularly those of Muslim Indian women, perhaps the outcomes of the Hindu–Muslim negotiation process would have been different.

The large and intriguing Indian democracy, however, has been characterized by a complex political game of "give and take". In the spheres of language and minority representation, in particular, where the need for group rights is most prominent, the relevant community leaders stopped short of violating the "rules of the game" of the delicate Indian minority–majority relationship. It is precisely the sphere of religious autonomy on which the community leaders were not willing to compromise. For its part, the irresolute Indian state did not insist on implementing the principle of equality before the law for all its citizens, the result of which would have benefited Muslim women.

Although dissenting voices were silenced in the conflict surrounding the state's failure to enforce the constitutionally guaranteed equality before the law of all its citizens, Muslim women in India did not wait for their elites to protect their rights. The more recent emergence of forums and associations of educated Muslim women marks an important step in facilitating a new public debate on women's rights (Basu 1993; Menon 1998b; Vatuk 2008; Agnes 2012). In addition, the formation of alliances between the diverse Muslim women's groups with the broader women's movement in India has been crucial in widening the struggle for women's rights in general and for Muslim women in particular (Sunder 1996; Basu 2003, 2008; Vatuk 2008; Hasan 2010). Indeed, several Muslim women's organizations have as their aim to challenge the Muslim conservative elite (Jones 2010; WLUML 2011).

In the mid to late 1980s, Muslim-led women's NGOs began to appear in India (Vatuk 2008; Harel-Shalev 2010; Jones 2010; Kirmani 2011), but they had very little influence on practical women's issues. For example, in the wake of the Shah Bano affair, hundreds of women rallied in Delhi to protest the policy advanced by the Indian Parliament, which summarily ignored the rallying women (Pathak and Sunder Rajan 1989). More recently, civil society was strengthened by a rise in Muslim feminism reflected in the formation of new women's groups (Jones 2010; Kirmani 2011), including, among others, the All-India Muslim Women's Personal Law Board (2005), the Muslim Women's Rights Network (1999), the Women's Research and Action Group (1993), and the Bharatiya Muslim Mahila Andolan (2005).

Among the most important concerns of Muslim women have been physical security, the legal age of consent in marriage, the legality of polygamy within the Muslim community, divorce and custody rights, abortion rights, and inheritance rights (Vatuk 2001, 2008; Kirmani 2011; Women's Research and Action Group 2008). However, negotiations over these issues have consistently been entangled with gendered elements. Common to feminist movements elsewhere, Muslim women's groups in India struggle with the question of how to cooperate without being co-opted and to participate without stepping beyond the boundaries of compatible values (Yuval-Davis 1999, 133). This perceived incompatibility may lead women to relinquish their struggle or to come to the realization that they must prioritize the rights of their community over their own rights as women. Therefore, ever since the right-wing Hindu forces co-opted the issue of the Uniform Civil Code for their political agenda, some women's movements have been rethinking the demand by Hindu groups for a Uniform Civil Code. But these movements have taken other actions to promote Muslim women, because demands for a Uniform Civil Code were perceived as supporting the Hindu nationalists' agenda for a homogenous public sphere dominated by majoritarian values (Menon 1998a, 251–264; Hasan 2003; Rattan 2004; Subramanian 2008; Agnes 2011). Similar to conflicts involving minority women in other countries (Stopler 2003), however, their attempts to resist gender-specific oppression often agitate members of their own community, who then single them out as traitors. Such inconsistencies – the secular state's decision to grant legal authority to the men "leaders" of a particular religious community despite the constitutionally guaranteed right to gender equality – are at the basis of gender relations in India. Not surprisingly, Muslim feminist objections were ignored.

The normalization of women's identity and experience speaks directly to the decision-making involved in determining "who is secure and who is not" (Hoogensen and Vigeland Rottem 2004, 166), who is a legitimate "side" in the conflict and who is allegedly less important in the "general picture" of the conflict. The current research suggests that conflict studies and conflict resolutions – both in practice and in theory – should be sensitive to in-group inequalities, including gender, class, centre-periphery, and so on. Following the streams of studies in critical communitarian and feminist analyses, the current study further advocates the inclusion of marginalized voices and women's perspectives at the negotiation table to promote just conflict resolutions. Given that cultures and communities are often internally torn by conflicts over their own rules (Benhabib 2002), a disaggregation of the varied preferences of the different players in the political game is called for. Additionally, the perspectives of marginalized groups, including various minorities, women, and others, should also be substantive elements of any mediation process. Indeed, as Narayan (2013) and Okin (1999) rightly stated, renegotiations over cultural religious legacies in post-colonial contexts should only take place if women are assured an equal right to participate under the newly defined religious norms (Narayan 2013).

In claiming that gender-blind analyses may be misleading and false, therefore, the current analysis interprets the aforementioned political compromises in India in a different light from previous studies. What Lijphart (1996) sees as a success story of power-sharing between a Hindu majority and a Muslim minority would elicit a markedly different interpretation were issues of gender incorporated in the core of the analysis. Theoretically, communities are central to the formation of human identity and are prime agents for the fulfilment of human needs. The implementation of group rights and differentiated citizenship rights, however, should be balanced by the principle of equality, such that women's rights and their preservation are understood to be equally essential to a just and democratic society.

Today, women and women's issues are still invisible in most conflict resolutions. But gendered analyses from the critical communitarian perspective can extend the discussion about multicultural legal systems, women's voices, and group-differentiated rights to ensure that these issues are acknowledged by the state. By their very nature, group-differentiated rights are sources of potential inequality that actually promote state-sanctioned discrimination against women due to group religious and cultural practices, making the state a willing accomplice in perpetuating inequality rather than a guardian of its weaker minorities. Feminist research and activism contribute both to people's awareness of gender injustices and to directly combating those injustices (Jeffery and Basu 2011). Accordingly, the scholarly agenda should be challenged. Conflict analyses must ask at the outset who among the players is being empowered and who is being disempowered. Likewise, the effectivity of solutions that attempt to enhance and expand the meaning of equality within the multicultural framework of divided societies must first concede that the reduction of physical casualties is only one of several dimensions of just conflict resolution. Women's voices should be brought into the main frame of conflict analysis (Harel-Shalev and Daphna-Tekoah 2016). The failure to incorporate women, particularly minority women, in conflict resolution and analysis is detrimental to women's futures and to attempts to create egalitarian societies.

As Hutchings eloquently claimed,

> Feminist scholars have long pointed out that the logic of masculinity, as a mechanism for framing our understanding of international politics, renders the thinking of the feminine and the feminized impossible other than in terms of lack or absence. Quite rightly, much feminist analysis has been devoted to tracing the practical effects of this logic for the ways in which international politics is practiced and understood and as a precursor to challenging masculine hegemony in its many different forms. (Hutchings 2008, 41)

In fact, not only is gender-blind analysis wrong and misleading, present-day academic analysis should do more than describe the social pitfalls of patriarchy and hegemony. One of the main purposes of this article, therefore, was to shed light on such blind spots in a way that links scholarly domains and that can lead to new and more fine-tuned interpretations of social life.

Notes

1. For a detailed description of Muslim representation in India and the limited Muslim eligibility for reservations, see The Sachar Report, 189–214.
2. The official languages of India are Hindi and English.
3. Although the main intercommunal conflict in India is between the Hindu majority (79.8 per cent) and the Muslim minority (14.2 per cent), there are other sizeable religious communities in India (Christians, Sikhs, Buddhists, Jains, etc.), all of whom enjoy the same legal rights as Hindus. Muslim women are the only group excluded from these constitutional rights.
4. The Hindu Code of 1955 introduced inconsistencies in the area of personal law by granting specific rights to Hindu women, which were denied to Muslim women on the grounds that Muslim personal laws are considered part of the religion of Islam.
5. Islamic family law is more often referred to as Muslim personal law in the South Asian context.
6. For a list of Supreme Court rulings pertaining to the Muslim personal law, including a description of the Shah Bano case, see Iyer 1986; Basu 2008. In fact, in response to the Shah Bano case, the Indian government enacted the Muslim Personal Law Bill, under which Muslims in India would continue to be governed by particular interpretations of Sharia law, thus reasserting Muslim women's position of legal inequality.

Acknowledgements

The research was sponsored by the "Sol Leshin Program for Collaboration between BGU and UCLA." The author wish to thank the Leshin program committee for their generous support, as well as the workshop participants for their feedback and constructive comments.

Disclosure statement

No potential conflict of interest was reported by the author.

References

Agnes, Flavia. 2011. *Family Law. Vol. 1: Family Laws and Constitutional Claims*. New Delhi: Oxford University Press.
Agnes, Flavia. 2012. "From Shah Bano to Kausar Bano: Contextualizing the Muslim Woman within a Communalized Polity." In *South Asian Feminisms*, edited by R. A. Lukose, and Ania Loomba, 33–53. Durham, NC: Duke University Press.

Alam, Arshad. 2008. "The Enemy Within: Madrasa and Muslim Identity in North India." *Modern Asian Studies* 42 (2/3): 605–627.

Asad, Talal. 1999. "Religion, Nation-State, Secularism." In *Nation and Religion*, edited by Peter Van der Veer, and Hartmut Lehmann, 178–196. Princeton, NJ: Princeton University Press.

Aslam, Mohammad. 1989. "State Communalism and the Reassertion of Muslim Identity." In *The State, Political Processes and Identity*, edited by Zoya Hasan, S. N. Jha, and Rasheeduddin Khan, 270–282. New Delhi: Sage.

Barry, Brian. 2000. *Culture and Equality*. Cambridge: Polity Press.

Barzilai, Gad. 2003. *Communities and Law: Politics and Cultures of Legal Identities*. Ann Arbor: University of Michigan Press.

Basu, Amrita. 1993. "Women and Religious Nationalism in India: An Introduction." *Bulletin of Concerned Asian Scholars* 25 (4): 3–4.

Basu, Srimati. 2003. "Shading the Secular: Law at Work in the Indian Higher Courts." *Cultural Dynamics* 15 (2): 131–152.

Basu, Srimati. 2008. "Separate and Unequal: Muslim Women and Un-Uniform Family Law in India." *International Feminist Journal of Politics* 10 (4): 495–517.

Baxi, Upendra. 1994. "The Shah Bano Reversal: Coup Against the Constitution." In *Inhuman Wrongs and Human Rights*, edited by Upendra Baxi, 89–94. New Delhi: Har-Anand Publication.

Benhabib, Seyla. 2002. *The Claims of Culture: Equality and Diversity in the Global Era*. Princeton, NJ: Princeton University Press.

Bhargava, Rajeev. 2007. "On the Persistent Political Under-Representation of Muslims in India." *Law & Ethics of Human Rights* 1 (1): 76–133.

Bhargava, Rajeev. 2011. "States, Religious Diversity, and the Crisis of Secularism." *Open Democracy*, March 22. https://www.opendemocracy.net/rajeev-bhargava/states-religious-diversity-and-crisis-of-secularism-0.

Brass, Paul R. 1991. *Ethnicity and Nationalism: Theory and Comparison*. New Delhi: Sage.

Brass, Paul R. 2005. *The Production of Hindu-Muslim Violence in Contemporary India*. Seattle: University of Washington Press.

Chatterjee, Partha. 1995. "Religious Minorities and the Secular State: Reflections on an Indian Impasse." *Public Culture* 8: 11–39.

Confortini, C. C. 2006. "Galtung, Violence, and Gender: The Case for a Peace Studies/ Feminism Alliance." *Peace & Change* 31 (3): 333–367.

Connor, Walker. 1987. "Ethnonationalism." In *Understanding Political Development*, edited by Myron Weiner and Samuel Huntington, 198–220. Boston: Little Brown.

Connor, Walker. 1992. "The Nation and its Myth." *International Journal of Comparative Sociology* 33 (1-2): 48–57.

Diaz, P. C. 2010. *Women's Participation in Peace Negotiations: Connections Between Presence and Influence*. New York: UNIFEM.

Engineer, A. A. 2009. "Why Codification of Muslim personal Law?" *Countercurrents*, May 2. http://www.countercurrents.org/engineer020509.htm.

Enloe, Cynthia. 2000. *Maneuvers: The International Politics of Militarizing Women's Lives*. Los Angeles, CA: University of California Press.

Esman, M. J. 1985. "Two Dimensions of Ethnic Politics: Defense of Homelands, Immigrant Rights." *Journal of Ethnic and Racial Studies* 8 (3): 438–440.

Etzioni, Amitai. 1995. *New Communitarian Thinking: Persons, Virtues, Institutions, and Communities*. Charlottesville: University Press of Virginia.

Farouqui, Ather. 1994. "Urdu Education in India." *Economic and Political Weekly* 14 (April 2): 782–785.

Galanter, Marc. 1989. "The Displacement of Traditional Law in Modern India." In *Law and Society in Modern India*, edited by Marc Galanter. New Delhi, 15–36: Oxford University Press.

Galanter, Marc. 1997. *Law and Society in Modern India*. New Delhi: Oxford University Press.

Galtung, Johan. 1990. "Cultural Violence." *Journal of Peace Research* 27 (3): 291–305.

Ganguly, Sumit. 2003. "The Crisis of Indian Secularism." *Journal of Democracy* 14 (4): 11–25.

Guelke, Adrian. 2012. *Politics in Deeply Divided Societies*. Cambridge: Polity Press.

Hansen, Lene. 2000a. "Gender, Nation, Rape: Bosnia and the Construction of Security." *International Feminist Journal of Politics* 3 (1): 55–75.

Hansen, Lene. 2000b. "The Little Mermaid's Silent Security Dilemma and the Absence of Gender in the Copenhagen School." *Millennium – Journal of International Studies* 29: 285–306.

Harel-Shalev, Ayelet. 2006. "The Status of Minority Languages in Deeply Divided Societies: Urdu in India and Arabic in Israel." *Israel Studies Forum* 21 (2): 28–57.

Harel-Shalev, Ayelet. 2009. "The Problematic Nature of Religious Autonomy to Minorities in Democracies – the Case of India's Muslims." *Democratization* 16 (6): 1261–1281.

Harel-Shalev, Ayelet. 2010. *The Challenge of Sustaining Democracy in Deeply Divided Societies: Citizenship, Rights, and Ethnic Conflicts in India and Israel*. Lanham: Lexington Press.

Harel-Shalev, Ayelet. 2013. "Policy Analysis Beyond Personal Law: Muslim Women's Rights in India." *Politics and Policy* 41 (3): 384–419.

Harel-Shalev, Ayelet, and Shir Daphna-Tekoah. 2016. "Bringing Women's Voices Back In: Conducting Narrative Analysis in IR." *International Studies Review* 18: 171–194.

Hasan, Zoya. 1993. "Communalism, State Policy and Question of Women's Rights in Contemporary India." *Bulletin of Concerned Asian Scholars* 25 (4): 5–15.

Hasan, Zoya. 2003. "Shah Bano Affair." In *Encyclopedia of Women and Islamic Cultures*, edited by Joseph Suad, 741–744. Leiden: Brill.

Hasan, Zoya. 2010. "Gender and the Perils of Identity Politics in India." *Open Democracy*, November 30. https://www.opendemocracy.net/5050/zoya-hasan/gender-and-perils-of-identity-politics-in-india.

Hasan, Zoya, and Ritu Menon, eds 2005. *The Diversity of Muslim Women's Lives in India*. New Brunswick, NJ: Rutgers University press.

Hechter, Michael, and Margaret Levi. 1979. "The Comparative Analysis of Ethnoregional Movements." *Ethnic and Racial Studies* 2: 260–274.

Hoogensen, Gunhild, and Svein Vigeland Rottem. 2004. "Gender Identity and the Subject of Security." *Security Dialogue* 35 (2): 155–171.

Hutchings, Kimberly. 2008. "Cognitive Shortcuts." In *Rethinking the Man Question: Sex, Gender and Violence in International Relations*, edited by Jane L. Parpart, and Marysia Zalewski, 23–46. London: Zed Books.

Irigaray, Luce. 1985. *Speculum of the Other Woman*. Ithaca, NY: Cornell University Press.

Iyer, Krishna. 1986. "Muslim Women Bill Unjust." *Indian Express*, New Delhi, March 4.

Jacobsohn, Gary J. 2003. *The Wheel of Law*. Princeton, NJ: Princeton University Press.

Jeffery, Patricia, and Amrita Basu. 2011. *Appropriating Gender: Women's Activism and Politicized Religion in South Asia*. New York: Routledge.

Jones, Justine. 2010. "'Signs of Churning': Muslim Personal Law and Public Contestation in Twenty-First Century India." *Modern Asian Studies* 44: 175–200.

Kirmani, Nida. 2011. "Beyond the Impasse: "Muslim Feminism(s)" and the Indian Women's Movement." *Contributions to Indian Sociology* 45 (1): 1–26.

Kukathas, Chandran. 1995. "Are There any Cultural Rights?" In *The Rights of Minority Cultures*, edited by Will Kymlicka, 228–255. Oxford: Oxford University Press.

Kymlicka, Will. 1995. *Multicultural Citizenship*. Oxford: Clarendon.

Kymlicka, Will. 2007. "The Internationalization of Minority Rights." *International Journal of Constitutional Law* 6 (1): 1–32.

Kymlicka, Will. 2012. "Multiculturalism: Success, Failure, and the Future." In *Transatlantic Council on Migration*, Migration Policy Institute. http://www.migrationpolicy.org/research/TCM-multiculturalism-success-failure.

Kymlicka, Will, and Wayne Norman. 2000. "Citizenship in Culturally Diverse Societies: Issues, Contexts, and Concepts." In *Citizenship in Diverse Societies*, edited by Will Kymlicka, and Wayne Norman, 1–41. Oxford: Oxford University Press.

Lijphart, Arend. 1977. *Democracy in Plural Societies: A Comparative Exploration*. New Haven, CT: Yale University Press.

Lijphart, Arend. 1996. "The Puzzle of Indian Democracy: A Consociational Interpretation." *American Political Science Review* 90 (2): 258–268.

MacKinnon, Catharine. 2006. *Are Women Human?* Cambridge, MA: Harvard University Press.

Mahajan, Gurpreet. 2005. "Can Intra-Group Equality Co-Exist with Cultural Diversity?"." In *Minorities Within Minorities: Equality, Rights, and Diversity*, edited by A. I. Eisenberg, and J. Spinner-Halev, 90–112. Cambridge: Cambridge University Press.

Menon, Nivedita. 1998a. "Women and Citizenship." In *Wages of Freedom: Fifty Years of the Indian Nation-State*, edited by Partha Chatterjee, 241–266. New Delhi: Oxford University Press.

Menon, Nivedita. 1998b. "State/Gender/Community: Citizenship in Contemporary India." *Economic and Political Weekly* 33 (5): 3–10.

Menon, Ritu, and Kamla Bhasin. 1998. *Borders & Boundaries: Women in India's Partition*. New Brunswick, NJ: Rutgers University Press.

Moran, M. H. 2010. "Gender Militarism and Peace Building: Projects of the Post Conflict Moment." *Annual Review of Anthropology* 39: 261–274.

Mullally, Siobhan. 2004. "Feminism and Multicultural Dilemmas in India: Revisiting the Shah Bano Case." *Oxford Journal of Legal Studies* 24 (4): 671–692.

Naraghi Anderlini, Sanam. 2006. "Mainstreaming Gender in Conflict Analysis: Issues and Recommendations." The World Bank: Special development papers, Paper No. 33/ February.

Narayan, Uma. 2013. *Dislocating Cultures: Identities, Traditions, and Third World Feminism*. New York: Routledge.

Newbigin, Eleanor. 2009. "The Codification of Personal law and Secular Citizenship: Revisiting the History of law Reform in Late Colonial India." *Indian Economic & Social History Review* 46 (1): 83–104.

Okin, S. M. 1999. *Is Multiculturalism Bad for Women?* Princeton, NJ: Princeton University Press.

Pandey, Gyanendra. 1994. "The Prose of Otherness." In *Subaltern Studies VIII: Essays in Honour of Ranajit Guha*, edited by David Arnold, and David Hardiman, 188–221. Delhi: Oxford University Press.

Pathak, Zaki, and Rajeswari Sunder Rajan. 1989. "Shahbano." *Signs: Journal of Women in Culture and Society* 14 (31): 558–582.

Peleg, Ilan. 2007. *Democratizing the Hegemonic State: Political Transformation in the Age of Identity*. New York: Cambridge University Press.

Raghubir, Malhotra. 1986. "Shah Bano Judgment and the Aftermath." *The Economic Times*, New Delhi, March 30.

Rajgopal, P. R. 1987. *Communal Violence in India*. New Delhi: Uppal Publishing House with Center for Policy Research.

Ramsbotham, Oliver, Hugh Miall, and Tom Woodhouse. 2011. *Contemporary Conflict Resolution*. Cambridge: Polity Press.

Rattan, Joyti. 2004. "Uniform Civil Code in India." *Journal of the Indian Law Institute* 46: 577–587.

Ross, M. H. 2000. "Creating the Conditions for Peacemaking: Theories of Practice in Ethnic Conflict Resolution." *Ethnic and Racial Studies* 23 (6): 1002–1034.

Sachar, Rajinder. 2006. *"Social, Economic and Educational Status of the Muslim Community of India Report."* New Delhi: Hereinafter The Sachar Report. http://berkleycenter.georgetown.edu/publications/social-economic-and-educational-status-of-the-muslim-community-in-india-sachar-committee-report.

Selznick, Philip. 1992. *The Moral Commonwealth: Social Theory and the Promise of Community*. Berkeley: University of California Press.

Shachar, Ayelet. 2001. *Multicultural Jurisdictions: Cultural Differences and Women's Rights*. Cambridge: Cambridge University Press.

Shachar, Ayelet. 2010. "State, Religion, and the Family: The New Dilemmas of Multicultural Accommodation." In *Shari'a in the West*, edited by Rex Ahdar, and Nicholas Aroney, 115–133. New York: Oxford University Press.

Shani, Ornit. 2010. "Conceptions of Citizenship in India and the 'Muslim Question'." *Modern Asian Studies* 44 (1): 145–173.

Sjoberg, Laura. 2013. *Gendering Global Conflict: Toward a Feminist Theory of War*. New York: Columbia University Press.

Sjoberg, Laura. 2016. "Feminist Reflections on Political Violence." In *The Ashgate Research Companion to Political Violence*, edited by Marie Breen-Smyth, 261–279. Farnham: Routledge.

Speake, Beth. 2013. "A Gendered Approach to Peacebuilding and Conflict Resolution." *E-International Relations Students*, February 11.

Steans, Jill. 1998. *Gender in International Relations: An introduction*. Cambridge: Polity Press.

Stein, Arthur, and Ayelet, Harel-Shalev. 2017. "Ancestral and Instrumental: Affect and Interest in the Politics of Ethnic Conflicts." *Ethnic and Racial Studies* 40 (12).

Stopler, Gila. 2003. "Countenancing the Oppression of Women: How Liberals Tolerate Religious and Cultural Practices That Discriminate Against Women." *Columbia Journal of Gender & Law* 12: 154–221.

Stopler, Gila. 2007. "Contextualizing Multiculturalism: A Three Dimensional Examination of Multicultural Claims." *Journal of Law and Ethics of Human Rights* 1: 309–353.

Strickland, Richard, and Nata Duvvury. 2003. *Gender Equity and Peacebuilding, from Rhetoric to Reality*. Washington: International Center for Research on Women.

Subramanian, Narendra. 2008. "Legal Change and Gender Inequality: Changes in Muslim Family Law in India." *Law & Social Inquiry* 33 (3): 631–672.

Sunder, Madhavi. 1996. "In a "Fragile Space": Sexual Harassment and the Construction of Indian Feminism." *Law & Policy* 18: 419–442.

Talbot, Ian, and Gurharpal Singh. 2009. *The Partition of India*. Cambridge: Cambridge University Press.

Tickner, J. Ann. 1992. *Gender in International Relations: Feminist Perspectives on Archiving Global Security*. New York: Columbia University Press.

Van Der Veer, Peter, and Hartmut Lehmann, eds 1999. *Nation and Religion – Perspectives on Europe and Asia*. Princeton, NJ: Princeton University Press.

Varshney, Ashutosh. 2002. *Ethnic Conflict and Civic Life: Hindus and Muslims in India*. Ann Harbor, MI: Yale University Press.

Vatuk, Sylvia. 2001. "'Where Will She Go? What Will She Do?': Paternalism Towards Women in the Administration of Muslim Personal Law in Contemporary India." In *Religion and Personal Law in India*, edited by G. J. Larson, 226–248. Bloomington: Indiana University Press.

Vatuk, Sylvia. 2008. "Islamic Feminism in India: Indian Muslim Women Activists and the Reform of Muslim Personal Law." *Modern Asian Studies* 42 (2–3): 489–518.

Weiner, Myron. 1997. "Minority Identities." In *Politics in India*, edited by Sudipta Kaviraj, 241–253. New Delhi: Oxford University Press.

Wilkinson, Steven I. 2000. "India, Consociational Theory, and Ethnic Violence." *Asian Survey* 40: 767–791.

Wilkinson, Steven I. 2006. *Votes and Violence: Electoral Competition and Ethnic Riots in India*. Cambridge: Cambridge University press.

WLUML (Women Living Under Muslim Laws). 2011. "India: "Indian SC Gives Hindu Women Equal Property Rights.'" *The News*, October 14. http://www.thenews.com.pk/TodaysPrintDetail.aspx?ID=9536&Cat=13.

Wolkowitz, Carol. 1987. "Controlling Women's Access to Political Power." In *Women, State, and Ideology: Studies from Africa and Asia*, edited by Haleh Afshar, 205–225. London: Routledge.

Women's Research and Action Group. 2008. "Position Paper on Reforms in Muslim Family Law." http://www.wragindia.org/publications/MPL_FINAL_POSITION_PAPER-11TH_October08.pdf.

Wright, Theodore P., Jr. 2002. "Strategies for the Survival of Formerly Dominant Languages." *Annual of Urdu Studies* 17: 168–186.

Yuval-Davis, Nira. 1997. *Gender & Nation*. London: Sage.

Yuval-Davis, Nira. 1999. "The "Multi-Layered Citizen'." *International Feminist Journal of Politics* 1 (1): 119–136.

Index

Note: Page numbers in *italics* refer to figures
Page numbers in **bold** refer to tables

9/11 attacks 107

Abd al-Majid Thnaibat 112
Abdur-Rahman, Muhammad 107, 108
Abu al-Futuh, Abd al-Mun'im 105
actors, categories of 22–23, *27*, 117,
    129–131
adat, local, violation of 122–123
affiliation 1, 5, 8; as a social group 4, 5–6,
    9, 25
Afghan Intra-Mujahedin War 81
African/Afro-Caribbean Christians 25, 30,
    32–33
al-Tawhid wa-al-Jihad 111
All-India Muslim Women's Personal Law
    Board 146
al-Nahda 98, 104
al-Qaeda terrorists 98, 99, 107
Alshech, Eli 97–115; "Changing Islam,
    Changing the World" 11
al-Takfir wal-Hijra 104
Ambon and Poso conflicts 117, 130;
    ethnic causes and 117–118
Ambonese Christians 124, 127
ancestral lands, loss of 120–122
Angstrom, Jan 41
Aoun, General 86, 87, 88
apostasy 100, 104, 105, 109
Arab Democratic List 67
Arab Movement for Renewal 67
Arab Upheaval 103–104
Arab-Palestinian political parties, seats of
    67
Aragon, Lorraine 126
autonomy: and ethnic conflict 13, 137;
    religious 12, 143, 144, 146

Balad 67, *67*, 68, 71
Banna, Hasan al- 101, 106
Basic Agrarian Law 5/1960 120
Basic Forestry Law 5/1967 120
Basic Mining Law 11/1967 120
Bates, Robert H. 7
BBM *see* Bugis, Butonese, and Makassar
    (BBM)
Bishara, Azmi 67
Boellstorff, Tom 119
Brubaker, Rogers 3, 8
Bugis, Butonese, and Makassar (BBM)
    119–120, 123–125, 127–128
Burdick, Eugene 6

Cairo Agreement 84
category sets 24–25
Chandra, Kanchan 63, 64
"Changing Islam, Changing the World"
    (Alshech and Hurvitz) 11
Christia, Fotini 81
Christian parties 87, 88, 89, 91
Christian–Muslim clashes 117
citizenship: conception of 48;
    construction of 5; identification
    and 5; laws 5; and Palestinian
    minority 66; rights 148;
    women's 139
civil wars 10, 41, 43, 93–94; in Lebanon
    80, 83–86, 90, 91–92; and militia
    organizations 80, 81, 83, 88–89, 94;
    and networks 81; and violence 13,
    78–79
cleavages 1–2, 6, 11–13; ethnic 29;
    horizontal 7; social 21, 24–25;
    sociocultural 21; vertical 11

communal competition, and ethnic conflict 10, 136
communal conflicts, in Indonesia 10, 116–118
conflict analysis: ethnic 139; gendering of 136, 144–149
conflict resolution 140–141; ethnic 135, 136, 139; and women and gender factors 136
conflicts 6; resolution of 137; support or intervention for 42–44; see also ethnic conflicts
consociational power-sharing, in Lebanon 84
constructivism: position of 6, 60; versus primordialism 3, 7–8
constructivists 3, 5, 9
Cook, Michael 110
Corstange, Daniel 87
Council for Development and Reconstruction 88
cross-generational affective ties 7; see also political parties
cross-national ethnic kin, and international conflict 43

Darul Islam (DI) rebellions 118
Davidson, Jamie 126, 130
Dayaks, ethnic mobilization of 126
democracies: and ethnic minorities 59–60; parliamentary 62
democracy 61; and Islamist political thinkers 102–103, 109
descriptive representation 60, 62–63, 64, 73
Devanagari script 142
divided societies, deeply: and ethnic conflicts 110, 136–137; power-sharing in 144–149
Divine law 102, 105, 108–109
dual identity issues 46

Egypt 98, 101, 103, 105, 108, 111
Egyptian state: and Muslim Brothers 98, 107–109; see also Muslim Brothers/Brotherhood
Egyptian-Israeli Peace Treaty 108
electoral design, in Israel 64–65
electoral reform, in Israel 65–66
electoral thresholds 61–62; in Israel 10, 61, 64, 65, 70, 73
Enloe, Cynthia 136
Esteban, Joan 7
ethnic and religious conflicts 2, 126–130; in India 135; see also religious conflicts

ethnic cleavages 29, 63; see also cleavages
ethnic competition 13, 42
ethnic conflicts 2; causes of 118–123; and communal competition 10; economic or rational choice approach to 7; and extraterritoriality 52; gendered aspects of 136; international dimensions of 41; and minority groups 136–149; and modern politics 40; and Muslim women in India 140–144; and partition 23, 32–36; patterns of 80; and post-coldwar world 136; and power sharing 13; versus religious conflicts 126–130; through gender lens 139–140
ethnic groups 9, 80, 109–110; statistics 42
" 'Ethnic' in Indonesia's Communal Conflicts, The" (Schulze) 10
ethnic minorities: and democracies 60; and descriptive representation 73; and representation 61–62
ethnic ties: and conflicts 43
ethnic violence 118, 123–126; see also ethnic conflicts
ethnicity 1, 4, 119; concept of 3; and extraterritoriality 52; politics of 8; as a social construct 4, 129–130
"Ethnicity, Extraterritoriality, and International Conflict" (Stein) 9
ethnicity and conflict regulation 12–13
ethno-national conflicts 66, 137
extraterritorial interests 1, 2, 9, 40, 45; and balance of power 50 – 51; pursuit of 51–52; and threats to 48, 50–51
extraterritoriality 48–50; and threats to 50–51

Fearon, James D. 42
Fiqh Council of North America (FCNA) 107
Future Movement (FM) 88

Galtung, Johan 137, 140
Gellner, Ernest 8
gender 11–12
gender-based security and insecurity 139
gendered analyses, and global politics 139–140
gendering conflict analysis 144–149
"Gendering Ethnic Conflicts" (Harel-Shalev) 11
genocidal conflict: and citizenship 5; in Rwanda 5
German racialism 51
Gleditsch, Kristian Skrede 43
Governance Law 65, 68, 69

group identity 1, 4, 6, 8, 13, 138
group-differentiated rights 138, 148

Habibie, BJ 126
Hadash 67, 68, 71, 72
Hansen, Lene 136
Harel-Shalev, Ayelet 1–20, 13, 135–154;
    "Gendering Ethnic Conflicts" 11
Hariri, Rafik 88, 90, 92–93
Hashid Tribal Confederation 111
Hezbollah 81, 83, 87, 89, 90–93; Shia 86
high-risk mobilization 80–81, 90
Hindu–Muslim conflict, and women's
    involvement 135–136, 140, 144
Holsti, Kalevi J. 49
homeland communities 121, 137
Horowitz, Harold 63
Hudaybi, Hasan Ismàil al- 100–101;
    Preachers . . . not Judges 100
Hurvitz, Nimrod 97–115; "Changing Islam,
    Changing the World" 11
Hutchings, Kimberly 148

identification 4, 5; categories of 7; nature
    of 4; primordial basis of 3; social 9
identity 3; categories of 24–25; as a social
    group 5
identity choices 9, 24, 30, 31
identity entrepreneurship 21, 23, 28
identity repertoires 24, 25, 32
India: ethnic and religious conflicts in
    135; ethnic riots 80; partitioning of
    140; status of Muslim women in 136
Indian Constitution 142, 143–144
indigenous communities see homeland
    communities
indigenous population, marginalization
    of 118–120
Indonesia 104; causes of ethnic conflicts
    in 118–123; communal conflicts in 117;
    ethnic conflicts in 130–131; ethnic
    violence in 123–126; violence in
    116–117
in-migration 118–120, 123, 130
inter-communal conflict 2, 12, 13, 41, 42,
    136
international conflict, and cross-national
    ethnic kin 43
international law: and Middle East 11;
    and Muslim law 107–108
international politics, and extraterritorial
    interests 40, 45, 48–50
international relations theory 44–45
internationalization 42–44
inter-state conflicts 43

inter-state wars 51
inter-tribal conflicts 111–112
Irigaray, Luce 139
Islam: past, views of 112–113; political 97,
    109–112
Islamic umma 110, 112
Islamists, militant 110–111
Israel 47, 108; electoral design in 64–65;
    electoral threshold 61, 72–73;
    Palestinian citizens of 66–68
Israeli–Palestinian conflict 84

Jemaah Islamiyya (JI) 128
Joint List (JL) 61, 68–70; "democratic
    elements" claims and 72–73;
    representational claim of 70–71
Justice and Development Party 104

Kalyvas, Stathis N. 41
Khawarij 99
Knesset 61, 67–68, 67–69
Kook, Rebecca 12, 59–77;
    "Representation, Minorities and
    Electoral Reform" 10

language 142
Laskar Jihad 117, 128, 131
Latuconsina, Akip 127
Law on Village Governance 122
Lebanese Army (Christian) 86; faction 88
Lebanese Forces (LF) 85, 87–88, 91
Lebanon: case study of 79; civil war
    83–87; May 2008 conflict in 90–91;
    party mobilization in 91–93; postwar
    developments in 87–88; postwar
    parties in 88–90
Lijphart, Arendt 60, 140, 144, 148
Lipset, Seymour Martin 21, 22
Livni, Tzippi 65, 68
Loveman, Mara 8
"Loyalty and Disassociation," doctrine of
    108
Lublin, David 63, 64

MacKinnon, Catharine 139
Ma'da – the Arab Democratic List 67
Madurese-Dayak conflict 129
Makdisi, Samir 85
Malay–Dayak offensive 117
Malay–Madurese conflict 126
Marzouki, Moncef 104
Middle East 2, 8, 106, 110
Milestones (Qutb) 100
militias: development 81–82;
    organizations 85, 88

minority communities 2, 135–136, 138, 143, 145
modern democracy 59
Morsi, Mohamed 103
multiculturalism 136, 138
multi-party system 62, 101, 109
Muslim Brothers/Brotherhood 97–98, 99, 100–101, 103, 104, 112; and democracy 102; and Egyptian state 107–109; Guidance Bureau 105; and international law 107–109; and nationalism 106–107; and political involvement 103; and state and global order 106–107
Muslim community 141; removal from 99, 104–105
Muslim law 110; and international law 107
Muslim League 140–141
Muslim movements 11; militant 99; and Muslim-majority states 97–98
Muslim societies: beliefs and future of 112–113; cleansing of 99; and multi-party system 101; past and 112
Muslim *umma* 109–110
Muslim women: gendered analyses of 140; gendering conflict analysis of 144–149
Muslims: and dual identity issues 107; elites 13, 143, 145
Mustafa, Shukri 104–105

Narayan, Uma 147
national security 40, 45–48
nationalism 1, 46, 106–107; and global political order 107–109; modern 5, 8
nationality 4–5
nation-states: as a political entity 107; rejection of 108
Netanyahu, Benjamin 68
networks, postwar migration of 82–83
Nikijuluw, Emang 127
Norris, Pippa 60
North Africa 11, 103, 110

Odeh, Ayman 68, 71, 72–73
Okin, S. M. 140, 147
old communities *see* homeland communities
"Operation Pillar of Defense" 108

Pakistan 33, 36, 140–141
Palestine 47, 67
Palestinian lists 68; representational claim of 71–72; unification of 73–74

Palestinian minority 60–61, 64; in Israel 66–68, 70, 73–74; representation of 72; voting rate of 70
Palestinian representation: in Israel 61; society 70–71
"Paradox of Powersharing, The" (Rizkallah) 10
Parkinson, Sarah Elizabeth 81
parliamentary democracy 64
partition 103; and ethnic conflict 21, 23, 32–36; of India 140–142; and inter-communal conflict 12, 13; in Kikuyuland divisions *34*
party mobilization, in Lebanon 91–93
partyism 101, 103
Patanga, Arief 127
political coalitions 9, 22, 24, 31
political competition 1–2, 9, 21, 130, 135
political Islam 97–98, 109–112
political mobilization 6, 13, 83, 94
political participation 61, 67, 82, 97, 99–103
political parties 6–7
political unification 68, 73
political violence 2, 41, 99–103, 105; and Muslim discussions about 99
Posner, Daniel 9, 10, 12, 22, 63, 64; "When and Why Do Some Social Cleavages Become Politically Salient Rather than Others?" 9
Posner, Daniel N. 21–39
Poso conflict 117–118, 124, 126, 130
postwar parties 82–83; in Lebanon 78, 88–90, **89**
power, balance of 50–51
power-sharing 74, 137, 140, 144, 148; solutions to ethnic conflicts 13, 61–63
power-sharing regimes 61; and ethnic conflicts 61; settlements 78–79
Preachers . . . not Judges (Hudaybi) 100
primordialism/primordialists: versus constructivism/constructivists 3, 4, 5, 7–8
Program of the Muslim Brother's Party, The 106
Prophet, age of the 112–113
Proportional Representation (PR) multi-party system 62

Qaradawi, Yusuf al- 100–103, 105, 107, 108–109
Qutb, Sayyid 100, 104–105; *Milestones* 100

Ra'am 67, 68
Raam-Taal alliance 66

race 3–4; classification 3; a social construct 3
Ray, Debraj 7
rebel organizations 80–81
religious conflicts 2, 411, 41, 49–50, 135–136; versus ethnic conflicts 126–130
representation 62–64; in Israel 65; *see also* Palestinian representation; *see also under* ethnic minorities
"Representation, Minorities and Electoral Reform" (Kook) 10
representative claims 64, 70, 73
Rizkallah, Amanda 10, 13, 78–96; "Paradox of Powersharing, The" 10
Rokkan, Stein 21, 22

Sacks, Harvey 24–25
Sadaka, Richard 85
Salafi-Jihadis 102, 108
Salehyan, Idean 43
Sambas conflict 116, 117–118, 123, 125, 129, 130
Saward, Michael 60, 64, 73
Scacco, Alexandra 80
Schattschneider, E. E. 22
Schulze, Kirsten 11; " 'Ethnic' in Indonesia's Communal Conflicts, The" 10
Schulze, Kirsten E. 116–134
Sen, Amartya 5
Shachar, Ayelet 136
Shah Bano affair 142–143, 146; verdict 144
Sharia law 105, 112, 143
Shoucair, Brigadier 91
Sinai Tribal Federation 111
Sjoberg, Laura 136
Sleiman, Aida Toma 68
social cleavages 9, 21–23, 24–25; *see also* cleavages
social conflict 21–22
social division 25, 29
social identities 9, 21, 22; conceptualization of 23–24
social identity matrix 22, 23, *26*, 26–29, *29, 32*; framework, aspects of, 31
social networks 80–81; and civil wars 93–94
Stamatov, Peter 8
state and global order 106–107
state survival 45–48
Stein, Arthur 1, 12, 40–58; "Ethnicity, Extraterritoriality, and International Conflict" 9

Syria 83, 86–87, 88, 90
Syrian army 86, 87, 90

Ta'al – The Arab Movement for Renewal 67, 68
Taif Agreement 84, 85, 86–87, 88
Tajfel, Henri 22
Tartusi, Abu Basir al- 105, 108–109
territorial state, and international relations theory 44–45
territory, controlling 47, 79, 81–82, 84
Tibi, Ahmad 66
Tickner, J. Ann 136
Tilmisani, Umar 103
transborder ethnic affinities/kin 43
transmigrants 118–120, 123
transnational ethnic alliances 43
transnational ethnic kin 43
tribalism 109–110
tribes, grievances of 109–112
Tumimor, Albert 123
Tunisia 98, 103–104
tyrannicide 104–105

"Uniform Civil Code for Citizens" 12, 142, 143, 147
Urdu language 141–142, 146

Van Klinken, Gerry 126
Varshney, Ashutosh 80
violence: mobilization for 78, 79, 81, 86; recurrent 78–79

Walt, Stephen M. 50
wars: causes of 50; source of **48**
wartime network: building 79, 82, 83; postwar migration of 82–83
Wattimena, Dicky 124
Weinstein, Jeremy M. 80
"When and Why Do Some Social Cleavages Become Politically Salient Rather than Others?" (Posner) 9
" 'which'-type sets" 25
women: divided societies 135–136; and ethnic conflicts 136–149; systematic maltreatment 139
women's rights 143, 146, 148; in India 11–12; and Muslim women 144–145

Yaari, Ehud 111
Yemen 111–112
Yuval-Davis, Nira 136

Zionist Camp 68, 70
Zuabi, Hanin 68

		Race		
		South Asian	African/Afro-Caribbean	
Country of Origin	India	47	0	47
	Pakistan	31	0	31
	Bangladesh	19	0	19
	Sri Lanka	3	0	3
		100	0	

	Race		
	African/Afro-Caribbean	South Asian	
Nigeria	50	0	50
Jamaica	28	0	28
Kenya	22	0	22
	100	0	

Figure 7. Homogeneity gives way to diversity post-partition.

would simply be displaced by another. The *depth* of conflict might be lessened (if for some reason racial conflict was more disruptive than national origin conflict), but the *fact* of conflict along group lines will remain, as long as there is a competition for who will control access to resources.

Figure 8 makes this point again in a different context. Here, the setting is Nakuru, a multi-ethnic district in Kenya that has witnessed significant intergroup violence in recent years (Gettleman 2008). The figure provides a social identity matrix for a hypothetical community that, for simplicity, is comprised of just two groups: Kikuyu and Kalenjin (Nakuru also contains significant numbers of Luo and Luhya). Would partitioning the community along tribal lines solve the problem? Perhaps. But as Figure 8 makes clear, the internal sub-tribe and clan divisions present within each seemingly monolithic

Pre-Partition

		Tribe		
		Kikuyu	Kalenjin	
Sub-tribe/clan	Nyeri Kikuyu	40	0	40
	Kipsigi	0	23	23
	Kiambu Kikuyu	15	0	15
	Tugen	0	12	12
	Turkana	0	5	5
	Nandi	0	3	3
	Keiyo	0	2	2
		55	45	

Post-Partition: A New Kikuyuland

		Tribe		
		Kikuyu	Kalenjin	
Clan	Nyeri Kikuyu	73	0	73
	Kiambu Kikuyu	27	0	27
		100	0	

Post-Partition: A New Kalenjinland

		Tribe		
		Kalenjin	Kikuyu	
Sub-tribe	Kipsigi	51	0	51
	Tugen	27	0	27
	Turkana	11	0	11
	Nandi	7	0	7
	Keiyo	4	0	4
		100	0	

Figure 8. A community in Nakuru, Kenya.

		Race		
		South Asian	African/Afro-Caribbean	
Country of Origin	India	47	0	47
	Pakistan	31	0	31
	Bangladesh	19	0	19
	Sri Lanka	3	0	3
		100	0	

		Race		
		African/Afro-Caribbean	South Asian	
	Nigeria	50	0	50
	Jamaica	28	0	28
	Kenya	22	0	22
		100	0	

Figure 7. Homogeneity gives way to diversity post-partition.

would simply be displaced by another. The *depth* of conflict might be lessened (if for some reason racial conflict was more disruptive than national origin conflict), but the *fact* of conflict along group lines will remain, as long as there is a competition for who will control access to resources.

Figure 8 makes this point again in a different context. Here, the setting is Nakuru, a multi-ethnic district in Kenya that has witnessed significant intergroup violence in recent years (Gettleman 2008). The figure provides a social identity matrix for a hypothetical community that, for simplicity, is comprised of just two groups: Kikuyu and Kalenjin (Nakuru also contains significant numbers of Luo and Luhya). Would partitioning the community along tribal lines solve the problem? Perhaps. But as Figure 8 makes clear, the internal sub-tribe and clan divisions present within each seemingly monolithic

Pre-Partition

		Tribe		
		Kikuyu	Kalenjin	
Sub-tribe/clan	Nyeri Kikuyu	40	0	40
	Kipsigi	0	23	23
	Kiambu Kikuyu	15	0	15
	Tugen	0	12	12
	Turkana	0	5	5
	Nandi	0	3	3
	Keiyo	0	2	2
		55	45	

Post-Partition: A New Kikuyuland

		Tribe		
		Kikuyu	Kalenjin	
Clan	Nyeri Kikuyu	73	0	73
	Kiambu Kikuyu	27	0	27
		100	0	

Post-Partition: A New Kalenjinland

		Tribe		
		Kalenjin	Kikuyu	
Sub-tribe	Kipsigi	51	0	51
	Tugen	27	0	27
	Turkana	11	0	11
	Nandi	7	0	7
	Keiyo	4	0	4
		100	0	

Figure 8. A community in Nakuru, Kenya.